Studies in Civilization

UNIVERSITY OF PENNSYLVANIA
BICENTENNIAL CONFERENCE

Studies in Civilization

By

ALAN J. B. WACE
OTTO E. NEUGEBAUER
WILLIAM S. FERGUSON
ARTHUR E. R. BOAK
EDWARD K. RAND
ARTHUR C. HOWLAND
CHARLES G. OSGOOD
WILLIAM J. ENTWISTLE
JOHN H. RANDALL, Jr.
CARLTON J. H. HAYES
CHARLES H. McILWAIN
ARTHUR M. SCHLESINGER
CHARLES CESTRE
STANLEY T. WILLIAMS

UNIVERSITY OF PENNSYLVANIA PRESS
Philadelphia
1941

Contents

v

The Mycenean Civilization

By

ALAN J. B. WACE, Litt.D., LL.D.*

Our conception of the Mycenean civilization is based mainly
on the results of archaeological exploration in Greece and the
Aegean, since Schliemann, as he said, discovered a new world
for archaeology at Mycenae in 1876, but much has also been
learnt from study of the surviving monuments like the walls of
Tiryns and Mycenae and tombs such as the Treasury of Atreus,
which have always been known and accessible. Since our knowledge of the Mycenean civilization is primarily derived from
archaeology there is a natural tendency among both archaeologists and historians to treat it too much from an archaeological standpoint. This is perhaps inevitable. Too much emphasis,
for instance, may be laid on pottery, the chronological value of
which is paramount, and other aspects of daily life are overlooked. Further, since their material remains are grander, the
palaces and treasures of kings and princes attract greater attention, and we are sometimes apt to imagine that everything
Mycenean was on that scale and of that standard. If there was
an Agamemnon there was also certainly a Thersites and, after
all, the kings and chiefs must have been numerically inferior
to their peoples, even if culturally superior. The object of this
survey of the Mycenean civilization is to envisage it as a whole,
to estimate its value, and to try to form some idea of the average
standard of life.

The Mycenean Civilization may be said to have occupied
the whole of the late Bronze Age in the Aegean, that is to say
from the rise of the Eighteenth Dynasty in Egypt soon after
1600 B.C. till the days of Ramses III of the Twentieth Dynasty
at the beginning of the twelfth century B.C. A period of four
hundred years is too long for the survey planned. We can
realize this from the tremendous changes in European civ-

* Laurence Professor of Classical Archaeology and Fellow of Pembroke College, University of Cambridge.

1

ilization between 1400 and 1800 A.D. We must limit the field, and I propose to discuss the Mycenean Civilization only of the last phase of the Aegean Bronze Age from about 1400 to 1200 B.C. when Mycenae was the dominant power in the Aegean, the period known to archaeologists as late Helladic III. This was the period when the civilization pictured by Homer's genius flourished, though it had passed away before he wrote, and valuable sidelights on some aspects of Mycenae and its culture may be drawn from Homer, though in using them we must not forget that Homer was a poet and not an archaeologist or sociologist. A period of two hundred years gives time for changes to be noted and for the general tendency of the evolution of the civilization under survey to be observed more closely. Though there are many excavated sites which illustrate the archaeology of this age, Mycenae is the typical site, and if I draw more on it than on any other it is perhaps natural because it has been my good fortune to have excavated there, following in the footsteps of two great archaeologists—Schliemann and Tsountas.

Let us first look at the buildings. Conspicuous among the remains of the civilization are the fortresses of Mycenae, of Tiryns, and of Goulas in Lake Kopais. These, however, were not towns or cities as they are sometimes called, but castles protecting the palace and headquarters of the king or prince. As in the case of the lower fortress at Tiryns and apparently of Goulas also, some of the area defended by these fortifications was intended to shelter the civilian population living outside the fortress and its flocks and herds in time of need. The people generally lived in settlements which do not seem as a rule to have been walled. They were set on low hills near a good supply of water and with fertile lands at hand. Many have been discovered in Greece and many more undoubtedly await discovery. On the flat land round Tiryns was a large town, the extent of which is not yet known. On the hills adjoining Mycenae stood settlements of varying prosperity. One on the Kalkani hill to the west of the citadel is comparatively small. A larger one has lately been identified on the top of the ridge above the Treasury of Atreus, where the houses were those of a high-class residential quarter. Before the Lion Gate were some small buildings which probably offered shelter and refreshment to man and beast as well as accommodation for shops or booths. Within the citadel was the palace of the King, equipped with every luxury and comfort the time could afford. Also within the walls were houses great and small, the great for other members of the royal family and the chief ministers and officers civil and military, the small for soldiers, craftsmen, scribes, and slaves who completed the social picture. All were equipped with ample storerooms for wine, oil, and grain, and by the Lion Gate was a special storehouse perhaps for the reception of dues paid in kind to the king. Merchants and traders would, for the most part, have had their own premises outside the walls. At Zygouries, between Mycenae and Corinth, in the basement of the largest house lay a big stock of unused pottery, presumably that of a retailer. Agricultural workers must obviously have lived outside the walls near their daily tasks. The herdsmen and shepherds, like those of today or Eumaeus in Homer, would have had their flocks and herds and their camps in sheltered glens among the hills. The slaves and the poor undoubtedly lived in one- or two-roomed huts of crude brick with flat roofs and earthen floors and only the bare necessities of life. On the other hand, the palace had a large court with a hall of state or megaron on one side, and on the other an audience room with a throne where the king would receive official visits. The megaron was nobly planned and well built and decorated. In front was a deep porch with two columns and a floor of gypsum slabs. Behind this was a vestibule floored with gypsum and stucco brightly painted. This led into the megaron proper, a large well-proportioned apartment floored in the same manner and with four columns in the center placed round a large circular, stepped hearth of painted stucco. The walls of all three sections of the megaron were covered with frescoes, and all had massive thresholds of sawn conglomerate. The doors, usually double, were of wood and set in wooden frames and swung on bronze pivots. The effect of the whole must have been rich and impressive. The palace was divided by long corridors, and off them on the ground floor were storerooms. The living and sleeping rooms would presumably have been on the upper floor, which was approached by well-arranged staircases. The roofs were flat and could serve as sleeping terraces or convenient places for drying grain and fruits. The loggia always seems to have been a popular feature. Attached to the living rooms and bedrooms were bathrooms. These had floors of painted stucco or of one gigantic limestone slab, as at Tiryns, and on them stood earthenware bathtubs for which water was probably brought by handmaidens as in Menelaos' palace in Homer. Sleeping arrangements were probably much the same as those pictured by Homer. Ordinary folk slept on rugs, skins, and blankets spread on the floor, but princes and distinguished guests slept on wooden pallets. Chairs certainly were in use, and low benches covered with stucco are found in porches and lobbies, but ordinary folk probably sat, as a rule, on rugs or cushions on the floor. What other furniture there was—tables, chests, cupboards —is not known.

Next to the palace come large houses such as the House of Columns lately planned at Mycenae. This had a colonnaded court approached by a cemented corridor from the main entrance. On the north of the court opened a megaron and another large room by the side of which a staircase led to an upper floor. South of the court was a basement where stores of various kinds were kept. Drains lead in two directions from the court, and since drains are a striking feature at both Mycenae and Tiryns we can conclude that their purpose was to carry away not merely rain water, but also waste water from baths and other domestic uses. Indeed it seems clear that the Myceneans were alive to the advantages of proper drainage.

Closely allied to the question of drainage and sanitation is that of water supply. The proximity of a plentiful supply of good water seems always to have been taken into account by the Bronze Age inhabitants of Greece, who usually chose for their settlements hills near a good source of water. Mycenae, for instance, has at hand just above the citadel the splendid spring of Perseia from which in the thirteenth century an underground conduit was led into a secret subterranean cistern outside the walls just to the east of the postern gate. This cistern was approached by a hidden passage through the thickness of the Cyclopean enceinte of the citadel, and ensured a constant supply of fresh water in case of siege. Two wells have been found within the walls, and there were probably rainwater cisterns, too. Outside the walls there are two springs today known as the Epano Pegadi and the Kato Pegadi, which lie between the Atreus ridge and the Kalkani hill and were doubtless the sources of water for the dwellers on those hills.

The next stage in the house can be seen in those south of the Grave Circle at Mycenae and at Korakou near Corinth. At the latter site the main house type seems to have had a porch facing south giving access to a vestibule which in turn led into the main room of the house. This megaron-like room had an earthen floor with a hearth of broken potsherds set in clay in its center, placed between two columns that supported the flat roof. Behind the megaron was a storeroom which was an indispensable part of the house, and if the house were one-roomed, part of it must have been occupied by store jars, great and small. Great skill was shown at Mycenae and at Zygouries in using the slope of the ground for the basements which contained the storerooms.

The usual method of building was of crude brick on a stone foundation set with clay. Doors, thresholds, and jambs were of timber with which the brick was strengthened. Doors, whether single or double, swung on bronze pivots and often, when shut, were barred at the back with stout timbers as in the Lion Gate and at Tiryns. In cases where an upper story was constructed above a basement, the stone walls of the basement were about six feet high and in their upper part was anchored a wooden framework which, projecting above the stone work, ran right up through the crude brick superstructure and held it together. For main doorways, stone thresholds were used which, when placed between solid jambs, were inserted on the wedge principle. Otherwise, the doors were set between vertical piers of rubble, bound with timber ties. If, as in parts of the palace at Mycenae, ashlar work was used, the interior of the wall consisted of rubble packed with clay and the facing blocks were held together by wooden clamps through the thickness of the wall. In basements and the humbler parts of the house, the walls were surfaced with mud plaster, but the megara and living rooms were stuccoed. Sometimes the stucco was painted a plain color, sometimes with decorative patterns of, it must be admitted, rather a Victorian character, and sometimes with elaborate friezes of men and women, hunting scenes, battle scenes, and chariots. Windows existed but were not large and of course not glazed, and so the rooms must have been both dark and draughty. At night, lamps for olive oil of stone or clay with one or more wicks gave light, and they were sometimes placed on stands. Heat was supplied by charcoal braziers, and in the megaron was a central hearth which in some cases, as in the palaces of

Tiryns and Mycenae, was probably more ceremonial than useful. In houses such as those at Korakou, the hearth was probably used for all purposes—cooking, heating and ceremonies. The flat roofs were of timber covered with brushwood and reeds overlaid with clay and hard earth packed tight, which as used today in the Archipelago make a good watertight roof.

The household equipment varied, of course, according to the social status of the owner. In the palaces gold, silver, and bronze were in frequent use. The upper classes used the same metals, but of course to a less extent than royalty, and the lower a man stood in the social scale the less he could afford of valuable metals. Lead was much used for large vessels and also employed for mending large jars or vases of earthenware when cracked or broken. All the metals were used for cups, jugs, saucers and bowls of many forms, knives, axes, swords and spears, as well as for ornamental and toilet articles, but bronze, lead, and earthenware were principally employed for household uses. Every kind of vessel almost for kitchen or domestic use can be found in Mycenean pottery, and many of the shapes are imitated from or influenced by metal vases. The earthenware for kitchen and ordinary household use was plain and undecorated, though some of the large store jars, which were often of great capacity, were strengthened with applied bands of clay decorated with simple incised or relief patterns. The finer pottery was well made according to a certain number of shapes which almost seem to have been standardized. The clay is well refined, the walls are thin, the forms are true, and the vases are surfaced with a smooth well-polished slip which makes them better adapted for holding liquids, and they are well baked. Kilns of the period have been found at Tiryns, Berbati, and Mycenae, and also clay discs on which the potter threw the pots. The finer vases are painted in a simple and abstract manner in a rich glaze paint with linear and curvilinear designs which, though often derived from natural subjects, floral or marine (octopus, argonaut, murex) are used in a formal style. On one class of vases occur representations of animals (oxen, horses) and of men and women driving in chariots or marching in single file. These may have been inspired by the frescoes on the stuccoed walls. The restraint with which the patterns are employed, the sense of design which pervades the decorative system, and the instinct by which for each shape of pot a pattern suitable for it is chosen, are in marked contrast to the practice of much later and more sophisticated potters. There is a style in Mycenean pottery (L.H.III) which shows that it is the product of a trained intelligence and a sensitive eye.

Food consisted of several forms of meat: mutton, goatsflesh, pork, and, more rarely, beef. These animals were domesticated, as were fowls also. Deer and wild boars provided game, which can include also hares and wild fowl, such as duck, geese, partridge. Fish was eaten, and shellfish of various kinds, especially oysters and mussels, were popular. Vegetables, grains, and fruits comprised wheat, barley, peas, beans, vetches, lentils, the vine and olive and their products, figs and wild vegetables such as are collected and eaten in Greece today. The pear, which is native to Greece, was possibly cultivated, and other fruits known were probably the almond, the plum, and the pomegranate. Other important natural supplies available were milk and honey and they must have been invaluable. Many of the vases found would seem to be well adapted for treating milk for cheese-making and similar processes, but most dairy vessels were probably of wood as they are today in Greece. Whether any other stimulant than wine was known we cannot tell. There is no hint as to the distillation of any kind of spirit. On the other hand herb infusions such as those made today from the mountain sage or camomile may well have been known and drunk.

Clothing is a more difficult subject because no remains except of a few small fragments of linen have been found. From the finding of loom weights and spindle whorls it is obvious that spinning and weaving were freely practised and that wool and linen furnished cloth for garments. Men wore loin cloths to which short tunics with sleeves were added. Women wore full ankle-length skirts, flounced and pleated, and small tight jackets with short sleeves and open bosoms. This costume was certainly that worn by women of the upper classes, but whether the lower classes and slaves also wore it is not known. A child, in a recently discovered ivory group from Mycenae, wears a long robe rather like a dressing gown fastened with a cord about the waist. Buttons seem to have been used. Whether the men's clothes were decorated we do not know, but the women's were certainly as richly decorated as means allowed. The skirts of the rich had gold discs of various patterns stitched on between the groups of flounces, and their hems and the borders of the jackets were trimmed with bands of thin sheet gold with embossed ornament. Those who could not afford gold used ornaments of glass or even of terra cotta which were often covered with thin gold leaf. Jewelry was much in evidence. Beads of all kinds, gold, stone, faïence, glass, and amber, were used for necklaces according to the means of the wearer and in many cases, for real gold beads, beads of glass or terra cotta covered with gold leaf were substituted. Head bands and diadems of gold were worn by the rich, and pins of gold, silver, bronze, ivory, or bone again indicate the owner's rank and wealth. The stones favored were carnelian, amethyst, lapis-lazuli (these three probably imported from Egypt), sard, agate, crystal, and onyx, and they were also used for engraved gems. The latter, which were sometimes worn on necklaces and sometimes on the wrist, seem to have served as signets for the illiterate who could not write. The art of writing was known, as we shall see, but the number who could sign their names must have been comparatively small, and consequently signets must have been in constant use. Gold signets were used, and many of these are of high quality as works of art and of great interest for the representations on them. Bronze signet rings plated with gold are also known.

The presence of foreign objects at Mycenae and at other excavated sites, and the discovery of Mycenean objects in other lands make it clear that overseas trade was carried on freely. Mycenean pottery (of course made at various local centers) is found throughout the Greek Mainland and its adjacent islands and throughout the Archipelago. It occurs on the coasts of Macedonia, Thrace, the Troad, and Asia Minor both west and south. It is common in Syria, especially at Ras Shamra, in Cyprus, in Palestine, and in Egypt during the period under review. In some islands such as Rhodes and Cyprus especially, Mycenean pottery may have been made locally, but in Syria, Palestine, Egypt, and Asia Minor it can hardly be other than imported, and the same applies to the Mycenean vases found in Sicily and Italy. We cannot even guess at what was exported in the vases, but it may have been some form of oil or unguent.

On the other hand, Egyptian objects of Eighteenth and Nineteenth Dynasty date are often found at Mycenae and other sites in Greece. A special type of bead—a lantern bead—occurs in

Mycenean Greece, Rhodes, Cyprus, and Syria in fourteenth-century deposits and thus links these areas together by what was probably a main trade route. Further in the same places carved ivory, probably from Syria where the elephant once existed, is common at the same time. Other products of Near Eastern or Levantine trade are amethyst, lapis-lazuli, carnelian, and flint, all of which probably came from Egypt. With these were presumably other goods of a perishable nature, such as foods, wooden objects, and textiles. From the north, amber reached Mycenean Greece, and there are other objects mainly of metal such as bronze which do not appear to be native and therefore were presumably imported, but their precise source is not yet determined.

This overseas trade must have been carried by sailing ships of not very great burden and probably the forerunners of the modern Aegean caiques. Such vessels could easily use sandy bays and small sheltered harbors just as do their descendants today. The frequent occurrence of Mycenean settlements at suitable ports such as Asine, Korakou, Aegina, Iolcus, and many another, all of which have easy communication with the interior, suggests that the outlets and entrances for goods were easy and unrestricted. There is, however, no archaeological evidence as yet to give us any picture of the vessels employed, or of their cargoes or methods of seamanship or destinations other than that provided by the overseas sites where Mycenean pottery is found.

On land there was, round Mycenae at all events, a well-organized road system. The roads were carefully laid out to take advantage of the contours of the hills and were supported by low embankments of huge stones where necessary. They were carried over small streams by low culverts and over deeper ravines by Cyclopean viaducts like that which lies on the road from Mycenae to the site of Prosymna by the Argive Heraion. This road system is more easily than elsewhere traced in the hills behind Mycenae, which must have been more thickly populated then than they are today. There are signs that the roads were protected by guard stations at selected points, and the silent evidence of this well-constructed system connotes not only a strong, but also an intelligent, central administration.

Travel by land must presumably have been carried on by mule or horse used as pack animals as has been the rule in

Greece for many centuries. Pack animals were probably the
normal method of transport for everything, for ordinary travel,
for shepherds moving camp, for traders conveying goods, for
military purposes. It is remarkable, however, that the frescoes
and vase paintings never picture men riding horses, though
scenes of men and women riding in chariots are not uncommon.
It would appear that the chariot was freely used for ordinary
travel as well as for the chase and for war. It cannot have been,
however, very comfortable to ride standing, as shown in the
frescoes and vase paintings, in wooden springless chariots over
the Mycenean roads which, though well laid out, must have
been, to say the least, rather bumpy.

We have assumed so far that the population of the Mycenean
world included traders and merchants, sailors and muleteers,
shepherds and farmers who would have grown grain, olives, and
fruit. Besides these there must have been skilled craftsmen such
as tanners, cobblers, smiths, potters, carpenters, masons, fine
metal workers (whom we might perhaps call jewelers), and lapidaries. Of these crafts that of the potter is well known from the
enormous number of Mycenean vases that has been discovered.
It is clear from these that the potters had full command of their
material and could produce vases of almost any shape and size
and for almost any purpose. The pottery is certainly of high
technical quality, is decorated with a sense of abstract design
unusual at that date, and is in shape well proportioned and
well constructed. The vessels of bronze are of equally good design, but the actual execution occasionally leaves something to
be desired, since the art of joining metals had not been completely mastered. Still, the bronze smith, whether in making
warlike weapons or vessels for household uses, was obviously
practising a craft perfected through long decades of experience.
Of the woodworker we know little but what we can deduce
from the traces of woodwork left in the walls of buildings and
the emplacements for door frames and thresholds. A few pieces
of carved wood have survived, but not enough to give any idea
of the standard of workmanship.

In masonry and stonecutting and dressing the Myceneans
attained a high standard. The construction of the Cyclopean
walls shows familiarity and skill in handling and dressing large
masses of stone. This is especially true of the huge blocks of

conglomerate used in the Lion Gate and adjoining bastions, the Treasury of Atreus and the other two beehive tombs of the third group, and in thresholds in palaces and houses. Conglomerate blocks from Mycenae are to be seen at Tiryns and Argos. Most of the conglomerate and limestone is hammer-dressed with great skill and uniformity, but much in the later constructions at Tiryns and in the Treasury of Minyas and the Tomb of Clytemnestra is sawn, and this indicates an advance in the methods of preparing stonework. The saws used would have been bronze blades, probably only slightly if at all toothed, and working with water and sand. The tubular drill probably of reed or hard wood and also working with sand and water was in common use throughout the period. With the saw, it was employed in carving the Lions of the Lion Gate. The chisel was, of course, known and freely used as can be seen from traces on stones. Stone vases were popular, and lamps, bowls, saucers, rhytons were made either of hard stone like *lapis Lacedaemonius* or of softer stone like steatite. They were drilled out with the tubular drill, chisel-dressed, and carefully rubbed down and highly polished. The accuracy and skill with which they were made show that Mycenean lapidaries were experts in this type of work. Some of the small stone vases are carved with delicacy and refinement with patterns in low relief and are beautiful works of art. The largest stone vases are some store jars, much broken, of steatite, but the greatest monument to the Mycenean stone workers' skill is the relief of the Lion Gate. The designer of this was a true artist, and the carvers responsible for its execution were unrivaled. With their rather primitive tools of bronze and reed they cut out of hard limestone one of the finest monuments of Greek sculpture. The artist's conception of the lions, their postures, their anatomy, and their life betray a mastery of material unsurpassed even in historic Greece.

Another form of the lapidaries' skill is to be seen in the engraved gems or sealstones, already mentioned, which are so marked a feature of Mycenean culture. The gems are admirably designed so that the device chosen fits the circular or oval field, and the cutting with fine drill and graver is minute and delicate, carried out with great economy of line.

Another favorite craft among the Myceneans was the casting in faience or glass or paste of ornaments of various kinds. Steatite molds for making them have been found, and it is clear from

the depth of some of the molds that the objects cast were made
of a material that shrank as it dried, for otherwise the depth of
the mold would have made it extremely difficult, if not impossible, to extract the object when cast. These ornaments were
often covered with thin gold leaf and were doubtless intended
as substitutes for ornaments in precious metals, necklaces, pendants, beads, dress trimmings and the like. There is consequently a certain carelessness about some of them and they are
more industrial than artistic in character, since they imitate
hand-wrought jewelry in precious metals.

✓ The craft of the jeweler, however, was one in which the
Myceneans excelled. We cannot judge their skill in silver work
because, owing to the bad condition due to oxidation of most
of the silver found, its technical accomplishment cannot be estimated. Gold work there is, however, in plenty, and it is of the
highest quality. Everything even the smallest object of gold is
beautifully and most carefully finished. The granulated work of
tiny beads of gold on rings, pendants, and other decorative work
is unrivaled in fineness and accuracy, for each little grain is attached separately. The soldering together of the two halves of
the hollow gold beads and the ring bezels is admirably executed.
Further, some of the gold work is chased with designs in low
relief produced by a combination of beating and graving. The
work of inlaying precious or semi-precious stones in gold and
silver mounts was also popular, and Mycenean metal workers
were especially skilled in setting one metal in another, gold and
niello in silver or bronze. The inlaid work of the daggers and
cups from Mycenae and Dendra is so exquisitely done that it is
difficult to believe that it is work of the Bronze Age and ante-
dates by nine hundred years Phidias' gold and ivory statue of
the Parthenos.

Having now considered the arts of peace we must glance at
the Mycenean equipment for war, which divides naturally into
the means of defense and offense. Prominent among the former
are, of course, the mighty fortifications, Tiryns, Mycenae,
Goulas, Mideia. As explained already, Tiryns and Mycenae at
least were large castles, somewhat like Edinburgh Castle or the
Tower of London, which were royal residences containing also
the administrative and military headquarters of the realm, together with the troops and civilian population necessary for

their protection and existence. It was obviously necessary to fortify the royal residence strongly in those days, so as to be ready to meet any sudden aggression by barbarian or pirate raiders or by unscrupulous neighbors. The fortifications are constructed with great skill. They occupy key points easy of defense and their walls are so planned as to give the defense the advantage of position. An example of this is the concealed sallyport at the southeast angle of the walls of Mycenae. Another instance of well-prepared defense against surprise or treachery is the postern gate at Tiryns with its oubliette. Further, no private houses seem to have been allowed to be built right up to the walls. There is always a gap between the defensive wall and the houses which follows the course of the wall directly on its inside. This seems to have been the rule too in classical Greek fortification. Its object was, of course, to guard against betrayal from within. A typical instance of this is the story of Rahab and the spies at Jericho. Careful provision was also made for water supplies, which were well protected. In addition to those mentioned, there are many other Mycenean castles, the Acropolis of Athens, the Kadmeia at Thebes, the Larissa at Argos, and the citadel of Las in Laconia. There were also forts in strong and lofty positions to serve as observation posts like that on the peak of Hagios Elias above Mycenae which was probably a station for fire signals such as Aeschylus describes. This has a magnificent outlook surveying the whole region between Corinth and Nauplia. I believe, therefore, that Aeschylus has preserved a Mycenean tradition. Small posts also seem to have existed for watching roads and passes which probably were partly for the defense of travelers but presumably also formed part of a recognized defensive system. The chariot was used for war and peace and must have needed these roads.

Defensive armor included shields, helmets, and greaves, and of such but little has so far been found. Greaves are known from Cyprus, and only in 1939 the first Mycenean bronze helmet known was found in a tomb near Mideia. Thus though corselets, breastplates, or thigh pieces have not been found, such may still come to light. Helmets of felt or leather covered with boar's tusks were common, and the remains of many have been discovered. They seem to have corresponded closely with the description given by Homer in the Doloneia. Shields, of which we have only illustrations in frescoes and on vases, were of two types. There were small round shields, perhaps of bronze over a backing of wood or hide, and large oval shields shaped like a figure of eight. The latter were of oxhide probably stretched on a wooden frame and pinched in at the middle so as to present a glancing surface to missiles.

Offensive weapons divide into those for close fighting and those for distant fighting. The former comprise long swords better suited for thrusting than cutting, daggers either for hand-to-hand work or for parrying, and spears. The latter include slings with bullets either of stone or terra cotta and bows and arrows tipped with barbed heads of bronze, flint, or obsidian. The obsidian came from Melos and the flint was probably imported from Egypt, for Greece is a flintless land.

Troops so armed could well have defended the walls of Tiryns or Mycenae, but how they would attack such walls we have no means of knowing. Blockade or beleaguer may have been preferred to direct assault, and this would explain the attention paid to the vital question of water supply and the provision of the great store chambers in the thickness of the walls of Tiryns.

Allied to war in its use of weapons is hunting, and the Mycenaeans, to judge by the illustrations they have left, were great hunters. The chariot was used to follow swift game. Deer, wild boars, and even bulls were trapped in nets into which they were driven by hounds. For attacking the prey, bows and arrows and spears were used, and probably also slings. For really dangerous game, such as lions, shields and swords were also brought into action. The game hunted included besides lions, which then apparently still existed in Greece, for they were found by Xerxes in Thrace, wild boars, two or three species of deer, and probably bears and wolves, for though these latter two are not represented in Mycenaean art they are native to Greece. The hills of Argolis must then have been much better wooded, probably with the prickly oak, which would have afforded excellent cover for the game. Other objects of the chase no doubt were hares, and birds such as partridges, wild geese, and duck, all plentiful in Greece. Thus it is natural that hunting both as a sport and as a means of helping the larder should have been a favorite pursuit among the Mycenaeans.

Among domestic animals the horse and the dog, man's companions in the chase, take first place. In several instances dog's skeletons have been found in tombs, and probably the dead man's favorite hound accompanied him by way of the tomb to the other world. Achilles, it will be remembered, slew Patroclus' hounds on his pyre, and his horses also.

So far we have discussed aspects of civilization that are mainly material and can be illustrated either by reference to actual archaeological objects or by representations on them. Now it is the turn of more abstract matters, as regards which we can only draw deductions from the archaeological material and our interpretation of it. The first and most important question is that of political administration. To judge by the evidence of the stately palaces, the great fortresses, and the beehive tombs together with the riches found in them, the system of government was monarchical. There would have been a chief, prince, or king in every state, and Greece was then—to judge by the Homeric Catalogue—divided into many states, though not perhaps so many as classical Greece. Perhaps too, as in Homer, one king like Agamemnon was overlord and superior to the others in some kind of feudal fashion. The organization of the state would have been rather elastic, as in Norman England before Magna Charta or as in the Holy Roman Empire before the rise of the Hapsburgs. The administration itself we cannot divine, though perhaps, as in Homer and Aeschylus, there was a council of elders or some similar means for public opinion to find expression. The arrangement and location of the cemeteries round Mycenae and other sites suggests that the civil population lived according to tribes, in separate settlements or small villages. This is of course conjectural, but it is by no means impossible that some kind of tribal organization underlay the regal method of government. The positions of the castles, the roads and the forts to guard them, and the signal stations suggest a well-ordered government that provided efficient protection to its subjects. The tablets found in Nestor's palace at Pylos appear to be for the most part inventories and lists, some of persons, slaves perhaps, and some of things. They are presumably official records of some kind, and probably concern dues or tithes paid or owed to the chief or king. Whatever they are, they indicate once again the existence of a well-organized central administration with a staff of scribes or some form of civil service or revenue officers. In the palace at Thebes a great number of large jars was found, many of which are inscribed, and no one who has seen them as they stand in the Thebes Museum can avoid the impression that here again is evidence of order and organization. We do not know the purport of the inscriptions on the jars, but their very existence implies method. When these inscriptions and the Pylos tablets can be read we shall doubtless know something more definite about the Mycenean form of government, but what we can derive from the silent evidence of the archaeological material suggests an orderly monarchical form of administration organized on some form of tribal basis.

The forms of justice are even more unknown and we can advance no theories.

One other question you may now well ask. What was the source of the wealth of Mycenae? Why was Mycenae in particular so strong, so great, so wealthy? This is borne out not merely by its ruins and the treasures of all kinds found among them, but also by the words of Homer. The country immediately around Mycenae is not outstandingly rich in agricultural products, oil, wine, or grain. Its wealth cannot have been derived solely from booty from military or piratical expeditions. Within its territory there must surely have been some natural product which gave it advantages its neighbors did not possess. Perhaps it was copper. Near Nemea not far north of Mycenae an ancient copper mine has been discovered. The Argive hills behind Mycenae are still insufficiently explored and it is possible that they hide in their recesses ancient copper mines which the lords of Mycenae exploited. Copper would obviously be a prime source of power and wealth in the Bronze Age, and such an explanation would fit most of the facts as we have them. The gold found at Mycenae presumably came from abroad, for gold is not known to occur in the Argolid, in noticeable quantities at least, and would, if the theory just advanced is correct, have been the price obtained by the Myceneans for their copper. Generally Mycenean Greece was probably self-sufficient so far as the necessaries of Bronze Age life were concerned. The area it covered is rich in land for grain, olives, vines, and timber, and further produced lead, copper, and silver. This gifted and energetic people, however, derived part at least of their wealth from overseas trade, exchanging their surplus products with Asia Minor, the Levant, and Egypt, just as did the Greeks of later days. They may even have acted as merchants and intermediaries, pursuits which have always appealed to the Greek character.

As regards the thought of this people, the first aspect to con-ᴗ sider is the religious. We know nothing or practically nothing definite about their religion. We can only set out the ideas presented to us by material remains from excavations such as the ruins of shrines or the tombs or by illustrations of religious subjects in gems, frescoes, vases, and the like. Two shrines are known, one at Asine and one in the palace at Mycenae, and both are small domestic sanctuaries. In the Asine shrine, a small simple cell-like room, was a ledge at the back where stood the cult objects, and these included several terra cotta figurines, mainly female. At Mycenae the shrine is not well preserved owing to the fact that a series of Greek sanctuaries was later built over its ruins, but it also was apparently a simple cell-like room. In its ruins were found remains of small circular altars of painted stucco such as are often found at Mycenean sites. It stood almost on the summit of the citadel. To it perhaps belonged the deposit found in 1939 on a rocky ledge just below it to the north. This comprised ornaments of gold, faïence, and glass, a painted stucco head, fragments of altars of painted stucco, and a most remarkable group carved in ivory representing two squatting women with a boy standing before them. The significance of this, if it is a cult object, we will discuss presently, but it may be observed in passing that this ivory group is the finest artistically of all the Mycenean carved ivories yet found in Greece or even in Crete.

There are two main difficulties in dealing with Mycenean religion, first what certainty we can place on the interpretations given to the representations of religious scenes and objects, and second how to determine what is Mycenean and what is borrowed from or influenced by the Minoan religion of Crete.

In addition to the circular altars of painted stucco, rhytons of various forms and materials for pouring libations were in common use as cult vessels. The double axe and perhaps the shield, pillars and columns, snakes, and terra cotta figurines mostly of women, for men occur but rarely, served as cult objects and may have been regarded as personifications of the divinity or rather of some of its aspects. Whether the terra cotta figurines of animals, usually oxen, are cult objects or votive

offerings is an open question, but for myself I would rather regard them as votives.

Their religion seems to have been polytheistic, and the principal figure in the Pantheon is a goddess. She appears in various
characters, as a snake goddess, with a double axe, and with lions
or other animals. She has thus many of the characteristics of the
later Cybele or Rhea who was, according to Suidas, associated
with the double axe and was as we know the mistress of lions.
This goddess seems to have had many attributes and natures
and also many localizations, so that she seems to be not so much
one individual goddess as a union of an almost indefinite number of local deities. She is connected with the heavens as well as
with the lower world and with animals as well as with trees and
vegetation. She is not, however, the only goddess, for with her
is associated another goddess, younger apparently and without
such marked characteristics. In any case, in the Pantheon the
deities are mainly female and the male gods who do appear are
young and less important. The ivory group from Mycenae, if it
really is a cult object from the shrine, may well represent the
two goddesses, the Great Mother and her younger associate, and
their young male companion. They may correspond to the Eleu-
sinian triad, and we may perhaps think of them by one of their
later Greek titles as the Mistresses or the Ladies. The view sometimes put forward that the Myceneans were monotheistic appears to be mistaken, and their Great Goddess like the Athena
or the Artemis of classical Greece seems to have united in herself many local cults and goddesses. To this worship of divine
beings the Myceneans almost certainly added the cult of the
dead. Their beehive and chamber tombs with the evidences of
the ritual of burial and the whole circumstances of the Grave
Circle at Mycenae, where the Royal Tombs were enclosed as a
sacred area for the practice of a cult, indicate more clearly than
words that there was a definite cult of the dead in Mycenean
Greece. What form it actually took we cannot tell, but it may
have been similar to the later classical cults of heroes. The ap-
paratus of their religion as we know it also suggests that it was
tinged with magic and superstition as are most early religions,
but it does not appear to have been of what might be called a
savage type. They worshipped a divine principle, in various
forms both anthropomorphic and symbolic, it is true, and they
believed apparently that the grave did not end all, but that the

spirit existed beyond the tomb and might even revisit this world to help or protect its descendants and worshippers.

From religion we may pass to the last aspect of Mycenean civilization with which we can deal, the intellectual side of life. Here again we can only deduce their intellectual powers from the material remains they have left, and there are some of their monuments that on inspection reveal much. The Myceneans were great builders, and to judge by the size of the stones they employed also great engineers. No one could build the Lion Gate and the adjoining walls or the corresponding gate at Tiryns and the great galleries there without a sound knowledge of engineering. The galleries of Tiryns are constructed on a cantilever principle with an elaborate system of counterweighting. This knowledge may have been obtained originally by empirical methods, but this system of construction was well understood and regularly practised. Again take the Treasury of Atreus, one of the great architectural monuments of the world, and analyze its construction. Here first of all there is a definite plan showing that before ever stone was cut or excavation begun a trained brain had considered the problems involved and found their solution. The plan of the tomb reveals clear thinking and a definite intention as well as bold imagination. Yet further it reveals that the mind behind the plan had also calculated weights and thrusts and stresses and taken the necessary steps to counteract them. The purpose of the tremendous hundred-ton lintel, the wedge principle in the setting of the threshold, the accuracy of the building all show that an intellect was at work. This unknown master of the Bronze Age who designed and built the Treasury of Atreus deserves to rank with the great architects of the world. He, however, was not alone. Other monuments such as the Tomb of Clytemnestra or the Treasury of Minyas and the lay-out of the palaces at Tiryns and Mycenae, the adapting of the site to the plan rather than the plan to the site, as in the megaron at Mycenae, all show that the architects at least were bold and good designers as well as thoroughly competent builders. The steps taken by the architect to make the walls and dome of the Treasury of Atreus watertight are being followed by the Greek authorities today in their repairs to that monument. Such building implies measurement and calculation, and measurement and calculation imply mathematical knowledge,

just as the study of thrusts and stresses and the use of the cantilever show a sound engineering knowledge, again mathematical.
Another instance of their engineering knowledge is to be seen in
the prehistoric dykes of the Kopais basin designed on much the
same lines as the modern drainage works to control the flood
waters and prevent the basin becoming a lake and to guide the
surplus water to the outlets provided by nature in the *katavo-
thras* or swallow holes. It was the blocking of the swallow holes
by falls of rock and the neglect of the dykes that flooded the
Kopais basin. Similarly at Tiryns recent research has shown that
Mycenean engineers diverted a stream which threatened the
lower town and turned it into a new course on the other side
of a hill. All such work connotes ordered thought by trained
minds, and further we know that they possessed a numerical
system which seems to have included fractions, founded on the
Minoan system. The existence of a numerical system shows that
calculations of a mathematical character were possible or at least
no more impossible than in classical Greece. A people who could
produce such buildings and such engineering works and could
figure cannot be described as unintellectual, and we know too
that they could read and write, in a form of the Minoan script.
The word groups in the clay tablets from Pylos show so little
correspondence with the Cretan word groups that we can only
conclude that the language of the Mainland differed from that
of Crete even though the script was much the same. A common
alphabet does not by any means even today denote a common
language. The Arabic alphabet, for instance, was common to
Arabic, Persian, and Turkish, three languages of totally different linguistic families. The same probably applied also to
Mycenean Greece. The tablets are mainly lists and inventories,
and we do not as yet possess anything in the nature of a text
either secular or religious. Inscriptions are also found on large
store jars (stirrup jars) and some other objects, from Tiryns,
Mycenae, Eleusis, Thebes, and Orchomenos, so that it is clear
that the knowledge of writing was spread all over Mycenean
Greece, though perhaps such knowledge was limited to scribes
and learned persons such as priests. Clay tablets, though so far
found only at Pylos, were apparently the usual material for writing, though it is possible that some perishable material was also
used. Still, clay was used for the sealings on store jars and was the

most natural and convenient material. Future discoveries will doubtless enlarge our knowledge of these subjects.

Till the writing can be read we cannot venture any further opinion about their intellectual attainments in other fields such as literature. Who knows whether the forerunners of the Homeric epics may not have already existed in the Mycenean Age? As to medicine, which may be classed as an intellectual aspect of civilization, we know little or nothing. In tombs, instances have been found of bones, arm or leg, which had been broken and mended, but there is no means of telling whether the cure was natural pure and simple or helped by medical skill. In another case in a tomb the condition of the teeth and jaw of a skeleton showed that the dead man had suffered from what was probably a septic wound on the jaw which had troubled him for some time. He had, however, completely recovered from it long before his death, but here again we cannot know whether the cure was natural or helped by some form of medicine. Since medicine was practised in Egypt and Syria and since the Myceneans were in touch with both countries, it is reasonable to suppose that they had some sort of medical faculty also, but whether it went much beyond the use of charms and herbs who can tell? Beyond this we pass completely into the realm of hypothesis.

What then is the impression of the Mycenean people and their attainments which we can form from this survey, admittedly rapid, of their civilization? The first point which emerges is that, though only in a Bronze Age state, they were far from being barbarians and on a much higher scale than the gifted savage. They must undoubtedly rank as a civilized race, and Aristotle would, I feel sure, have hailed them as political beings. They were skilled craftsmen, imaginative artists, capable organizers, able engineers and architects, all signs of considerable intellectual power. I have laid special stress on this intellectual ability as we can deduce it from the monuments they have left and also on the signs of order and organization that can be discerned in their civilization. These characteristics are most marked among the classical Greeks of later date. With many other archaeologists, I believe that the first Greeks to enter Greece reached that country at the beginning of the Middle Bronze Age about 2000 B.C. Their descendants, the Myceneans of the last phase of the Late Bronze Age (the period under survey) between 1400 and 1200 B.C. were thus according to our view Greeks. This is confirmed by the tablets of Pylos which suggest that the language of Mycenean Greece differed from that of Minoan Crete. As the Cretan language was almost certainly non-Greek, the probability that the language of the Myceneans was Greek is much strengthened. We can thus look on the Myceneans as Greeks, the ancestors of Homer's Achaeans, and on their civilization as the earliest expression of the Greek genius. Indeed, the more we study the monuments they have bequeathed to us and the more we realize the implications of those monuments, the more we feel that it is right to recognize in the Myceneans the same Greek spirit which led the world in art, in science, and in literature.

Exact Science in Antiquity*

By

OTTO E. NEUGEBAUER, Ph.D., LL.D.†

IF HISTORY is the study of relations between different cultures and different periods, the history of exact science has a definite advantage over general history. Relations in the field of science can be established in many cases to such a degree of exactitude that we might almost speak of a "proof" in the sense of mathematical rigor. If, for instance, Hindu astronomy uses excenters and epicycles to describe the movement of the celestial bodies, its dependence on Greek astronomy is established beyond any doubt; and the dependence of Greek astronomy on Babylonian methods is obvious from the very fact that all calculations are carried out in sexagesimal notation. However, the fact that the center of interest in the history of science lies in the relationship between *methods* requires a new classification of historical periods. In the history of astronomy, for instance, concepts such as "ancient" or "medieval" make very little sense. The method and even the general mental attitude of the work of Copernicus is much more closely related to that of Ptolemy, a millennium and a half before, than to the methods and concepts of Newton, a century and a half later. It may seem, therefore, a rather arbitrary procedure in the following report on exact science in antiquity to take into consideration only the period before Ptolemy (ca. 150 A.D.). On the other hand, Ptolemaic astronomy climaxed the development of ancient science in its widest sense and we must therefore consider his work at least in a few lines,

---

* In this paper I have, very much against my general principles, refrained from giving any kind of references. The simple bibliographical collection of texts, papers, and books consulted would require about the same space as the text of this paper; and even such a bibliography would be of very restricted use for the reader without often very long discussions in order to justify the special conclusions drawn here. I am still hoping to publish lectures on ancient astronomy which will discuss in detail problems which are touched here.

† Professor of Mathematics, Brown University.

in order to be able to understand the influence of the preceding phases on all following development.

Ptolemy (ca. 150 A.D.) was undoubtedly one of the greatest scholars of all time. He left three large works, any one of which alone would place him among the most important authors of the ancient world: the *Almagest*, the *Tetrabiblos* and the *Geography*. The influence which these works exercised on the world-picture of medieval times can hardly be overestimated. Other works, such as his *Music*, *Optics*, investigations on sundials and geographical mapping, in addition to discussions on logic, theory of parallels, etc., show the extremely wide range of his interest.

This is not the place to discuss Ptolemy's works in any detail. It must be remarked, however, that the *Almagest*, for instance, shows in every section supreme mastership and independent judgment, even if he is presenting, as in many cases, results already obtained by earlier scholars. Furthermore, we must emphasize that the modern contempt for the *Tetrabiblos*, the "Bible of the astrologer," is historically very much unjustified. Today we know it to be an error to conclude any influence of the positions of the planets from the obvious influence of the position of the sun on the life on the earth. We must, however, not forget that the instrumental facilities of ancient astronomy were by far insufficient to reveal any idea of the fantastic size of the universe. I, at least, can see no reason why, for example, the theories of earlier Greek philosophers, Plato included, are praised as deep philosophy in spite of the fact that they are hopeless contradictions to facts well known in their own time, while, on the other hand, an attempt to explain the difference between the characters of nations as the result of the difference in the respective inclination of the sun's orbit, the clima, should simply be disregarded as astrological error. The overwhelming historic influence of the *Tetrabiblos* can only be fully understood when we realize that this work is methodically the highest development of the first naturally simple world-picture of mankind, in which earth and universe still have a comparative order of magnitude.

The importance of Ptolemy's *Geography* is generally much more recognized. Hence we do not need to point out the rôle of this work for the knowledge of the inhabited world, but we should, on the contrary, direct our attention to the surprising inaccuracy of the geographical coördinates of almost all places. The method of determining latitude and longitude by astronomical means was known at least as early as Hipparchus (ca. 150 B.C.). The fact that his plan for exact mapping by astronomical methods could never be carried out in practice touches a very essential point in the general situation of ancient science. The determination of geographical longitudes requires the simultaneous observation of a lunar eclipse. All the details of this method are described in a book on optics written by Heron of Alexandria (first century A.D.), but Heron's example shows that not even for Rome were such observations available. Obviously the number of scholars in the ancient world was by far too small to undertake any kind of program based on systematic organized collaboration. One of the reasons for the rapid decline of ancient science lies in the fact that the deeper knowledge of science was then confined to an extremely small number of scholars.

A second element is equally important: the tendency to popularize science in accordance with the taste of the ruling class and to adapt it to the teaching level of the schools. This tendency is clearly evidenced in the extant fragments of ancient scientific literature; I need only to mention the commentaries on the *Almagest* (Pappus ca. 320 A.D., Theon ca. 370 A.D.), the astronomical poem of Manilius (time of Augustus) or the purely descriptive geography of Strabo (same period), which entirely neglected the fundamental problem of exact mapping. Such works were well adapted to create a superficial kind of general education but ill suited for producing an atmosphere of serious research. There was almost nothing left to destroy when the collapse of the Roman Empire fundamentally changed the social and economic structure of the ancient world.

We have not yet mentioned mathematics outside of its applications in astronomy and geography. Actually we have to go back to the Hellenistic period in order to find that kind of mathematics which we have in mind when speaking about "Greek mathematics," and which is most clearly represented by Euclid's *Elements* (ca. 300 B.C.). This type of mathematics covers a very short period indeed, beginning in the time of Plato (Theaetetus and Eudoxus, ca. 400 B.C.), condensed in the *Elements* and appearing for the last time in the works of Archimedes and Apollonius (200 B.C.). The main reason for this early interruption of pure mathematics can be found in the purely geometrical type of expression which was adopted in order to gain the higher degree of generality which the geometrical magnitudes represent, in contrast to the field of rational numbers, which was the exclusive concern of oriental mathematics and astronomy. This geometrical language, however, very soon reached such a degree of complication that development beyond the theory of conic-sections was practically impossible. As a result, the development of theoretical mathematics ended two centuries after its beginning, one century before the cultivated world became Roman.

I think that the influence of this pure mathematics on the general standard of mathematics in antiquity has been very much overestimated. Even Euclid's own works, other than the *Elements*, are on a very different level; this can be simply explained by the remark that the *Elements* are concerned with a very special group of problems, mainly concentrated on the theory of irrational numbers, where the exactitude of definitions and conclusions is the essential point of the discussion. The main part of mathematical literature, however, was less rigorous and represented the direct continuation of Babylonian and even Egyptian methods. The Babylonian influence is, for instance, mainly responsible for the general character of other groups of Greek mathematical literature, as e.g., the work of Diophant (perhaps 300 A.D.). This situation in the field of mathematics corresponds very much to the general character of the Hellenistic culture, with its mixture of very contradictory elements from all parts of the ancient world. One of the most typical elements in this process is the creation of astrology, in the modern sense of this word, and of all kinds of mantic, number-symbolism, alchemy, etc., which became elements of highest importance for both Christian and Arabian thinking.

The different components in the creation of Hellenistic culture are especially visible in the field of astronomy. Mathematical astronomy can be traced back to Apollonius and, in much more primitive form, to Eudoxus. Both men were concerned with the development of kinematical theories for describing the movement of the celestial bodies. The lifetime of both of them is well known as a time of intimate contact between Babylonia and the Greeks. In particular, Apollonius was closely related to the rulers of Pergamon, at whose court one of the Babylonian astronomers, Sudines, well known from Greek sources, lived at the same time.

It is highly probable that this early Hellenistic astronomy was also the source of the Hindu astronomy, from which almost one thousand years later the Arabian astronomy originated. I think that this relationship between the Greek form of Babylonian astronomical computation and the older Hindu decimal number systems explains the creation of a decimal number system with place-value notation, which was transferred by the Arabs to Europe and finally became our number system.

The Babylonian mathematical astronomy which had so much influence on the Hellenistic science is in itself of very recent origin. Although no exact dates can be given, all available source material agrees with a date of about 300 or 250 B.C. for the lifetime of the founder of the oldest form of this theory, Naburi-anu. The most important feature of this late-Babylonian astronomy is its mathematical character founded on the idea of computing the very complicated observed phenomena by addition of single components, each of which can be treated independently. Here for the first time in history we meet the fundamental method for the investigation of physical problems by using purely mathematical idealizations, a method which determined the course of all future science.

Astronomy of this kind requires highly developed mathematics. Babylonian astronomy contains enormous numerical computations, which could never be carried out with such primitive methods as the Egyptian rules for calculating with fractions or the Roman and medieval abacus methods. Furthermore, every mathematical theory of celestial phenomena must fulfill conditions given by observations or, in other words, requires the solution of equations. The existence of such a mathematical astronomy would therefore be sufficient to justify the conclusion of the existence of corresponding Babylonian mathematics. Hence it is not in itself surprising that we actually have many mathematical texts in cuneiform script which show a development of mathematical methods to the point mentioned above. The surprising fact, however, is that these texts do not belong to the last period of Babylonian culture, as astronomy does, but that they appear as early as in the period of Hammurabi (the so-called First Babylonian Dynasty, about 1800 B.C.).

This leads to one of the most interesting groups of problems in the history of ancient science: Why does the origin of Babylonian mathematics precede the origin of astronomy? Why does such a mathematical astronomy appear at all, if not in direct development from mathematics? And finally: Why is there no parallel development in Egypt, where both mathematics and astronomy never went beyond the most elementary limits? In the following final section I shall try to call attention to some of the conditions which may answer these questions by tracing some main lines of the development of ancient science in chronological order.

The very few old texts of mathematical character which we have from Mesopotamia belong to the latest Sumerian period, the so-called Third Dynasty of Ur (ca. 2000 B.C.). These texts are simple multiplication tables using the already fully developed famous sexagesimal number system. The most important feature of this system is the fact that the powers of sixty, such as 60 itself, or 3600 or 1/60th, and 1 are all denoted simply by "1." This notation makes multiplication or division as simple as in our method of calculation (or even simpler, because the probability of needing infinite fractions is smaller in a system having a base with more divisors). The introduction of this notation is doubtless not a conscious one but is the result of the influence of the monetary system, which was used for the notation of fractions in the same manner as in Roman times. In the beginning the different units were written with number signs of different size, but later this careful notation was omitted and thus the "place value" notation originated. This process is closely related to the economic development of this period, from which we have thousands and thousands of texts which carefully record the delivery of sheep, cattle, grain, etc., for the administrative offices. Hence the first and real decisive simplification in mathematical notations is merely due to the writing practice of generations of business scribes.

The next group of our source material comes from the First Babylonian Dynasty. Those texts are pure mathematical texts, treating elementary geometrical problems in a very algebraic form, which corresponds very much to algebraic methods known from late Greek, Arabian, and Renaissance times. The origin both of a mathematics obviously independent of direct practical needs and of its algebraic form can be explained by the same historical event, namely the complete replacement of the Sumerians by a Semitic population, although in very different senses. The main point is the fundamental difference between the languages of the two types of populations and the fact that the Semites used the Sumerian script to express their own language. The Sumerian script operates with single signs for single concepts (so-called ideograms), derived from a picture script. The Semites used these signs in two different ways: first, in their old sense as representations of single concepts, and secondly, as pure sound symbols (syllables) for composing their own words phonetically. The first possibility of expression corresponds in the field of mathematics exactly to our algebraic notation: instead of writing "length" by six letters, it is sufficient to write l; instead of writing "plus" or "addition," it is sufficient to use one sign $+$. We see here again how an entirely unconscious external influence caused the second fundamental invention of "Babylonian mathematics," the "algebraic" notation. Without such a deep linguistic difference such a powerful instrument as ideographic notation for mathematical operations would never have been introduced, as the parallel with Egypt clearly shows.

The second effect of this contrast between Sumerian and Semitic languages was the creation of systematical philological schools, whose existence is made evident by large collections of texts containing word lists, grammatical rules, etc. Exactly the same thing happened at the very same place in Arabian times, at the school of Baghdad. The new rulers had to study carefully the language and script, religion and law of the preceding culture. This school of language and theology created an atmosphere of general learning, supporting large numbers of well-educated scholars. In these circles Arabian mathematics and astronomy were created, and this corresponds certainly to the *milieu* for the origin of mathematics in the First Babylonian Dynasty.

There is no doubt that some kind of astronomy was cultivated in the same period. The unification of the many different local calendars of Sumerian times was accomplished under Hammurabi's rule, just as he reorganized preceding laws. The first lists of stars and the first rough observations of the disappearance and reappearance of Venus belong to this same period.

Babylonian history knows only short periods of comparative peace. The struggle with and between eastern and northern neighbors kept the country in continuous warfare for many centuries, until finally Assyria succeeded in constructing a powerful kingdom reaching from Persia to Egypt. Corresponding to this shift of power from southern Babylonia to Assyria we find an increasing interest in astronomy in Assyrian texts, where the astrological component, in particular, was developed, if not created.

The Assyrian empire paved the way for the Persian empire and its Hellenistic successors. Babylonia itself lost all political influence, but the cultural tradition was still extant and fully recognized in every part of the ancient world to which Assyrian influence reached. The world of Persian times, however, was very different from the world in the little country around the estuary of the Euphrates and the Tigris, in which Babylonian culture originated. Politically powerless, Babylon became an admired cultural center of a world-wide empire, comparable to the position of Rome in medieval times. The thousand-year-old uninterrupted tradition attracted the admiration of the younger cultures and created the myth of Babylonian wisdom; the main object of admiration was astrology, the "Chaldean" science, which opened inexhaustible new possibilities to religious speculation. Now Persian priests, Jews, and Greeks lived in Babylon, and an international idiom written in simple characters, the Aramaic, made general communication easy. Precisely this actually existing internationalism created competition between national cultures. Zarathustra, Abraham, and Pythagoras were each proclaimed as the inventor of all science and creator of astronomy, astrology, and number-wisdom, and each group asserted itself to be the oldest, and consequently, the teacher of mankind.

In this atmosphere of intellectual competition the Babylonian school of scribes and priests had to defend their authority. Thousands of texts of New-Babylonian, Seleucid, and Parthian times are the evidence of a Babylonian renaissance, returning even in linguistic aspects to old Sumerian traditions. This revival of intellectual centers, this new intellectual activity, where Babylonian priests went to Asia Minor to teach their wisdom to the Greeks, resulted in the last period of Babylonian astronomy. The two mathematical achievements of the old Babylonian period, mentioned above, place-value-notation and algebraic symbolism, became the foundation of a theoretical astronomy of purely mathematical character which deserves more of our highest admiration the more we are able to understand its structure. This astronomy is not based on age-old observations of miraculous exactitude, as usually pretended, but on the contrary reduces the empirical dates to the utmost minimum, mainly period relations, which are easy to observe and almost unaffected by the inexactitude of single instrumental observations. The enormous power of purely mathematical construction was fully recognized here for the first time in the history of mankind.

On the background of the remarks made at the beginning of this lecture we may perhaps resume our discussion with the statement that the development of exact science cannot be adequately described as a systematic step-by-step progress. In any case where we are able to disclose the conditions of essential new development, the contact between highly different cultures appears to give the initial impetus. On the other hand "culture" is in itself equivalent to tradition, which unifies large groups of populations into a common type of opinion and action. However, the same force, tradition, which defines a culture as an individual being, becomes an increasing impediment to further independent development and creates the long periods of "dark ages," which cover by far the largest part of all human history.

The Artistic and Intellectual Contribution of Greece

By

WILLIAM S. FERGUSON, PH.D., LL.D., LITT. ET PHIL.D.*

THE sponsors of this program desired, I am sure, to isolate for particular attention the activities of the ancient Greeks which have had most enduring influence and acknowledged value. By common consent these were displayed in the production of works of art and in the quest and testing of ideas pertinent to human life. It is manifestly unwise on this occasion to try to assess individually or collectively the contributions in art and science made by the Greeks in their long and eventful history. Given the space at my disposal, the issue of such an undertaking could only be a dry catalogue of names and titles or a bare epitome of movements and events. To limit discussion to a single development in art and a single chain of thought would yield a partial and distorted picture of the whole. Rejecting, therefore, these methods of handling the subject, I shall try to elevate for your consideration the ways of life and attitudes of mind germane to my theme which are generally acknowledged to be basically Hellenic. In the sequel I shall touch briefly on the historical continuities; and I shall conclude with a number of concrete examples of Greek thinking which will serve at once to attest and to controvert my generalizations.

"What do we owe to the Greeks?" inquires a remonstrant. "The Romans gave us the arch, but what did the Greeks give us? I grant you beauty, but . . ." This is a prodigious concession, yet it does not go far enough. "Blessed are the poor in spirit, for theirs is the kingdom of heaven;" so runs the Christian beatitude, and it has its points. It affirms the inwardness and, by implication, the universality of religious satisfactions.

* McLean Professor of Ancient and Modern History and Dean of the Faculty of Arts and Sciences, Harvard University.

The Greek beatitude,[1] "Blessed is he who has learned to search into causes" and "discerns the deathless and ageless order of nature, whence it arose, the how and the why," has its points also. It affirms the intelligibility of things and the blessedness which comes from effort in making them intelligible. As Butcher well says,[2] " 'Let us follow the argument whithersoever it leads' may be taken not only as the motto of the Platonic philosophy, but as expressing one side of the Greek genius."

The cultivation of art and the cultivation of intelligence complemented each other; and both were fostered not only by the native bent of individuals but also by the will of communities, and especially during the period when the Greeks led the world by the strong will of the Athenians. In huge loosely knit societies such as ours, creative artists, whatever their medium, can much more easily become obscure and eccentric than could their Greek confreres in their small city-state societies. These societies linked appreciation with understanding and surrounded innovators too closely to make excesses easy. Greek art, whether decorative, plastic, or monumental, told a clear story to contemporaries. It appealed to their minds as well as to their senses.

Clarity was a persistent quality of the best Greek compositions. Universality was another. Artists, like poets, achieved success by representing what was in "widest commonalty spread," and since the societies comprehended in their view were in each age composed of many kinds of men, what master craftsmen formed in marble and in speech was rich in ideas and feelings common to all mankind. They made it their aim while dealing with a particular, whether it was an athlete or a struggle of gods and giants or a war or a drama, to treat it as the embodiment of a general. Fundamentality of substance and lucidity in its treatment combined to give an ageless quality to their masterpieces, so that Greek art, like Greek drama and philosophy, is today among the oldest of living things. Our Great Tradition in art and literature, philosophy and science, stems from the Greeks. That is a conclusion to which modern

[1] Euripides, *frg.* 902 (Nauck). Trans. by Butcher, *Some Aspects of the Greek Genius,*[2] p. 2.
[2] *Op. cit.,* p. 2.

thinkers who have themselves "learned to search into causes" inevitably arrive.

The legacy of Greece, bequeathed with significant modifications to the Romans and then handed down to us, grievously attenuated, by the Middle Ages, was the accumulation of thirty generations and at least five well-defined periods of continuous endeavor. This we can say now that modern scholarship— philosophical, historical, archaeological, aesthetic—has broken up the accumulation into its successive strata. Each period had its special characteristics—of mind, interest, and problem. It is difficult enough to determine these for any one period. It is still more difficult to determine what is common to all five. Nor does this exhaust the catalogue of difficulties. During all periods the Greeks were subdivided into many states, each seeking, to the best of its ability, its own salvation in its own way. What is true of men in a state at any epoch is at best only partially true of their contemporaries in other states. To speak of Greek peculiarities in art and science is therefore as perilous as to speak of European peculiarities.

Yet the Greeks possessed a centralizing agency which Europeans have lacked—substantially since the fall of the Roman Empire, completely since Latin ceased to be their *lingua franca* in the seventeenth century—a common language. Thanks to this and to the untrammeled intercourse it enabled, ideas of all kinds, techniques, and forms of composition in whatever medium spread rapidly from one city or area to another so as to merge in a common Hellenic core. The formation of this core was assisted by the emergence successively in Greece of active cultural foci, to which were drawn men of artistic talent and creative minds and whence were disseminated widely the techniques and ideas there developed. Ionia, Athens, and Alexandria were each in a particular period the effective unifiers of Greece, the creators of something which we may regard as typically Hellenic.

The process by which the one was formed from the many (*e pluribus unum*) may be illustrated by a few examples. The ten most illustrious historians came from eight different Greek states, all of them were widely traveled, and six of them lived at least for a time in Athens. The sophists, for whom the bounds of their homelands were normally too narrow and who flocked to Athens in the latter half of the fifth century, were the purveyors of ideas originated or elaborated by them in many different localities. Sculptors, too, rooted though their styles may have been in local schools, served an international clientele, and in the great age of temple building and the later age of theatre building, both widely Hellenic in scope, sculptors and architects profited from one another's improvements and collaborated to establish and maintain a certain uniformity of general taste.

We may concede the existence of certain traits broadly Hellenic. Two of these have been indicated already: (1) An instinct for the beauty indwelling in natural objects. The humblest specimens of Greek art which have reached us—and these in great abundance—are vase-paintings. Yet of them in their lustiest period the critic who knows them best writes:[3] "For all its variety, humour, and unconcern this art is not naturalistic: apart from some very old persons, crookbacked and borne-over, from a fat belly or so, a wrinkled brow, a bald head, a bad beard, or a blobby nose; god and man, Greek and barbarian, athlete, drinker and amorist have the same well-formed bodies and the same untainted vigour." In other words the subject was not represented artistically if the representation lacked beauty. (2) A passion for making things intelligible. The Greeks were curious about everything seen on land and sea when first we meet them, and they held fast to their birthright throughout the ages. Homer fills in lovingly the contours of his numerous similes with details uninvoked by the imagery. A yearning to see for himself is ascribed to Alexander the Great by his best ancient interpreter[4] as an impelling motive for great enterprises which transcended his military objectives. And in the days of their degeneracy St. Paul conciliated his Athenian listeners by an allusion to their eagerness "to hear some new thing." Curiosity, however, can be idle. With the Greeks it was not. Among them it bred reflection, and reflection fructified in two, often unrelated, attitudes of mind, the one critical and subversive of traditions, the other imaginative, constructive—eventuating in the framing of hypotheses. The appeal of each was to reason and its postulate the rationality

[3] J. D. Beazley, C A H, V., p. 425.
[4] Arrian, Anabasis, passim.

of things. Men endowed with the critical attitude did not shrink from assailing again and again even the citadel of knowledge —the capacity of the human mind for ascertaining truth and the adequacy of human speech for its transmission, and again and again men endowed with the constructive attitude scored victories for absolutes by receding from the world of phenomena to the world of ideas or subjecting logical proofs to the rigors of mathematics. Both attitudes, nurtured by freedom of speech, penetrated ever deeper and deeper into the consciousness of the Greeks. Formidable residuums were of course left at all times—ancient pieties, primitive rituals, crude superstitions, brutal customs, untested maxims, instinctive loyalties, and the like. But, however dear these relics may be to students of anthropology, folklore, religion, and to all good historians, they do not constitute "the greatness that was Greece." That resides rather in the free play of intelligence and the rule of reason. The apostle to the Gentiles, Paul of Tarsus, announced a self-evident truth when he affirmed that "the Jews require a sign and the Greeks seek after wisdom."

An instinct for the beauty indwelling in natural objects and a passion for making things intelligible are, then, two persistent Greek traits. A third may be entitled a conviction that well-being and well-doing spring from liberty ordered by law. All Greeks would have agreed with Mazzini that the minimum which comports with human dignity is national liberty. Yet their history was such that most of their city-states lost political self-determination to one another under the successive hegemonies to which they were subjected; but they did not lose it wholly or irretrievably till the Roman conquest was complete. Until then the subjected nations lived on hope of independence and with minds set, often foolhardily, on revolt. It can scarcely be an accident that Greek creativeness ended with the destruction of this hope. Thereafter Hellenism was simply a legacy—a glorious legacy—to the later Greeks and to the Romans and their other subjects.

Full political liberty meant for the Greeks more than national independence. It meant also civil liberty. The extent to which this was enjoyed varied with the types of polity established in the various states. There were nations like Sparta in which it was denied to a large majority of the free population, others like the Bœotians in which it was limited to owners of specified amounts of property, others like Athens in which it was possessed in equal measure by all free males, and yet others like Macedon in which it consisted simply of loyalty to the crown. It accords with the freedom of inquiry and discussion characteristic of the Greek spirit that both during the development of these commonwealths and after their maturity fierce controversies raged as to the relative merits of these various types of polity; and it accords with the rationalistic temper of the people that outside Sparta, which went totalitarian and consequently sterile, the theoretical properties of polities were searchingly investigated and marvelous attempts were made, as in Plato's *Republic* and Aristotle's *Politics*, to determine which polity was ideally best or best in given circumstances. The first great period in the history of political theory is the Greek period, and its primary concern was justice. The justice even of slavery was questioned and, alas, vindicated, on grounds which remained unchallenged until the advent of the machine age. In his *Republic* Plato argued that rulers, when properly selected and seasoned in philosophy, when rid of selfishness through being denied private property and families, would rule without laws more justly than with them; but in a later work he acknowledged that lawless rulers belonged of right only in a world of gods or sons of gods, and conceded that laws were essential in any permissibly imaginable community of human beings. Aristotle agreed with him. Liberty under law was more generally esteemed by the Greeks than equality under law, which was a postulate of democracy alone. Liberty under law was indeed elevated into a universal, and it became an operative principle of literary and artistic composition. There were rules for building a temple, planning a tragedy, constructing an oration, founding a state, of which the worshippers, the auditors, the citizens, were the custodians; and it was only in Hellenistic times when the world was rebuilt on larger patterns, when societies, as in Alexandria, for example, developed heterogeneity of nationality, speech, and faith, and city-states, no longer masters of their own destinies, ceased to control, as theretofore, the lives and activities of their citizens, that literature became obscure and recondite, literary types confused, taste in art capricious and flamboyant, and the spirit of the age scientific. With the passing of the Greek city-states, such as they were, grave as were their defects, the most effective

guardians of their inherited wisdom, the most stimulating fos-
terers of their individuals of genius, the most potent agencies
of their popular education, went, fighting even in retreat, out
of their life. Faced with a similar crisis in their national affairs,
the Jews had turned to the consolations of religion and produced a great religious literature. The Greeks indulged their
natural passion for knowledge and produced a great scientific
literature. Each people bore fruit after its kind.

There are those who would make moderation a fourth component of Hellenism. All would agree that it is a persistent
characteristic of Greek style in the literary and other arts and
hence a persistent Greek ideal; but as a guide of life the slogan
in which it found terse expression, μηδὲν ἄγαν ,[5] appeared
first at an epoch when its opposite governed most men's actions. The self-restraint of the artists is generally in marked
contrast with the abandon of the livers. As Aristotle himself
admits, there was little in the internal or external history of
the Greek communes to support his thesis that a middle course
between two extremes was the best. The fury of factional strife
(*stasis*) and the inveteracy of wars attest abundantly the Greek
penchant for violent solutions. Strenuousness, rather than pla-
cidity, was the distinguishing quality of the Athenians at their
greatest. In real life moderation was a virtue frequently praised
but seldom practised. It seems to have been a reaction of the
Greek spirit against realities, or a mode of escape from them. To
my way of thinking it was an aspect of the idealism of Greek
art, not a basic Hellenic trait.

Each of the five periods of continuous endeavor already mentioned, while addressing itself to the tasks sensed as immediately important, added its quota to the legacy of Greece. Let
us dwell on them for a moment in turn.

As Carneades, following Aratus, began with Zeus, we begin
with Homer, who rates a period all to himself. The Iliad and
the Odyssey, descriptive poems, epic in quality, campaigns and
adventure in a bygone Heroic Age their theme, combine in an
unique oral style simplicity, rapidity, and nobility. In them
were fashioned with plastic clarity the features and traits of
the great gods and goddesses of Olympus and the heroes and
heroines who held converse with them, to be caught and fixed

[5] Pindar, *frg.* 216; Theogn., 335.

again and again in marble, bronze, line, and color by subsequent generations of Greek artists; and in them were found at all times touchstones of literary taste, sure guides in matters of diction to poets and laity alike. It mattered not a little for the emancipation of Greek thought from religious control that Homer humanized so completely the national deities.

The second period was one of revolt and reconstruction. Tyrants wrecked ancient social fabrics and replaced them with new. Poets and poetesses voiced in new melodies their emotions and reflections. Stimulated by fresh knowledge and broader horizons, "clear-eyed men of Ionia," contemning sacred absurdities, with magnificent faith in the powers of human thought and intuition, sought to discover, one this way, another that, "the deathless and ageless order of nature, whence it arose, the how and the why." The age of archaic art, progressing steadily toward limited objectives in painting, sculpture, and architecture, achieved its heights in the great Doric temples, in which the peoples, while housing worthily their gods and goddesses, asserted their enduring ideals, as they did in the codes of law prepared for their guidance.

The next two periods, embracing first an age of poetry and then an age of prose, are the epoch of Classicism and the ascendancy of Athens. Classicism needs no lengthy definition: it is essentially a harmony of form and matter, a subordination of the particular to the general, and self-restraint in representation and composition. Primarily it was a reality of the mimetic arts. Sophrosyne was its motto, Sophocles and Praxiteles its exemplars. The richness of each of these ages in ideas and in art-forms defies summarization. Every analyst will stress something different. I shall content myself with an allusion to the genius of Aristophanes, prince of comedians, and to the State of the Athenians, each locally and temporally conditioned, yet unrivaled as manifestations of the spirit of the age. It was the democratic idea fructifying in Athens which quickened the political thinking of the two periods of Classicism, evoking enthusiasm and imitation on the one hand, and criticism, fiercely or tolerantly destructive, on the other. In its own way the Athenian Commonwealth was, I believe, a masterpiece of art, comparable in detailed execution and singleness of idea with the Parthenon itself. As completed by Pericles, it seated common men, who were in reality very uncommon citizens, collectively or in rotation on the seats of the mighty, and organized the only direct government of the people, for the people, by the people which history records.

The predilection of the second age of Classicism was for the social sciences or, to use the Greek term, city-state sciences. Cosmological speculation, initiated by the Ionians, had run its course; and the immediacy of political problems and awareness of their significance and difficulties set thinkers on a new course. The city-state sciences languished in turn with the decay of the city-states. Yet the passion for research and the organization of knowledge persisted. In the last period of our five, ethics had to be divorced from politics and geared to the individual, no longer the πολιτικὸν ζῷον (city-state-minded animal) of Aristotle, but the "friendly" animal of Epicurus, or the κοινωνικὸν ζῷον (cosmopolitan animal) of the Stoa. The essence of the Greek city-states was Hellenism and the fruition of Hellenism proved thus to be humanism.

Hellenistic historiography also adapted itself to the spirit of the time. A branch of literature hitherto, it now studied to be scientific. Polybius, its most influential representative, did not have the gift of style; but he had the ambition to make events intelligible and the insight to perceive that what the world needed most to have made intelligible to it was the march of the Romans to world power. Like Aristotle he felt that the stronger were always superior in respect to some "good." He made it his business to determine what this was in the case of the Romans; and in its exercise by them he represented them as striving to become the masters of others but the protectors of the Greeks. World power thus evoked interest in world affairs. Scientific interest in the *cosmos* was also revived. The sphericity of the earth, apprehended already, invited computations of the earth's size, and methods were devised for determining its circumference which yielded approximate, and were capable of yielding, precise accuracy. The immobility of the earth, instinctively assumed by all mankind, and deeply grounded in Greek myth and religion, had hitherto been a postulate of astronomy. Aristarchus of Samos now denied it, and submitted an interpretation of astronomical observations in substantiation of the theory that the sun was immobile, that the earth turned on its own axis and revolved around the sun. His audacious argumentation failed to convince his co-workers, and the orthodox theory of geocentricity held possession of the field and bounded the horizons of man till Copernicus and Galileo, a millennium and a half later, advanced convincing proofs that Aristarchus was right. Like several among his contemporaries, he lived too soon. Archimedes of Syracuse, a mathematical physicist of the first rank, came as near to the calculus of Leibnitz and Newton as was possible without algebra. The craft of the physician, inheriting from Hippocrates a sound clinical method, made such significant progress in anatomy and physiology that "modern medicine may be truly described as in essence a creation of the Greeks."[6] Philology, the science which seeks to save the literary treasures of the past for the edification and enjoyment of the present, resumed its task after ages of neglect—where the Alexandrians left off.

The transition from what has preceded to what is to come I let Gilbert Murray make for me.[7]

There is [he says] hardly any type of thought or style of writing which cannot be paralleled in ancient Greece, only they will there be seen, as it were, in their earlier and simpler forms. Traces of all the things that seem most un-Greek can be found somewhere in Greek literature: voluptuousness, asceticism, the worship of knowledge, the contempt for knowledge, atheism, pietism, the religion of serving the world and the religion of turning away from the world: all these and almost all other points of view one can think of are represented somewhere in the records of that one small people. And there is hardly any single generalization in this chapter [and in my address] which the author himself could not controvert by examples to the contrary. You feel in general a great absence of all fetters: the human mind free, rather inexperienced, intensely interested in life and full of hope, trying in every direction for that excellence which the Greeks called *arete*, and guided by some peculiar instinct toward Temperance and Beauty. The variety is there and must not be forgotten.

To make sure that it is not forgotten, I close by presenting a series of excerpts picked at random from extant Greek writings, which, even when divorced from their contexts, will, I

---

[6] Sanger, in R. W. Livingstone, *The Legacy of Greece*, p. 248.

[7] "The Value of Greece to the Future of the World," in Livingstone, *op cit.*, pp. 18f.

hope, illustrate at once the range and the sharpness of Greek thought and observation.

Much learning does not teach understanding. . . . This one thing is wisdom, to understand thought, as that which guides all the world everywhere.[8]
Man is the measure of all things, of things which are, that they are, and of things which are not, that they are not.[9]
The movement of events is often as wayward and incomprehensible as the course of human thought, and this is why we ascribe to chance whatever belies our calculation.[10]

Those who would rightly judge the truth must be arbitrators and not litigants.[11]

If cows and lions had hands and could fashion things like men, they would make gods in their own image.[12]
For of the gods we believe, as of men we know, that by a law of their nature wherever they can rule they will.[13]
In regard to the gods I cannot know that they exist nor yet that they do not exist; for many things hinder such knowledge—the obscurity of the matter and the shortness of human life.[14]
Furthermore, if you decide to go forward with the plan, I should advise you to send to Dodona and Delphi, and inquire of the gods whether such a design is fraught with weal for the state both now and in days to come. And should they consent to it, then I would say that we ought to ask them further, which of the gods we must propitiate in order that we may prosper in our handiwork.[15]

The secret of happiness is freedom and the secret of freedom is a brave heart.[16]
If a man is good, nothing evil can befall him either here or hereafter.[17]

We regard a man who takes no interest in public affairs, not as a harmless, but as a useless character; and if few of us are originators, we are all sound judges of a policy.[18]

[8] Heracleitus, quoted by *Diog. Laert.*, IX, 1. Trans. by Hicks, Loeb Classics.
[9] Protagoras, cited by Plato, *Theat.*, 152 A.
[10] Thucy., I, 140. Trans. by Jowett.
[11] Aristotle, *De Caelo*, I, 10 (279b, 11).
[12] Xenophanes, *frg.* 6 (Karsten, *Philosoph. Gr. Vet.*, I, p. 41).
[13] Thucy., V, 105. Trans. by Jowett.
[14] Protagoras, cited by *Diog. Laert.*, IX, 51.
[15] Xenophon, *Ways and Means*, VI, 2. Trans. by Marchant, Loeb Classics.
[16] Thucy., II, 43. Trans. by Zimmern, *The Greek Commonwealth*,[2] p. 205.
[17] Plato, *Apol.*, 33.
[18] Thucy., II, 40. Trans. by Jowett.

There is but a very small remnant of honest followers of wisdom, and they who are of these few, and who have tasted how sweet and blessed a possession is wisdom, and who can fully see, moreover, the madness of the multitude, and that there is no one, we may say, whose action in public matters is sound, and no ally for whosoever would help the just, what are they to do? They may be compared to a man who has fallen among wild beasts; he will not be one of them, but he is too unaided to make head against them; and before he can do any good to society or his friends, he will be overwhelmed and perish uselessly. When he considers this, he will resolve to keep still, and to mind his own business; as it were standing aside under a wall in a storm of dust and hurricane of driving wind; and he will endure to behold the rest filled with iniquity, if only he himself may live his life clear of injustice and of impiety, and depart, when his time comes, in mild and gracious mood, with fair hope.[19]

The love of honor alone is not staled by age, and it is by honor, not, as some say, by gold that the helpless end of life is cheered.[20]

The whole earth is the sepulchre of famous men.[21]

The masses strive for economic advantages rather than distinction.[22]

[Social] evils are due not to the want of community of property but to the depravity of human nature.[23]

We cannot desire to walk for the sake of health and to be healthy for the sake of happiness, and that again for the sake of something else and so on *ad infinitum*. . . . Those who set up an infinite do not see that they are destroying the Good. Surely no one would ever set about doing anything if he were never to reach any final result. There would be no sense in such action. For all men of sense act for the sake of something, and that something is a limit; for the end is a limit.[24]

Therefore, while our eyes wait to see the destined final day, we must call no one happy who is of mortal race, until he hath crossed life's border, free from pain.[25]

Any claim, the smallest as well as the greatest, imposed on a neigh-

---

[19] Plato, *Republic*, VI, 10. Trans. by Matthew Arnold, "Discourses in America," p. 9.

[20] Thucy., II, 44. Trans. by Zimmern, *op. cit.*, p. 206.

[21] Thucy., II, 43. Trans. by Jowett.

[22] Aristotle, *Politics*, VIII (VI), 4, 3.

[23] Aristotle, *Politics*, II, 5.

[24] Aristotle, *Met.* 994a, 1, 994b, 9. Trans. by Burnet, *The Ethics of Aristotle*, p. XLVI.

[25] Sophocles, *Oedipus Rex*, 1528. Trans. by Jebb.

bor and an equal when there has been no legal award, can mean nothing but slavery.[26]

I allow that for men who are in prosperity and free to choose it is great folly to make war. But when they must either submit and at once surrender independence, or strike and be free, then he who shuns and not he who meets the danger is deserving of blame.[27]

Military successes are generally gained by a wise policy and an accumulation of money. It is accumulated money and not taxes levied under stress that sustains wars.[28]

No friendship between man and man, no league between city and city can ever be permanent unless the friends and allies have a good opinion of each other's honesty and are similar in general character.[29]

To maintain our rights against equals, to be politic with superiors, and to be moderate with inferiors, is the path of safety.[30]

But you and we should say what we really think and aim only at what is really possible, for we both alike know that into the discussion of human affairs the question of justice only enters where the pressure of necessity is equal, and that the powerful exact what they can, and the weak grant what they must.[31]

The one party holds that justice is equality; and so it is, but not for all the world but only for equals. The others hold that inequality is just, as indeed it is, but not for all the world but only for unequals.[32]

Dictatorship is a fair field, but it has no exit.[33]

Always curry favor with the people by sugaring them with appetizing speeches. The other demagogic arts are yours already: you have a "blood-shot" voice, a base birth, and the habits of an agorasnipe.[34]

Graft is the glue of democracy.[35]

Every government enacts laws beneficial to itself, a democracy to benefit the masses, a dictatorship to benefit the dictator.[36]

Law is reason without desire.[37]

[26] Thucy., I, 141. Trans. by Jowett.
[27] Thucy., II, 61. Trans. by Jowett.
[28] Thucy., II, 13.
[29] Thucy., III, 10. Trans. by Jowett.
[30] Thucy., V, III. Trans. by Jowett.
[31] Thucy., V, 89. Trans. by Jowett.
[32] Aristotle, *Politics*, III, 9. Trans. by Welldon.
[33] Plutarch, *Solon*, 14.
[34] Aristophanes, *Knights*, 215ff.
[35] Demades, quoted by Plutarch, *Plat. Quaest.*, 1011 B., Trans. by Shorey.
[36] Plato, *Republic*, I, 12 E.
[37] Aristotle, *Politics*, III, 16, 5.

There is no real state where the laws are not supreme. Law ought to be above all else.[38]

Zeus takes from a man the half of his virtue when the day of slavery comes upon him.[39]

Slaves need to be filled with good hopes even more than free men in order to keep them at their posts.[40]

The art of war, so far as it is natural, is in a sense a branch of the art of acquisition; for it includes the art of the chase which we are bound to use against beasts and human beings who will not submit to the rule ordained for them by nature.[41]

God made all men free: nature has made no man a slave.[42]

If you go security, ruin stands by your side.[43]

'Tis money makes the man.[44]

To avow poverty is no disgrace: the true disgrace is in doing nothing to avoid it.[45]

If a man is really and truly ignorant that confidence is the best capital for commercial enterprise, he must be ignorant of everything.[46]

All commodities which can be exchanged must in some degree be comparable, and it is to this end that money has been invented and serves as a sort of medium. . . . Money, then, is a kind of conventional exchangeable representative of demand. . . . Money is affected in the same way as other commodities, that is to say, its value fluctuates; still it is a great deal more stable than other things.[47]

The surface of any fluid at rest is the surface of a sphere the center of which is the center of the earth.[48]

[38] Aristotle, *Politics*, VI (IV), 4, 31.
[39] Homer, Od. XVII, 322.
[40] Xenophon, *Oecon.* V, 16. Trans. by Zimmern, *op. cit.*, p. 391.
[41] Aristotle, *Politics*, I, 8. Trans. by Welldon.
[42] Alcidamas, quoted by Scholiast on Arist., *Rhet.*, I, 13.
[43] Thales, quoted by Stobaeus, 3, 1. 17c.
[44] Alcaeus, *frg.* 49; Pindar, *Isthm.* 2, 15.
[45] Thucy., II, 40. Trans. by Jowett.
[46] Demosthenes, XXXVI, 44. Trans. by Zimmern, *op. cit.*, p. 307.
[47] Paraphrase of Aristotle, *Eth. Nik.* V, 10; IX, 1. *Politics*, I, 9.
[48] Archimedes, *On Floating Bodies*, I, 2 (Heath, p. 254).

The Heritage of the Roman Law

By

ARTHUR E. R. BOAK, Ph.D.*

It is extremely fitting that a great university, dedicated to the preservation and advancement of human knowledge, on the occasion of its bicentennial should pay tribute to the cultural legacy of Rome by selecting the Roman Law as a subject of discussion at one of its conferences, for in so doing it commemorates the fact that university life in Western Europe had its beginnings in faculties dedicated to the study of the Civil Law.

We may take it as generally admitted that the Roman Law is the outstanding creation of the Roman genius. To western civilization the Roman Empire bequeathed, as its two greatest legacies, the Christian Church and the Civil Law. But the former was not Roman in origin and only partially so in spirit, whereas the latter was not only Roman in origin but also predominantly so both in form and spirit. This will be abundantly clear from a brief perusal of its history from the codification in the form of the XII Tables in the fifth century B.C. to the Justinian codification of the sixth century A.D. Doubtless the idea of codifying the law was derived from contact with the Greeks, presumably those of South Italy, but the law of the XII Tables itself is substantially the customary law of a simple agricultural community, much more primitive in character than that of the contemporary Greek city-states with their diversified economic life and highly developed political institutions. And if the XII Tables, the *fons et origo* of the Civil Law, were thoroughly Roman in character, no less so was the manner of its growth during the period of the Republic.

Whereas other states have, in general, made good the inadequacies of their legal systems by passing new laws and amending existing codes, the Romans of the Republic resorted but little to legislation and neither made any additions to the

---

* Richard Hudson Professor of Ancient History and Chairman of the Department of History, University of Michigan.

XII Tables nor supplanted them by an improved codification. Instead, they resorted to interpretation and to the edictal power of the magistrates to repair injustices in the old law and to provide means of dealing with newly arising legal situations. These two methods deserve our consideration, for not only were they typically and uniquely Roman in character, but also they gave to the Roman Law certain of its strongest qualities. In Rome, the interpretation of the law was not left to the trial judges but became the prerogative of a special class of persons who held a position of unofficial, yet recognized authority in the community. These were the *iuris consulti* or *iuris prudentes*, men "learned in the law." At first, the right to give disinterested advice in legal matters was a prerogative of members of the college of pontiffs. Down to the middle of the third century B.C., such advice was given only to parties directly concerned in some dispute, but thereafter it was offered publicly to all who sought it. The right of interpretation ceased to be a monopoly of the pontiffs and passed to other citizens of experience, proven knowledge, and established reputation. In addition to giving advice upon request, these "jurisconsults' also offered informal instruction in the law to those who cared to listen to them through the discussion of practical legal problems and the elucidation of obscure provisions of the code. Finally, they proceeded to publish collections of responses to consultants, commentaries on the Civil Law, and other works which laid the foundations of an extensive juristic literature. Opinions of the jurisconsults came to have the weight of rules of law because judges deferred to them when cited by parties to a suit and the judges themselves could and did take counsel with the *prudentes* with respect to cases over which they presided. Here we see a group of men belonging to the governing class of the state, experienced in public life through the holding of magistracies and memberships in the Roman senate, devoting themselves to the study of the law and the disinterested dissemination of their knowledge not for purposes of gain, for they received no fees for their services, but from a high conception of duty and public responsibility, with honor as their sole reward. No parallel development is to be found in ancient or modern times. There is no doubt that from the latter part of the second century B.C., the jurisconsults as educated Romans were more or less influenced by Greek philosophic

concepts and that this influence made itself felt in their writings. But it affected their general ideas about the nature of law
and their attempts to systematize the Civil Law without caus-
ing them to introduce into it substantive provisions of Greek
law or Greek methods of legal procedure. Jurisprudence, the
science of law, was Roman in its origin, and remained predominantly Roman in theory and practice. Well might Cicero
boast of the superiority of the Roman Law and legal science
over those of all other peoples, and of the Greeks in particular.

Pari passu with the rise of Roman jurisprudence came the
development of the *ius honorarium* or magisterial law. This
took the form of edicts issued by certain magistrates, in particular the urban praetor and his colleague the *praetor peregrinus,* who administered the law for aliens in Rome. In these
annual edicts, the praetors set forth the rules which they would
follow in the administration of justice, stating the circumstances under which they would grant legal remedies for the
redress of grievances. By providing remedies not recognized by
the older law, the praetors both simplified the methods of legal
procedure and established rights that previously had been ignored. Since the incoming praetors regularly incorporated in
their edicts such parts of those of their predecessors as had stood
the test of experience, and since the edict of the praetor in
office was the only one which was effective, the praetorian edict
came to be a body of law of considerable magnitude, passed on
(*tralaticium*) from year to year and capable of indefinite growth.
This praetorian law was designed expressly, as Pomponius in-
forms us,[1] "to aid, to supplement, or to correct the civil law."
Here, again, we must recognize the activity of the jurisconsults.
For, apart from the fact that they themselves were one-time
holders of the praetorship, we may assume with confidence
that a good many of them sat as advisers on the *concilia* of other
praetors. By the end of the Republic, they were writing commentaries on the edict as well as upon the rest of the law. In
general, we may say that the tendency of the interpretations
of the *jurisprudentes* and of the provisions of praetorian law
was from strict adherence to the formalism of the earlier law
towards a higher conception of justice expressed in the term
aequitas, "fairness" or "equity."

At this point we must consider the influence exerted upon

[1] *Dig.* I. 1, 7. 1.

the Roman Law by legal practices and theories of law prevalent among other civilized peoples with whom the Romans came into contact as the result of their political expansion. Both the *praetor peregrinus* in Italy and the Roman governors in the provinces administered law to foreigners and had to decide what law they would enforce. Strictly the Civil Law applied to Roman citizens only, and could not be made use of in its entirety for aliens. Therefore the Romans had to devise a set of rules which could be enforced between Romans and foreigners and between foreigners of different states who appeared in the court of a Roman magistrate. The want was met by the magisterial edicts which developed a system of law applicable to free persons irrespective of their citizen states. And this system became part of the Civil Law by the incorporation of its rules in the edict of the urban praetor, particularly when this absorbed that of the *praetor peregrinus*. Here we see the origin of the Roman concept of the *ius gentium*, or Law of Nations, which appears in its definition as "that part of the law which we apply both to ourselves and to foreigners." There can be no doubt that this part of the Roman law incorporated ideas and practices of Greek or other foreign origin, but in the process they became thoroughly assimilated and did not remain an alien, intrusive element in the Civil Law. The case is somewhat different with the philosophic concept of the *ius gentium* as the law which "is common to all mankind." Whether in this view the *ius gentium* is to be identified with the Aristotelian Law of Nature (*ius naturale*) or to be interpreted as emanating from the latter, it was a concept lifted bodily from Greek philosophy. But, allowing that it influenced Roman thinking about the origin of certain legal and moral ideas and sanctions, it always remained extraneous to the body of the rules of Civil Law and did not affect them in a practical way.

By the close of the Republic the Roman Law had developed the main features which it retained throughout the Principate, which is known as the classical period of the law, because it was then that the law attained its highest degree of perfection in organization, in content, and in expression.

Under the Principate, praetorian law continued to exercise its influence in favor of equity alongside of statute law until the codification of the edict in 131 A.D. And after this date the imperial constitutions, in the form of *edicta, decreta,* and *responsa* continued the tradition, if not the form, of the earlier *ius honorarium*. But by far the greatest contribution was made by the jurisconsults. Their influence was enhanced by the recognition of an official right of giving legal opinions (*ius respondendi*) which was conferred by the emperors upon a select number of jurists. The replies of these men, delivered in written form, were recognized as authoritative and to them judges had to conform, whether they were requested by a party to a suit or by the judge himself. As before, the jurisconsults for the most part continued active in public affairs, occupied in the administration of justice and, particularly since Hadrian, serving as members of the imperial council. But the best part of their work was incorporated in their voluminous writings which included introductory manuals, commentaries on the Civil Law, on the Edict, or on the whole law, and collections of responses or opinions given on specific cases, real or hypothetical. How great was the output of legal writing in this period we may surmise from the statement that the works of the thirty-nine select jurists cited in Justinian's *Digest* were twenty times as voluminous as the *Digest* itself, and they constituted only a fraction of the legal literature published between 27 B.C. and 250 A.D. The jurists also extended their influence through instruction in the private law schools of the period, of which the most famous were at Rome and at Beirut. On the whole, we may say that the jurists of the Principate continued the practical traditions of their forerunners. They wrote case law, but at the same time they made a great advance in the appreciation and formulation of abstract legal principles and in logical organization, and developed an unsurpassed lucidity in the expression of legal ideas. They continued to liberalize the law by breaking down its formalism and relaxing its rigidity. Thus they gave to the Roman law the form and the quality which have provoked the respect and admiration of later ages.

From two main sources foreign ideas and usages continued to affect Roman Law. They were Stoic philosophy and the local law of the Hellenistic world. Stoic philosophy supplied the governing circles of Roman society with a practical code of ethics. It offered them a moral sanction for rules of law, and its broad humanitarianism is reflected in the increasing humaneness of the law as interpreted in Roman juric writings as well as in imperial constitutions. The gradual removal of the distinctions between Italy and the provinces, and the admission of large numbers of men from the Greek East to administrative positions in the imperial government and to the senate, inevitably produced a more liberal attitude towards legal practices of Greek origin. This showed itself specifically in the increased recognition of written documents in legal transactions, not merely as evidence but also as establishing certain contractual obligations.

While the Roman Law through its internal development was thus acquiring the character of a law adapted to universal use, it actually became in a very real sense a world law. Strictly speaking, it remained as it had been in early days the law for Roman citizens. But the conferment of Roman citizenship upon the whole of Italy by the time of Julius Caesar, and its subsequent extension to the provinces culminating in the *Constitutio Antoniniana* of 212 A.D., practically gave the Roman Law universal scope within the frontiers of the Empire. Granted that in certain regions Roman officials continued to recognize local law to a limited extent, we still can say that the Roman Law was the law of the civilized world to the west of the Parthian Empire.

In the middle of the third century A.D., the development of the Roman Law through the agency of specialists in the science and practice of law came to an end, and with the decay of jurisprudence legal literature ceased to be produced. The causes are to be found in the political anarchy of the third century, the accompanying economic and cultural decline, and the emergence of a totalitarian state in the form of a highly centralized autocracy. But the Roman Law which has come down to us is by no means the classical law contained in the voluminous juristic writings extant in the third century. A large part of this rich literature gradually disappeared in the following centuries for lack of interested and competent users; the rest lost its practical value as the result of Justinian's codification and so passed into oblivion. For the Middle Ages and recent times, therefore, the heritage of the Roman Law has been transmitted essentially in the *Institute*, *Code*, and *Digest* of Justinian, known collectively since the sixteenth century as the *Corpus Iuris Civilis*, a term which also includes Justinian's

Novels. To what degree, then, can we regard this codification as preserving the essential features of the earlier law?

In the first place we must admit that the *Digest*, which consists of extracts from the works of leading jurisconsults on the old Civil Law, the *ius honorarium*, and special legal topics, does not always reproduce the cited texts in their original form. In many cases the citations have been abbreviated, or have suffered interpolations at the hands of the board of editors working under the direction of Trebonian. Secondly, it is quite clear that the Justinianean law differs in many points from the Roman Law of the classical jurists. There is no longer any distinction between the *ius civile* and the *ius gentium;* the formalism of the old law has disappeared and along with it many antiquated usages; in family law the principle of agnatic relationship is no longer effective and the *patria potestas* has been broken down; intent takes precedence over form; the principle of equity is carried to unreasonable extremes; Christian influence is seen in the tendency to protect the weaker party even when in the wrong; and Greek practices have been adopted in respect to the wife's interest in her dowry, in the emphasis on written as against oral contracts, as well as in other respects.

How are we to account for these changes? Do they signify that we have in the *Corpus Iuris* a new legal system, predominantly oriental in character, dominated by Hellenistic practices and Christian ethics? Before answering these questions we must see by what process innovations were introduced into the law under the Autocracy of the fourth and following centuries. Almost the sole agency for affecting changes in the letter or the spirit of the law was imperial legislation issued in the various forms of constitutions. The *ius respondendi* had ceased to be granted, the jurisconsults as a class had disappeared, and no other group had come forward to carry on their tradition. Legal science had sunk to so low an ebb that even the use of authorities in judicial decisions had come to be regulated by the imperial law of citations issued in 426 B.C. which practically made the writings of Papinian, Paul, Ulpian, Gaius, and Modestine the only sources of effective Roman Law outside of the imperial constitutions. It is true that schools of law flourished at Rome (later at Ravenna), Constantinople, Beirut, and for a time also at Athens, Caesarea, and Alexandria. But these produced no legal literature worthy of note, and so they could not have affected directly the course of legal development Only when students of these schools attained to high administrative positions could they have influenced the tenor of imperial legislation in accordance with precepts enunciated by their former teachers. And so far as we know, it was only through the appointment of professors from the schools of Constantinople and Beirut to Trebonian's commission on codification that members of the faculties of the schools were ever in a position to introduce new doctrines into the body of the law. It is frequently assumed that the eastern schools were active agencies in the permeation of the law with Hellenistic ideas, but the general tendency of law schools is to be conservative, and it is possible to argue that they were responsible for the preservation of the inherited Roman features of the law as much as for their modification. After all, Papinian and Ulpian were both from Syria, and we do not look upon them as active agents in the Hellenization of the classical law. Such changes as were made must, therefore, be attributed to the legislation of individual emperors on the advice of the chief officers of state who were members of the imperial council, in particular the quaestors and the praetorian prefects. These men would doubtless be affected by the spread of Christian ethics as well as by practical problems arising in the administration of justice. But as a class bureaucrats are apt to be conservative rather than radical, and we can hardly see in them conscious innovators serving as protagonists of oriental as opposed to Roman legal principles and practices.

Nor can we credit the emperors themselves with a generally Hellenistic rather than Roman point of view. Even those who ruled from Constantinople regarded themselves as the heirs of a great Roman tradition and, although they had to express their ideas in terms of the changing culture of their own times, they regarded the preservation of their inheritance as the supreme aim of their government. And of this inheritance which distinguished the Roman from the barbarian world Roman Law necessarily formed a large part. This attitude certainly was that taken by Justinian. He sought to revive the Empire as it had been prior to the barbarian invasions; Latin was his native tongue and he maintained it as the official language of government; the *Code, Digest* and *Institutes* were all published in Latin, although he had to yield to existing conditions so far as to issue his later constitutions (*the Novels*) in Greek. In codifying the law, Justinian had to meet the practical needs of his day, and consequently he must include institutions and ideas which were actually recognized in the courts of the Empire. But at the same time he felt himself the guardian of the legal treasures of the past, and hoped to preserve them for future generations by incorporating them in the impregnable citadel of the *Digest*. There is no trace here of any intention to transform the classical law or supersede it by another of different origin and spirit.

It is a mistake, I believe, to label the period from Diocletian to the death of Justinian as "Byzantine," if by that term we mean something predominantly Greek rather than Roman, although it applies well to the East Roman Empire from the end of the sixth century. And I believe that the same objection holds in the case of the Roman Law to the date of the codification of the *Corpus*. In recent years there has been a tendency to overemphasize "oriental" elements in the Autocracy as organized by Diocletian and Constantine, and a justifiable reaction is now taking place. A parallel occurs in the case of Roman Law, where Riccobono and his followers have succeeded in showing that a great deal in the *Digest* that formerly was attributed to Hellenistic influences is only a logical evolution of the classical Roman Law as interpreted by the jurists of the early third century, and modified by the abolition of the formulary process in favor of that of the *cognitio*.

If this point of view is correct, the law of the Justinianean *Corpus*, which experienced a miraculous revival in Western Europe and has so profoundly influenced the development of later legal thinking that it has become an ineradicable element in our modern civilization, embodies to a predominant degree the highest achievements of Roman jurisprudence.

SELECT BIBLIOGRAPHY

Declareuil, J. Rome the Law-giver. New York, 1926.
von Ihring, R. Geist des römischen Rechts auf den verschiedenen Stufen seiner Entwicklung, 5th ed. Leipzig, 1891.
Jolowicz, H. F. Historical Introduction to the Study of Roman Law. Cambridge, 1932.

Riccobono, S. "Fasi et Fattori dell evoluzione del diritto romano," Melanges Cornil, II (1926), 237-309.

Sherman, C. P. Roman Law in the Modern World. Boston, 1917.

Vinogradoff, P. Roman Law in Mediaeval Europe. London and New York, 1909.

de Zuleuta, F. "The Science of Law," in The Legacy of Rome, ed. by Cyril Bailey. Oxford, 1924.

The Medieval Pattern of Life

By

EDWARD K. RAND, Ph.D., LL.D., Litt.D.*

MEDIEVAL culture, like most cultures, is both a unity and a blend. The period in which it is displayed, like all historical periods, has a definite character, easily recognized when it is in full flower, but the more one defines its essence, the more its essence oozes away. The more exactly one sets its beginning and its end, the more one will erase such demarcations and try again.

One delimitation I shall have to make at the start, in ruling out from our medieval itinerary the Eastern world and the culture of Byzantium. That is a most summary proceeding. East and West, despite their eventual, but by no means complete, separation are but different facets of the same gem. They present in a novel and complicated and most interesting form, the antithesis, and the synthesis, of Greece and Rome. Beginning with the Emperor Hadrian, we have one Roman Empire and one Roman literature comprising two sorts—Greek and Latin. Beginning with Constantine, the Roman Empire located itself in the East, at Byzantium. Its character was Roman, its language Greek; and its citizens were ʽΡωμαῖοι. Its culture was Graeco-Oriental; its literature was startlingly conservative. The great tradition crushed popular themes in the vernacular, such as ultimately flourished in the West. And yet great works appeared in history, in theology, in scholarship, and in the poetry of liturgy. The old Greek classics, poetry and prose, which excepting certain philosophical works had vanished in the West, reposed in the East on library shelves and still were read and studied, though without vital effect on the literature of the day. The Byzantine Period came abruptly to an end—here is indeed one date of demarcation—in 1453, when Constantinople fell before the Turks, and scholars brought the treasures

* Pope Professor of Latin, Harvard University.

of Greek letters to Italy, there to come to life again and to give a fresh impulse to the movement that revived them.

But our theme is centered in the West. Here some who sadly follow the decline and fall of the Roman Empire in its original abode and think of Alaric, the Völkerwanderungen, and the rise of the Papacy, are apt to regard the Middle Ages as the period when the civilization of ancient Greece and Rome sank to an evening bed beyond the horizon, when religious intolerance held liberal thought in an iron grip, when scientific investigation was chiefly concerned with the number of angels that could dance on the point of a pin. I have heard medieval philosophy defined as a parenthesis in the history of thought. Your typical scholastic is pictured once for all in the immortal Hudibras:

> He could raise scruples dark and nice
> And after solve 'em in a trice,
> As if Divinity had catched
> The itch, on purpose to be scratched.

And Mr. Santayana, more delicately, but no less pungently, likens the schoolman's ratiocination to

> A dream's trouble or the speech of birds,

and finds nothing in his volume now but

> The garnered husks of his disuséd words.

Such a period of human civilization would appropriately be ushered in by Goths and Vandals and Pope Gregory the Great, who thought his Bishop Desiderius indulged too much in Virgil and who declared that the Word of God was not subject to the rules of Donatus the grammarian. Thus the period might end for the West, as for the East, with the fall of Constantinople in 1453, when those learned exiles to whom I have referred brought Greek literature once more to Italy. Or, since a certain amount of Greek had infiltrated into the West before that time, one might with some call Petrarch "the first modern man" and place him on the boundary line. He had, indeed, although no knowledge of Greek, a pathetic hankering for it; his *Tenth Eclogue* contains eulogies of some of the famous Greek authors, phrased in terms that he culled from Roman critics like Quintilian.

Supposing that Petrarch heads the Renaissance, one who accepts the picture of the Middle Ages that I have sketched might well regard the wealthy culture of Greece and Rome as the legacy that they received, the impoverishment of all that wealth as their own contribution to humanity, and as their bequest to us, merely a dreadful accumulation of absurdities that cried for reform, and got it in the humanism of the Renaissance and the rise of modern science. The unfaithful servant had hidden all ten talents in a napkin, and now in our enlightened age he is cast out into utter darkness.

But such a view of medieval civilization, although in some quarters it still does thrive, has in our day become rare. It fades before the poetic humanism of Dante, whose subject, as he said, was man, and whose poetry, like his imaginative *mise-en-scène*, sounds the depths and rises to the heights of the human spirit. It fades before the literary humanism of a John of Salisbury, who cites his ancients in the free and easy fashion of an essayist of the age of Anne, and before the philological and scientific humanism of Roger Bacon, who consulted original texts in Greek, Hebrew, and Arabic, and anticipated the laboratory in his simple experiments in physics. It fades before the jovial verse and the exquisite lyrics of the Goliards, disciples of wine, women, and song, and before the beauty of Catholic liturgy, fitted to the music called Gregorian as hand to glove. It fades before Chaucer's universal stage of human joys and griefs, ribaldry and devoutness—a mirror of our life second in scope and brightness only to that of Shakespeare, with true reflections of both Griselda and the Wife of Bath, portraits by an artist self-possessed, who viewed them both with sympathy.

With these discoveries as a start, one may course the Middle Ages and make many more, in letters, in philosophy, in poetry, and in art. One will find, for example, in certain satirists of the age of John of Salisbury, like Walter Map, and Nigel Wireker and John himself, meet companions for Aristophanes and Horace and Ovid, for Rabelais and Erasmus, for Fielding and Thackeray at a banquet of the wits. A satirist of another type, Jean de Meun, presents, in his part of the *Roman de la Rose*, a deep debate on nature, in which the contestants are medieval counterparts of Ovid and Boethius.

In philosophy greater names will follow the subtle Irish thinker John the Scot, but none excel him in the poetry of his

Neoplatonic flights into the realm above existence. Like Cicero he wrote verse and, like him, even Greek verse, but the poetry of soul which both of them at times possessed finds its normal vehicle not in verse but in a melodious prose. In the middle of the period is the vain and daring Abelard, composer of love-songs in his native French and of human letters to his Eloise. In works of literary charm he proposes novel solutions of theological questions, collects the opposing opinions of the Fathers in a treatise called "Yes and No," and mediates in philosophy between the Realist and the Nominalist schools. The Age of Abelard sees a new birth of Platonism, about which, and about Aristotle's influence, we are learning more and more. The twelfth century with its stirring thought and its merry poetry, is, as our beloved Haskins taught us, another Renaissance; indeed, so numerous are these oases of Renaissance becoming that for them one can hardly see the medieval desert. No part of the field of medieval culture calls forth more fruitful publications year by year than the philosophy of the Schoolmen. We are given new views of its entire stretch from Boethius, who sets the method, to St. Thomas Aquinas, who completes its terminology in a fashion begun by Cicero, makes over Aristotle in a gigantic system of Christian philosophy, and shows himself a poet in his hymns and in his Mass for Corpus Christi.

To turn to poetry, if one misses in the whole range of French or English letters of modern times something to match the epic strength of Homer, it will be found in two medieval poems, *Beowulf* and the *Chanson de Roland*, which, like the poems of Homer are not primitive lays, but the works of artists of deep and tragic feeling, who knew their Virgil and who can set forth in an ancient episode, the one the vigor of ancient Britain, the other the heroic soul of France.

In art we need not dwell on the glories of architecture Gothic or Romanesque, equally fit houses for religious awe, nor on the master-painter of Dante's day, his Giotto, with whom the course of a great art starts from the heights. In reality Giotto and his precursor Cimabue stand also at the end of a long development, preserved to us not on canvas and only rarely on a wall, but in sculpture and the inside of books. For manuscripts from the beginning of the Middle Ages delight the eye with pictures and decorative borders and initials which often harbor figures of great beauty, or solemnity, or mock solemnity, or grotesque humor, a companion for that of gargoyles. Or a monk's fancy may make his fingers stray to the margins to embellish them with impromptu designs or figures of human beings, fair women not neglected. All this was but an escape for the fixity of his normal mind, even as the merry parody of solemn hymns in Goliardic songs or that of the sacred liturgy in a very financial Gospel of Mark, the German mark, is but the other side of piety. The medieval mind, like that of Aristophanes and that of Homer could play as well as pray. It is a balance hard to keep; the Puritans could make too much of one and Ovid of the other.

In the art thus treasured for us in medieval books the script must not be forgotten, or distinguished from ornaments and pictures as though they were the art and it were but the writing. That makes it trivial and makes them false. They both are part of the complete art of the book. On a page in the Gospels of Lothair, one of the masterpieces of the School of Tours in the middle of the ninth century, we find only the words of the beginning of the *Gospel of St. John,* written in the shortest of lines: *In principio erat verbum et verbum erat apud Deum et Deus erat verbum.* At the left, running from top to bottom, stands in a graceful figure the initial I; at the right two medallions are put and two at the bottom, to guard the text. The whole is an act of adoration. The words are its soul and the ornament its liturgy. The script, in a stately beauty and simplicity, with monumental capitals for the first line and large rounded uncials for the rest, is all thought out in terms of art and worship.

This script of Tours is an irrefragable proof of the reality of what some scholars have been reluctant to admit, the Carolingian Renaissance. The poets of the day thought of their age as a return to ancient Rome and of their monarch as a second Augustus; and so he aimed to be. With the help of competent masters, Paulus Diaconus, Alcuin, Theodulf, he sought to recover good Latin style, to find true texts of the ancient authors, of Holy Scripture and of the monastic rule of St. Benedict; he sought both to weed the liturgy of its accretions and to enrich it with new offices. His efforts are pictured for us in the script of Tours.

For all over France the form of minuscule employed for the

body of a work, based on the ancient Roman cursive, was gaining in clarity and beauty and insensibly losing its cursive traits; but at Tours, I think most probably under Alcuin, when he retired to the monastery of St. Martin's for the last eight years of his life, a deliberate attempt was made to replace the current forms of the larger sorts of letters—capitals and uncials— with those observed in ancient books and on ancient monuments. For capitals, those of early imperial inscriptions and the earliest manuscripts of Virgil and other ancient authors were studied. Uncials were no longer of the debased and decorated sort that flourished in the seventh and eighth centuries; they regained at a bound the large simplicity of the ancient style. Semiuncials, too, were reformed with the help of the oldest manuscripts containing this variety. In all these forms, the new creations equaled and even surpassed the beauty of their models. They were used not for the text, as before, but in a stately hierarchy at the beginning of works or of their main divisions. For minuscules, which had no ancient prototype, a large and elegant form was perfected from which all cursive traits were banished; one may dare to say that this is what ancient minuscule would have looked like had there been a real minuscule then.

The achievements of Tours were paralleled by similar, yet different, successes in other scriptoria of France. An intense and fruitful rivalry prevailed. The genus of the sorts developed in these different centers is aptly called by paleographers Caroline. It proceeded to a quiet conquest of the varieties in other lands, no less significant in human history, and far more pleasant to contemplate, than the devastating progress of a Genghis Khan. Germany, North Italy, the British Isles, and Spain successively yielded to the peaceful penetration of a style of script. This Caroline hand, with its finished rotundity, accompanied and illustrated the growth of Romanesque art, until at the end of the twelfth century it felt the new spirit of Gothic and of the new philosophy of the Schools. Its letters shot up, like tiny Gothic spires; later they yielded to the tendency to elaborate and over-adorn. They then were brought back to their ancient simplicity by scribes of the Renaissance. Again we see a title for an age, disputed by some today, which, as in Charlemagne's time, is written plain in humanistic manuscripts and the Roman style of early printed books. Here is indeed a conspicuous legacy contributed by the Middle Ages to our times; for the forms of letters, large and small, in books and papers today depend in direct lineage on a happy invention, a re-creation, of early medieval France. The most fiery critic of the Middle Ages is courteously furnished by them with the necessary letter-forms for penning his indictment.

With these scant suggestions of the fertility and the humanity of arts and letters in the Middle ages, let us revert to our initial quest of the boundaries and the character of medieval culture. It all becomes easy if we consider our Middle Ages as a tree that waxed from a tiny seed.

The seed was the Christian faith, sown by Jesus of Nazareth. It produced what John Buchan, one of the noblest men of our generation, declared in his book on Augustus the greatest of historical convulsions. The Savior of mankind brought no new plan for human government or for human society. His followers rendered unto Caesar the things that were Caesar's, serving God and honoring the King when the King was Nero. But by being citizens of a kingdom not of this world, they found that their new allegiance insensibly transformed all life and settled human problems. As the Church spread, it had to justify itself before the state of Rome, to whom it seemed a band of traitors. Tertullian asserted its higher loyalty to the monarch when, refusing to worship him, it prayed for him to God. Its spokesmen reckoned more and more with a growing class of enlightened men who admired its unshakable faith, but who could not forego the noble way of life and thought transmitted to them by the poets and philosophers of ancient Greece and Rome. Clement of Alexandria and Minucius Felix, Lactantius and Ambrose, Jerome and Augustine, Basil, Gregory of Nyssa, Gregory of Nazianzus, and a host of others chronicled in a memorable letter of St. Jerome, followed the example set by St. Paul in his sermon on Mars' Hill and proved to their pagan friends that Christian doctrine depends in part on great human truths that "some of their own poets" had also proclaimed. Step by step a new and Christian humanism was formed, which reinterpreted the liberal arts and enlarged them with new literary works of pagan form and Christian contents. The goal, as in the old days, was philosophy, the training of the mind to think with the help of the best thought of old, but to preserve at all costs the truths that in the light of the Incarnation and with the guidance of the Holy Spirit, the Church had with increasing clarity proclaimed. This harmony of old and new was the achievement of the great fourth century, which laid the foundation in many ways for medieval culture.

The ancient liberal arts and the Christian Catholic Church— these in a word were the great bequests of antiquity to the western Middle Ages. What were these liberal arts? Implicit in Plato's teaching, described most liberally and attractively by Cicero, they were at last precisely defined; they were embraced in the familiar seven, a *trivium* of grammar, rhetoric, and dialectic, a *quadrivium* of arithmetic, geometry, astronomy, and music. This program of arts has been variously misunderstood.

First, it has seemed to some a dry affair, and today most superficial. But *grammatica* included not only grammar but the reading of the best literature and the understanding of its historical background. Rhetoric is a term so repulsive today that it is hardly mentioned in our college programs, except in Catholic colleges, where it thrives as lustily as it did in Puritan Harvard of the seventeenth century and our other colonial colleges. Dialectic is likewise a distasteful term, though once most innocent and most enlivening. It means conversation, philosophical conversation, laboratory practice in philosophy, truly a most wholesome discipline; it is the Socratic method of stirring young minds to think and to formulate their thoughts.

In the mathematical and scientific *quadrivium*, music appears with the rest, because of its close association with mathematics since Plato's time. The famous *De Musica* of Boethius would be understood, or enjoyed, by few musicians today, and yet it was the accepted textbook on music at Oxford down into the eighteenth century. Astronomy of course left much to do for Galileo and Kepler and Copernicus and Shapley, yet at least the heliocentric theory was not unknown in antiquity, and John the Scot, as has recently been shown, has interesting deviations from the geocentric doctrine. This science of the stars, or heavenly bodies, was not divorced from a general philosophy of nature, or what we call science today. The crown of the arts was philosophy, which was broad enough, as Cicero defines it, to include the quest of all things human and divine; ethics and political science and physics as well as metaphysics lay within its scope. It was accompanied at every step by rhetoric, which had been reconciled with philosophy by Aristotle and by Cicero, who followed in his steps. Let us, to be modern, speak not of dialectic and rhetoric, but of thought and expression. In the lists of Commencement theses at Harvard College, some few of which have survived from the seventeenth century, one category of subjects is called technology, which embraced not the useful sciences pursued at the Massachusetts Institute of that name, but studies of the significance of the τέχναι, the liberal arts; in a word, technology meant the principles of education. In more than one of these theses the idea is emphasized that the pursuit of the arts will train the mind to think and the tongue to speak—an unexcelled ideal of education, particularly since for the ancients and our forefathers thought and expression came not from the void, but were fed by great poetry, oratory, history, and philosophy.

Moreover, philosophy was not merely the goal towards which the arts conducted the learner, not merely a promised land of milk and honey after dry stretches of "factual" information had been wandered through. When Boethius wrote his treatises on arithmetic, geometry, and music, he was not turning aside from his higher studies, in the manner of a scholar today, who sometimes, to perform a public service or replenish a cobwebbed purse, will lend his authority to a set of school textbooks. Boethius was dealing with subjects that were of the very woof of philosophy itself, without an intimate knowledge of which nobody could be said to think straight. This conception of the immediate relation of the arts to the process of philosophic thought was transmitted by Boethius to the Middle Ages.

Another authority was Martianus Capella, who quaintly called his treatise on the liberal arts "The Marriage of Mercury and Philology," meaning thereby that very partnership of philosophy and rhetoric inherent in the liberal arts since Aristotle. In his commentary on Martianus, a work which we at last, thanks to a young American scholar, may read in its complete form, John the Scot explains the phrase *perceptae artes* as those that are estimated by the common perception of the mind (*communi animi perceptione*). They are learned for their own sake that they may end in a habit of the mind, or mental condition (*ut in habitum mentis perveniant*). And while they are being thus learned, these very disciplines are perceived by the mind alone and are not taken from any other source but are naturally

understood in the mind.[1] Thus, we see, the arts are all transmuted into mental texture. Whether this description will prove
acceptable to modern paedogogical psychology or not, it suits
my present purpose admirably, an innocent purpose, after all,
merely to show that education as practised in the Middle Ages
was no affair of rote but was designed to stimulate the learner's
mind to thought. Alcuin could even profess to inebriate his
pupils with the wine of the seven arts.

It has also been thought that the *trivium* and the *quadrivium*
included in a nutshell the sum total of all that there was to
know—the *omne scibile*. That is not so. The arts were not an
encyclopedia, but a preface to further inquiry. The mind was
trained by them to think and the tongue to speak. Worlds of
thought remained for exploration, and worlds of language to
chronicle the new discoveries. Encyclopedias there were, by St.
Isidore and Hrabanus Maurus, and comprehensive works like
the several *Mirrors* of Vincent of Beauvais, including his *Mirror
of History*. There were collections of opinions or judgments of
matters legal and theological, of which the names of Gratian
and Peter Lombard, Abelard's less dangerous pupil, are typical.
There were collections of fine bits of poetry or noble philosophic thoughts culled from authors ancient and modern, Christian and pagan; one of these is exalted in Chaucer's *Meliboeus*
into a Canterbury Tale.

Although we may sometimes regard the Middle Ages with a
bit of envy, as a very simple age, unaware of the intellectual
complexities brought by the very wealth of science of which we
are justly proud, the medieval mind contemplated a mass of
problems quite as intricate, which are well mirrored in a chapter
of John Livingston Lowes' golden little book on Chaucer. When
we say that the Middle Ages possessed no science, we are thinking of the science of our day or of the early days of the University of Pennsylvania, guided in part by your Prometheus, who

eripuit fulmen caelo sceptrumque tyrannis.

But we must not forget the medieval preoccupation with astrology, which to them had its serious as well as its sensational as-

[1] Perceptae igitur artes dicuntur liberales quoniam propter se ipsas adipiscuntur
et discuntur, ut in habitum mentis perveniant; et dum perveniunt ad habitum
mentis antequam perveniunt, ipsae disciplinae sola ipsa anima percipiuntur nec
aliunde assumuntur sed naturaliter in anima intelliguntur.

pects, and indeed might be called the pure or speculative branch, with an immediate relation to the body's "humors" and thus to physiology, whereas astronomy was the humbler, descriptive affair. Though the science of one age may become the myth of another, it feeds the scientific mind with plenty of complexities so long as its reign endures.

Let us also not forget—indeed let us put in the foreground of medieval intellectual activities—the pursuit of allegorical interpretation not only of the Scriptures but of pagan literature and of the whole world of nature, its birds, beasts, and fish, and stones—verily there were sermons in stones abundantly. All this seems child's play to the enlightened scientific intellect of our time, nor do many Classical scholars find profit—at least there is amusement—in *Ovide Moralizé*. But although reason can discern no Jacob's ladder connecting stones with the upper realms of thought, the medieval mind leaped nimbly from one to the other and on arriving was free to roam.

Gone is that irrecoverable mind

indeed, but it was not a shackled mind. It operated under a set of large and controlling scientific assumptions, like the human mind in any age, as Henry Osborn Taylor has brilliantly set forth. The process of observing facts, or what looked like facts, and of drawing conclusions on the basis of their evidence was the same then as now. And the motive for philosophic thought, then as now, was proclaimed by Lupus Servatus, an eminent humanist back in the ninth century; *propter se ipsam appetenda sapientia*—seek philosophy for herself alone.

Beyond the arts, with philosophy their crown, lay theology for the learned clerk of the Middle Ages, as the life of the statesman was the normal career for an educated gentleman in Cicero's day. For cultivated laymen, who had no thought of Holy Orders, the faith and practice of the Catholic Church preceded, accompanied, and completed the training of the gentleman. For all of these life had a meaning, because it offered unity, though not a static unity, and progress without a tearing up of the foundations. The guidance of the Church in every land of Europe and its use of Latin for the liturgy provided a common basis for works and faith and worship everywhere. The Latin language also secured this feeling of community among writers in the different countries. It was the age of wandering scholars and cosmopolitans. Literature in the vernacular did not grow in a field separate from Latin, though it is sometimes so treated in our university programs. It was no protest against Latin, but, in the main, a resort to a free and popular and romantic treatment of themes both ancient and modern which appeared just as clearly in certain works in Latin. Above all, the Middle Ages were, indeed, in the traditional phrase, the ages of faith, when Plato's dream seemed to have come true—not that all kings were philosophers, but that both the minds of the cultivated and the souls of humbler folk had a vision of the one in the many as a part of normal living. Was everybody obedient unto this heavenly vision? By no means. It was a human age. In the medieval panorama, as Coulton has learnedly set forth, transgressions against the virtues cardinal, both pagan and Christian, abounded. Lowly motives went into the construction of sacred things. Bigotry and obscurantism thwarted the humanity of the liberal arts. These black spots we must not blink. But they were transgressions of ideals; the ideals transgressed remained. And ideals rather than transgressions, to my thinking, are the historian's ultimate concern. At least nobody in the Middle Ages proposed, as has today been proposed and terrifically exemplified, a new philosophy of life, a "realism" most unmedieval, in which *superbia* has been replaced by *humilitas* as the most deadly of the seven deadly sins.

This, then, is the legacy that the Middle Ages passed on to the coming generation, a pattern of life based upon ancient culture and the Catholic faith. This pattern lacks features conspicuous in the life of Greece and Rome, but it possessed beauties, thanks primarily to Christianity, that antiquity had lacked.

It is well that my instructions did not require me to consider what has become of this medieval legacy today. That would be a large order for the minute that remains. Perhaps I might have suggested for your contemplation two great figures of somewhat similar greatness—Martin Luther and President Eliot. Let me venture to suggest that if modern civilization is to endure, it must either return to the medieval plan or work out some new pattern of life on the basis of the old-time virtues, in which human eyes amidst the clouding of the many may still make out the one.

The Institutional Pattern of the Middle Ages: Inheritance and Legacy

By

ARTHUR C. HOWLAND, Ph.D., Litt.D.*

THE combination of change and continuity in all history makes it impossible to set definite time limits to such periods as ancient, medieval, and modern history. The beginning and the end of the Middle Ages cannot be fixed by mere dates. A geographical division of European history is in many ways as satisfactory and as accurate as a chronological division, and on that basis one might define ancient history as dealing with the affairs of the Mediterranean basin only; medieval history, with the interests of central and western Europe; and modern history as concerned with the affairs of the whole world.

Such geographical categories, like those based on years or centuries, lack definiteness and precision; but considering the Middle Ages as the period of a thousand years or more following the decline of the Roman Empire, it is obvious that what survived of that empire constituted the institutional heritage of the following age.

In the political realm the legacy of Rome was the conception of a universal state, including all civilized mankind, possessing absolute authority over all its subjects and exercising the right to control and direct all their activities not only in secular affairs, but also, when necessary, in religious matters. The Roman Empire was, in fact, a totalitarian state including the whole Mediterranean area. This institution was unable to survive the impact of another type of society, the tribal organization common to the barbarian peoples outside the empire. The tribe exalted the interests of a small, related group above the interests of all others and hence sought the extension of its own power over neighboring groups. It was a self-centered and parochial, not a cosmopolitan, society. The tribal concept led to

* Curator of the Henry Charles Lea Library and Emeritus Professor of History, University of Pennsylvania.

the establishment of a variety of barbarian kingdoms in western Europe and to the collapse of the elaborate administrative system that had enabled the government of the empire to exercise its authority. Politically, the establishment of these Germanic kingdoms marks the beginning of the Middle Ages.

But the ideal of a universal state still survived and found expression in two ways: through the medieval empire and through the Christian church.

As to the first of these, Charlemagne's revival of the Roman Empire was a genuine but vain attempt to reëstablish a common political organization for western Europe. The second attempt to revive the empire, that undertaken by Otto in the tenth century, rested, however, on a different basis—the superior power of a single tribal kingdom. This destroyed its claims to universality by identifying the empire with a racial group in central Europe. The later Germanic emperors pursued two irreconcilable aims, a universal state and a German national state, and they failed in both. Though later ages inherited a simulacrum of the Roman Empire it became only one, and that not the strongest, of the various political divisions of Europe.

The principle of universality found more effective expression in the Latin or Western church, which came to embody many of the characteristics of the old empire: such as the union of all people in a single organization, the exercise of absolute authority over its members, an elaborate system of administration culminating in a supreme head, a common legal and judicial system, and even territorial divisions based on those of the empire. So, too, a totalitarian principle analogous to that of the Roman Empire was adopted by the church. Far from confining itself to the religious field, the church put forward the claim to supervise and control secular government as well, thus envisaging the ultimate political direction of all Europe. This ideal, expressed so clearly in the bull *Unam Sanctam* of Boniface VIII, was shattered by the power of the rising national states of Europe and suffered the same fate as did the Holy Roman Empire. Thus the ideal of a universal state remained peculiar to the Middle Ages and was not passed on to later times.

In its place a new political pattern was taking form in the later Middle Ages, that of the national state—an hereditary monarchy governing a restricted territory whose inhabitants recognized certain common interests and loyalties at variance

with those of neighboring states. The genesis of this later form
of political organization is found in the old tribal kingdom
whose ruler, supported only by followers pledged to personal
fidelity, had attempted to govern his territory without any efficient administrative system. Hence this type of tribal kingdom
had broken down under attacks from without and rivalries
within. The tribal king did not disappear entirely. He retained
his royal title, but what political power survived fell into the
hands of feudal nobles, each governing the tenants of his own
estate. Though the royal office survived in name, the king in
reality became merely a feudal noble with a primacy of honor
rather than of authority.

The minute subdivisions of government characteristic of the
feudal régime remained endurable only so long as society continued to be almost exclusively agricultural. But the revival of
other forms of economic activity in the later Middle Ages created a class of people whose interests were no longer purely
local. Townsmen required a broader political organization than
that furnished by feudalism and so turned to the old tribal
kingship, not yet extinct, as the basis for that larger organization. With the support of the new industrial classes and with
the help of the money revenues they provided, a new and wider
political organization grew up around the king. As usual when
looking for the origins of an institution, it is possible to indicate
a variety of elements which contributed to the growth of the
new national kingship: the king's early claims to tribal loyalty;
his later claim, as feudal suzerain, to the fidelity of his vassals;
the memories of sovereignty handed down from Roman times—
all these supported by the power derived from a hired soldiery
and an administrative system of his own devising.

The satisfactory functioning of this new type of state was
measured by the number and quality of the royal officials whose
duty it was to bring the central government into direct contact
with the individual. The growing need of money revenue for
administration and for war brought the state into competition
with the church, whose vast organization also required large
revenues from the same sources of wealth. In no other respect
did the rivalry of the universal church and the national state
become so bitter as in their competition for an adequate income.
In this struggle the victory of the state not only marked the
end of the church's claim to control secular governments, but

led ultimately to the formation of separate state churches in many parts of Europe.

Thus the medieval inheritance of a unified society was lost. A common religious organization was replaced by rival churches; a universal empire was transformed into a group of independent and rival states whose disputes were not subject to settlement by a superior power, but only to the arbitrament of war. Certain parts of Europe, however, failed to attain national statehood by the close of the Middle Ages: such as Germany, where tribal psychology retained too great a vitality to permit the growth of a central government; or Italy and the Netherlands, where city life became too vigorous to require royal support, while economic rivalries prevented union on any other basis.

Turning to the economic aspects of the Middle Ages, we find but one important institution carried over from Roman times to a later period—the great landed estate, which continued to shape the pattern of nearly all economic life for centuries and underwent little change until the advent of a money economy at a later time. The old Roman estate had been cultivated as a unit by a body of dependent tenants partly slaves and partly freemen, but both subject to the complete control of the landlord. As city life declined, these estates had become self-contained areas which provided for all the needs of their inhabitants, only the proprietors having contacts with the outside world.

It required but few modifications to transform such an institution into its medieval counterpart. The Roman villa becomes the medieval manor; the Roman proprietor, the feudal lord. The two classes of workers, slave and free, tend to merge into the single class of serfs through recognition of the slave's right of possession of his holding, and the freeman's loss of even that shadow of protection once furnished by the imperial government. The entire body of tenants become subject to the lord's exploitation, limited only by his own interest and the custom of the manor. Another change in the Roman institution is the final disappearance of the profit motive in agriculture and the adoption of cultivation for subsistence only. On the legal side a different conception of ownership also emerged. In place of the Roman principle of the proprietor's complete *dominium* over his land, subject only to the claims of the state, there grew up in the Middle Ages the conception of joint rights of ownership of land, rights shared by tenants, landlord, and suzerain.

The Roman and modern conception of absolute ownership disappeared.

Such changes, though modifying, did not materially alter the pattern of agricultural life from Roman days down to the time when new forms of economic activity, by introducing the use of money, gradually broke down the manorial organization.

The more varied activities of the later Middle Ages led to the creation of new economic institutions, some peculiar to that period and others of great importance in modern times. The cessation of barbarian inroads into Europe in the tenth century, and the greater stability of feudal relations after that time, permitted a slow but steady growth of population. More settled conditions, combined with certain technological advances in agriculture, freed an increasing number of the population from the cultivation of the soil and turned their energies to the satisfaction of less immediate wants, both intellectual and material. The revival of learning and the revival of industry go hand in hand. The production of goods for sale rather than for the use of the producer created a new economic class free from the feudal lord's control, though not entirely free from his exploitation. The distribution of these goods over a wide area required a common medium of exchange and introduced the use of money to supplement the older nature economy, thereby setting in motion new impulses that affected all aspects of medieval life.

The early lack of government protection forced the producers and distributors of goods in self-defense to devise their own form of organization, which took the shape of the medieval guild. The guild presents three important characteristics, all closely related: absolute monopoly in a particular industry in a given town; restriction in numbers; and equality among the members of the same guild. These characteristics conform to the medieval ideal of a non-competitive economic society, an ideal exemplified in the internal organization of the manor as well as in that of the guild. The restraint of competition tended to secure the solidarity of the group and to maintain the principles of mutual responsibility and mutual support necessary for the protection of guild interests. Moreover, it conformed to the attitude of the church, whose doctrine of brotherly love condemned the idea of gaining personal advantage out of the needs of one's neighbor; whose insistence on contentment with the lot assigned each man by Providence seemed incompatible with personal ambition; and whose ideal of poverty appeared inconsistent with exceptional economic prosperity. Thus both self-interest and religion joined in condemning competition among those following the same occupation.

This non-competitive form of society was able to survive only as long as economic conditions remained relatively stable. The increasing demand for goods and the rapid expansion of markets which took place toward the close of the Middle Ages created opportunities for greater rewards to individual enterprise than to group activities. The advantages awaiting superior energy and ability overcame the ideal of equality within the guild. Consequently, the competitive instinct could not be restrained, and money began to accumulate in the hands of fortunate individuals. This wealth was used in ways that weakened and ultimately destroyed the guild system. In some cases a minority of guild members secured privileges giving them a disproportionate share of the profits of an industry and reducing the majority of the workers to the status of wage-earners. Among the merchants, whose wide contacts had always made guild control difficult, great family fortunes led to the private organization of commerce or to the establishment of banking houses that undertook the transfer of funds from one country to another, collected taxes for the church and for secular rulers, and financed the wars of the period. Before the close of the Middle Ages economic life had already lost many of its medieval characteristics and had become highly competitive. It had, in fact, acquired many of the forms of a capitalistic society, and it was these forms, rather than the guild organizations, that constituted the economic pattern carried over from the medieval to the modern world.

In looking at those institutions that are regarded as specifically medieval, one characteristic may be noted that was common to most of them—the greater significance of the whole than of any of its parts, the emphasis on the group instead of on the units of which it was composed. This is seen in the persistence of the ideal of the universal state in face of the disintegration of feudalism and in spite of the growth of separate kingdoms in Europe. It is seen in the church, a single, corporate body whose absolute spiritual authority could not be questioned by the independent judgment of any of its members. In the economic field the same emphasis on the group rather than the individual is seen in the organization of work on the manor and in the rules governing the activities of the guild.

As the medieval gradually merged into the modern world, the sense of mutual responsibility within a group, and the obligation of its members to conform to a common pattern, began to give way before the attractions of individual initiative and personal ambition. Politically, the decline of the medieval spirit is shown by the development of the independent kingdoms of Europe; in religion, by the breaking away of the various Protestant churches from the universal church of earlier times. The same weakening of medieval ideals is seen in economic life. In agriculture, the use of money enabled the peasant to pay a money rent instead of personal services for his land. This freed him from the direct supervision of the landlord as well as from the fixed routine of manorial cultivation previously dictated by his fellow tenants. In western Europe serfdom began to disappear and the capable peasant seized the opportunity of improving his own condition without regard to the fortunes of his fellow workers. Similarly, the craftsman of the town, long bound by the rules of his guild, finally broke through its restrictions. In the resulting competition some members rose to wealth while a majority were reduced to an inferior status. A pattern of life once followed by a whole group became a struggle of individuals for their own advancement.

In such ways as these the institutions of the Middle Ages were profoundly modified in their transition to modern times. The result was a rapid advance of material civilization; but, at the same time, something of value in medieval life was lost, for the equality once existing among members of the same group disappeared and self-interest became the predominant motive in state and in society.

Literature and Learning

By

CHARLES G. OSGOOD, Ph.D.*

LITERATURE and Learning! What a charming, happy, congenial
pair! Where should literature be at home, if not in the ivy-clad
House of Learning? What a beautiful subject for an allegorical
mural in a college library—two tall, fair, bovine female figures
in studio Greek costume, with arms amiably intertwined, gazing
vacantly out across a campus, where in reality Humane Letters
and Humane Learning are rapidly being evicted by the applied
sciences and social studies, so called.

Dr. Johnson boasted of the number of poets produced by
Pembroke College in his day. "Sir," said he, "we are a nest of
singing birds." Dr. Johnson was a learned man, if anyone ever
was, in all the learning of the schools. But he was also a literary
genius. He stretched his wings and left the nest. Restive and
recalcitrant under academic restraint, he preferred the greater
world of London as an ampler and more fitting field for his
powers. And as we review the long and noble roster of English
Men of Letters, we find him no exception, for by far the greater
number have either openly rebelled against the learned disciplines, or have refused to accept them with complete sub-mis-
sion, or have dispensed with them altogether. Shelley was ex-
pelled; Milton was suspended, and later, like Lord Tweedsmuir,
declined flattering academic preferment; Chaucer, Shakespeare,
Keats, Browning, with the prehensile mind of genius, found
their own magnificent erudition without putting on the gown.
Learned Ben Jonson saw little if anything of a university;
Wordsworth, Tennyson, Byron, and many others read, not by
academic prescription, but following their own preference and
appetite. Indeed Gray and Arnold are the only exceptions that
come readily to mind, and it may be that the genius of both was
in a measure frustrated by too much University. Those among
you who teach—have you never felt the embarrassing incon-

* Professor of English, Emeritus, Princeton University.

venience of finding in your class one who had received a touch
of the divine fire, to whom neither the contents of the course,
nor the processes of the classroom, nor the mediocre students to
whose capacities the course was modulated, were hospitable?
And yet he, more than all the rest, seemed to belong there,
though he also seemed bent on getting himself eliminated as
soon as he could. Strange that men of literary genius should
always hunger for the thing we call learning, and yet when
they encounter it in prescribed and concentrated form, pur-
veyed in college courses, texts, and lectures, they relish it not,
and in disgust turn to seek it in more natural undigested forms.

Are we then to conclude that the disciplines and learning of
the Liberal Arts can neither nourish nor fertilize literary
genius? Is it possible, as some think nowadays, that Learning is
actually inimical to Literature, that it arrests the fine, naïve,
careless rapture of composition—damps her intended wing?

Evidently the journeyman decorator who designed our mural
for the college library had not given much thought to the matter. For the entente between Literature and Learning has never
been settled nor assuredly happy. Its history is a history of un-
easy domestic relations.

Some fifteen hundred years ago a resourceful and ingenious
teacher of things in general—for in those blessed days there
were no specialists or departments—devised a most entertaining
textbook which was to edify generations of youngsters for centuries after its author was gone. (Ten years, I hear, is the can-
onical lifetime of a modern textbook.) The author's name was
Martianus Capella and his book is known by the title, *De Nuptiis
Philologiae et Mercurii—The Marriage of Philology and Mercury*. Martianus shrewdly chose for what he had to say the
medium of allegory which was just then entering upon its long
career of high medieval favor. Together with gay threads of his
own genial fancy, and with patches of uninspired and difficult
verse, he interwove many a drab filament of what every educated youth of the day should know—mythology, rare and
learned words, a shred of Greek here and there, a bit of ancient
philosophy, and in fact the encyclopedia of the Seven Liberal
Arts, which in the fifth century and for a long time thereafter
was all the secular lore you needed.

This wedding of Philology to Mercury we may understand as
the wedding of Learning to Literature. For Philology in those

days meant far more than mere gerund-grinding. It embraced the whole round horizon of secular knowledge, the encyclopedia of humane learning.

According to Martianus, Mercury, being amorously inclined, goes in search of a wife. First he burns with passion for Sophia (Wisdom), but she has forsworn marriage, and evidently means it. Then with equal ardor he turns first to Mantice, that is, Prophecy, and then to Psyche, both of whom, it appears, are already engaged. Then Virtue suggests to the undiscouraged bachelor that he consult Apollo, who recommends the beautiful bluestocking Philologia, daughter of Phronesis, for whom Mercury instantly conceives the most incendiary passion. But formalities must be observed, and here the instructive Martianus finds his grand chance. The party sail off to the music of the spheres, solo and chorus, in search of Jove, who properly consults his wife. She, true to her sex, likes a wedding (*dehinc nuptiis Iuno non solita refragari*), and advises Jove to hurry up before Mercury changes his mind. They call a council of all the gods, who consent to the marriage of course. And so to the end of Book One.

When the curtain rises again, Philology is attended to her wedding by her mother, by the nine Muses singing lustily to a full band of wind, strings, and water-organ, and by the Four Cardinal Virtues, and the Three Graces. Nobody, not even the bride, seems to be embarrassed when at the emetic touch of Athanasia, with an exhausting effort, Philology exgurgitates a *bibliothecalis copia*, a perfect flood of books, letters, scrolls. Indigestible bibliographies, it appears, are nothing new.

Chaperoned by Juno she rises along the Milky Way with all the gods Martianus can think of in her train, to Jove's palace, where she is to be married. The groom's brothers, Bacchus and Apollo, act as best men; Hercules, the Twins, and others are ushers; Linus, Homer, and Virgil join in the wedding-song to the lyres of those virtuosi, Orpheus and Aristoxenus. In short all the best connection of both Literature and Learning were among those present. So ends a second book.

But seven more follow, each consisting of a lecture on her subject by one of the Liberal Arts—Grammar, Logic, Rhetoric, Geometry, Arithmetic, Astronomy, Music—till all have had their tedious say. Martianus seems to have expected that the momentum of the first two books would carry the unwilling pupillary

mind through the more desiccated but disciplinary stretches of
the rest. And, judging by the book's thousand-year run, he was
right.

At the end of the story Martianus does not say: "And so they
lived happily ever afterwards." Perhaps it sounded too obvious.
Perhaps he knew better. For Literature and Learning, as we
guessed, have lived an uneven, at times inimical, life together.
The present is one of those times.

Possibly Martianus realized the situation far better than he
would say. He calls his allegory an old man's tale—*senilis
fabula*. An old man's tale indeed. Perhaps in his ripe erudition
he looked wistfully back along a thousand years or so; and
when he quoted a snatch of Homer, as he likes to do, wondered
how that king of poets had managed to breathe such uncanny
magic into a few simple familiar words without the advantage
of the modern, post-Alexandrian learning of Martianus's own
late Roman times. Just as *we* wonder at the magic of a single
phrase or line of Chaucer or Shakespeare, who knew less than
the modern Freshman, far less than that odious schoolboy of
Macaulay's. How naïvely do they confess this wonder who cannot believe that Shakespeare was Shakespeare because forsooth
he did not have enough booklearning to be Shakespeare.

Poor Martianus, replete and rotund with the encyclopedia of
his day, with the Seven Liberal Arts containing the encyclopedia
of literature and science and their practical application, the inherited and overripe philosophies of Greece, the old pagan religion rotted down from faith into a complicated allegory—poor
Martianus, with his blackboard distinctions between the terms,
letters, literature, literary, and *literate*! I wonder if, as he laid
down his pen, he sadly reviewed the long cycle from Homer to
himself. Was he aware of the progress of literature through its
vigorous and creative youth in Homer, Sappho, Aeschylus; into
its learned and middle-age sophistication of Alexandria, still
grandly productive through such poets as Theocritus, Apollonius
of Rhodes, and the great Romans, consciously richer and richer
by inheritance; then clever and cynical in Lucian, till now in
its senile and learned impotence it can only discuss its infirmi-
ties, studiously avoid the obvious, resort to learned allusion,
affect a recondite vocabulary, interweave snatches from old poets,
hint secondary meanings to make the reader quiz, discuss, and
advertise the author—anything but understand him? That

phrase at the end, "an old man's tale," suddenly is lurid with the eternal tragedy in the household of Mercury and Philology, of Literature and Learning. For Literature is getting old; Learning, now grown fat and world-wise and unromantic, is turning out to be the gray mare. About all she can do is to talk about the children of her better days, now much admired in the world, luxuriate in her own sophistication, and await the day when she and Mercury are again happily restored to their youth.

Ah yes, we can sympathize with Martianus; we can understand his *senilis fabula.* We look back upon our Hesiod and Homer in the *Beowulf* poet and Chaucer and Spenser; upon our Attic Three in Marlowe and Shakespeare and Ben Jonson; upon our sophisticated Virgil and Horace in Milton and Donne, in Dryden and Pope; upon our cynical decline in the eighteenth century, and so to our present comparatively uncreative state. Books, yes, by the million, but most of them informative, not creative. And our efforts at creation, clever, skilful, necromantic with all the inherited, tried, and perfected ingenuities of literature, fall short of greatness; sometimes in their despair writers affect to scorn it, and cultivate instead the *mot juste,* the rare word, the erudite allusion, artificial obscurity; or by perverse and desperate revolt, they revive the mannerisms of the primitives without their virtues.

Perhaps Macaulay after all was near the fact in his easy caption: "As civilization advances, poetry declines." Perhaps these relations of Learning and Literature are cyclic. In the first arc of the cycle Homer and Cynewulf and Chaucer, soul-hydroptic with a sacred thirst for all the learning they can get, increasing, regulating, economizing their creative power by it. In the second, as the available learning has increased and methodized itself, as literary tradition has grown richer and knowledge more multifarious, its demand upon literary genius is proportionately increased. For poetry obviously must transcend and control its learning, and make it subservient to greater ends than those of mere learning itself.

The two best examples I could cite of success in this stupendous feat are Virgil and Milton. Both were Alexandrians. Both were passionate patriots. Both were men of single faith, but sorrowfully conscious of the disintegrating of communal faith throughout their world. Both felt an insatiate hunger for knowledge, yes, for learning in the academic sense—for Grammar,

Rhetoric, the philosophies, Music, and Mathematics. And both knew how to use it.

I have elsewhere, more than once, attempted to show the actual reinforcement and enrichment and *approfondissement* of his poetry which Milton achieved in a hundred different ways by his mastery of his vast encyclopedic learning. Virgil wrought in like manner. It is easy for anyone to recognize Virgil's imitations of Homer, Theocritus, Apollonius, Ennius. It is not impossible to trace currents from various of the ancient philosophies which mingle with his mighty stream. Scholars point out the signs that he studied Roman archeology, and collected Roman folklore. He still clung to his practical boyhood knowledge of the art of agriculture. But it is not so easy to measure the subtler effects of all he knew upon his matchless song; its grand diapason blending many a voice long silent; its elevated, unsentimental *lacrimae rerum*; its utterance of things unutterable for sixty succeeding generations of men of many tongues, and for how many more no one can tell; its power to refine and civilize millions of young barbarians—a power which the world at present seems likely to forget; its encyclopedic concentration of the culture of preceding centuries into a poetic potential which has insensibly directed the praxis and behavior of millions; its strange, irresistible enchantment which has charmed thousands of poets into song, minim poets and poets as great as Dante and Petrarch, Chaucer and Spenser and Milton. For Virgil's Latin, elemental and universal, reverberated in their ears from childhood, inevitably attuning the cadence and accent of their native tongues. Yes, let Virgil stand as the highest and purest example of what Learning has done, and may do, for Literature.

In the same twilight years of the ancient world in which Martianus set down his old man's tale, a group of learned but genial friends came together during the Saturnalia or Roman Christmas for a season of good living and most erudite discussion. The talk, as reported by Macrobius, touches upon this and that, and seems at first to ramble casually and delightfully from inquiry to inquiry. But as it proceeds a centripetal force begins to assert itself, and that is the adoration of the memory of Virgil. Not only was he, in the sophisticated eyes of these scholars, the preëminent poet, but the referee of all learned dispute, *omnium disciplinarum peritissimus*; and they cite him as final authority, not only for his knowledge of rhetoric and jurisprudence, but also of philosophy, literature, liturgy, and theology. From that time till the day of Dryden, no serious discussion of poetry and the poet fails to insist that learning is a primary and indispensable part of the poet's equipment.

But this happy equilibrium, this fruitful coagency between Literature and Learning as realized by Milton and Virgil, is an unstable adjustment. The creative imagination has a tendency to overload, to become embarrassed and overwhelmed by accumulating fact and formula, achieving at best the poetry of Statius, then Claudian, and at last the amusing pedantry, the *senilis fabula*, of Martianus.

But the modern cycle of nine centuries is in some respects riding to a different close from that of the ancient. With an eye to the fact we recognize two modifications of the cycle, perhaps discernible also in the ancient instance, but not so dominant. I mean the so-called Romantic Movement, and the Rise of Science. Neither Romance nor Science has done much toward a happy adjustment of domestic relations in the household of Mercury and Philology, though they have interfered enough, to be sure.

For example Romance, urging the return to Nature, has for two centuries tried to alienate Mercury from his lawful spouse, and free him from the inherited and formal learning of the schools. Romance has gone in heavily for natural genius, unsoiled and unspoiled by the artificialities of Academe. The bachelor Mercury, wild and promiscuous, is the Mercury for the Romantics. Accordingly they once sought out the milkmaid poet, the blacksmith poet, the poet below stairs. Lo, at length the Aurora over Scotland, the apotheosis of the peasant-poet, supposedly the love-child of Mercury and Nature. For Burns, although he sneered that college-classes turned out asses, crept instinctively back to his lawful mother Learning for the nourishment necessary to his genius.

Have we the right to laugh at these vagaries of our fathers, at their romantic faith in natural genius—we who romantically admire the painting of the taxi-driver, the cowboy's verse; who cherish the literary, or artistic, or musical output of the tender years before adolescence begins to stale, and Mrs. Philology lays her chastening hand upon the natural instinct to create? Yes, romance has even swayed the equitable minds of us scholars, Philology's favorites, and colored our conclusions. Ever since

Bishop Percy's day pundits have excitedly scoured the wilds for old ballads, songs, charms, superstitions, folklore, dialect, customs, often with touching indiscrimination prizing the rubbish equally with the treasure. In the scholarly criticism of the *Beowulf*, for example, authorities have long admired the poem as a sturdy, primitive, heathen work, a proper son of Mercury, untainted by Learning's degeneracies, and marred only by a few easily separable blemishes contracted from the Christian Faith. They have been astonishingly slow to accept the inescapable evidence of the poet's learning acquired in the seventh-century monastic English schools, where the study of Virgil, and perhaps of Homer, was going on. The available evidence would have convinced them on any other subject; but they could not bear to relinquish their romantic conception of the *Beowulf* as a rugged primitive.

Of course these romantic enthusiasms have had their uses as well as their extremes. They are the instinctive recalcitrations against the Alexandrian formalities of our latter-day culture, against the signs of senile weakness in Mother Philology.

The other modification of the modern cycle is the break-up of the encyclopedic conception of formal learning—that conception in the mind of every intelligent and aspiring man down to Milton's time that Learning is One.

To us Learning, under the centrifugal force of Science, has become a distracting myriad plural, without focus or singleness of Idea. The encyclopedic learning from Roman times embraced essentially the Seven Liberal Arts, included in time the two ancient cultures, Greek and Hebrew, and for a thousand years found the focus of its cycle in the creed of the Christian Church. If such compass seems irksome to our modern mind, yet we must admit that within this scope there was abundant room and sustenance for the genius of Dante, Shakespeare, and Milton. Nay, this unity of culture both in themselves and in their hearers was indispensable to poetry of such grandeur as theirs.

But Learning cannot pause at any happy moment in her course and continue to live. The modern mind is not static; and with Lord Bacon to inaugurate its new technique, the scientific method has led to acquisitions of knowledge by no means merely confined to the physical world, acquisitions which have grown out of all cesse. So great are they, so multifarious—and often so tentative or so soon invalidated—that no single mind can comprehend them, no intellect has yet appeared powerful enough to compress them into a new encyclopedia or unity. And until this can be done and is done, not only by one super-mind, but so that in some form all men can comprehend it, we are unlikely again to behold such grand manifestations of creative genius in literature or the arts as have come to fruition in the encyclopedic learning of the past. Creative genius, men point out, is today deploying itself in more material forms of expression.

Scientia, Science, is a parvenu amongst the Olympians. Yet she is old enough to have known Plato and Aristotle and Thales and Pythagoras. She had acquaintance even in ancient Egypt and Babylonia. But it is only through the last three hundred years that she has triumphed over all the other Olympians. She has usurped the whole-hearted adoration of both unlearned and learned. She is the Giver to men of all the modern means of convenience, pleasure, safety, and of the wholesale destruction of life and civilization. Nor is she, as commonly supposed, concerned only with the physical world. She has affected every remotest detail in the Household of Learning, or Philologia in old Martianus's sense. So that Philologia, under the domination of this pushing Science who has moved in next door, this all-efficient, unerring, unmoral, unhuman, ruthless neighbor—Philologia is a changed woman and a changed mother. Latterly she has presented Mercury with a new and numerous generation of offspring. Studies of sources and provenance, semasiology, classifications and sub-classifications by schools and isms, bio-graphical research, genealogies of ideas and influences, lexicons, concordances (God forgive me!), bibliographies—a sturdy, plain, truthful, serviceable, well-disciplined brood they are, perhaps more so than their older brothers and sisters; but they are neither well favored nor charming. Their mother dresses them in becoming, practical, dull gray or brown, and marshals them to take the air in monographs, learned journals, and series. Though latterly, I notice, some of them, wistfully aping more popular members of the family, affect the cosmetics of a pretty style, or the smarter costume of modish print, binding, and jacket. Alas, is it not sometimes painfully evident to a discern-ing world that these precocious and capable children, though they are up on all the facts about their father, their mother, and their older kin, do not know them at all?

And so, it seems, Learning and Literature did not live happily ever after. Why not, in the name of common sense? They have always sought each other out. Each yearns for the other, and languishes when alone. Why should not their domestic relations be perfectly and permanently happy? Why are poets no longer at home in Academe? Why should not the University implant, nourish, and cultivate the seeds of new poetry, furnishing from its rich stores the materials which will fertilize such, as obviously once it did for Cynewulf and Virgil and Dante and Marlowe and Milton? What do we, the professional attendants of Philologia, we academic and scientific men, we disillusioned doctors of philosophy with more learning than philosophy, what do we really care about great literature? What confidence have we in it as an agent for regeneration in the modern world? Less and less, I fear, if one may judge by the fate of the humanities at the hands of know-it-all educators these last few years.

I admit that Learning has shown some signs of pity for her old man Mercury, some hope that by taking thought she might bring him back to a semblance of his old-time vigor. She has been setting up and proclaiming courses in "Creative Writing." She has tried to domesticate in her own academic bower her wilder children with a trace of their father in them, possibly with some notion that the old Mercurial manners may be revived and propagated. She has added professed poets to her domestic staff or faculty. Sometimes they are looked upon askance by more academic colleagues; usually they don't stay long. She has even advertised Schools of Letters, with graduate study for writers, and she gives degrees in "Imaginative Writing." Martianus probably would approve. I wonder, however, what Virgil would say. Would he look for a literary revival?

Is it possible that we have advanced far into the autumn of this cycle of civilization, that the revolution into which we seem to be passing is the November of the winter we must endure, as men once endured the long stretch of four or five dark centuries, before a flowering new spring, a renewal of the glorious romance between Learning and Literature? If so, there is not much that we can do about it except recognize the fact.

But at our modern pace four centuries have shrunk almost to so many years. Let us remember that at the dawn of the Elizabethan heyday, when the east was already brightening with the coming sun of Shakespeare, no less a prophet than the learned

Sir Philip Sidney was in despair for English letters. Shall we, then, also despair?

We must, to be sure, resign any illusive hope that we can, once for all, settle domestic relations between Learning and Literature. Whatever our zeal for the case of Learning, however wistfully we may covet the favor and good graces of Mercury, we cannot do much by courses in Creative Writing, nor by courses of any kind, as courses. I have heard Mercury himself say as much.

But we should first of all know and understand the distinguishing marks of the greatest geniuses in days of happier relations between Literature and Learning. We should distinguish Genius from mere talent. We should be aware that Learning alone cannot make Genius prolific. Yet from all that has happened, Learning possesses that which is useful, even indispensable to Literature. But Genius insists upon appropriating it and using it in its own way, not submitting to the creeping pace of the multitude. Let us remember above all that creative Genius is instinctively in search of some encyclopedia of life, and that its modern despairs are the despair of finding one. Genius does not therefore readily warm to a dispassionate, impersonal presentation of Learning, however scientific that presentation may be, but to living incarnation. Such incarnation of Learning in the teacher gives Learning at least the encyclopedic form of a personality, even though the greater unity which comes from a common creed is at this point in history suspended.

I am sorry that after all these years I cannot present some immediate and glorified prospect of insured happiness in the household of Mercury and Philologia. It might help to illuminate so grand an occasion as this proud anniversary. But the light would be false and artificial. It is better, is it not, to transcend our illusions, to review the ups and downs of these domestic relations so important to our spiritual welfare, and to carry on as wisely as we can until the hour strikes, as God grant it will, of the new consummation, the greater Renaissance, a happier and nobler fruition in the Household of Mercury and Philology.

The Search for the Heroic Poem

By

WILLIAM J. ENTWISTLE, M.A., LL.D.*

THERE must be some truth behind the Epic Poem. Some wind-swept Troy, some Hellas unified by far-ruling kings must have existed if the *Iliad* is to be sung to believing ears; and if there were no Homeric Agamemnon, there were, at least, Agamemnons before Homer. The hearers' assent is uncritical and inert, but, as in the case of the *Odyssey*, the appeal is weakened by too palpable fabling. But from *some* truth it is a natural step to demand *all* truth, or at least the truth *essential* to any age or society. Such a demand belongs to a reflective age, and is made of none of the great autochthonous epics of ancient or modern times. It was met for the first time by Vergil in his *Aeneid*, which "sings for ever of imperial Rome," and it is possible that his answer was less convincing in his own age than it has since seemed to be. He reduced to verse and symbol the Augustan formula, which concealed under the appearance of liberty and pristine virtue far more savage realities. These realities doubtless became yet more stark as the Julian tyranny gave place to the formalism of the Antonines and the military despotism of the third century produced the rigidity of the Constantines. In time Rome passed away, leaving only a visible Church and a legend of civilized unity. This unity had one sole expression: the *Aeneid*. The *Aeneid* sings of Rome (in Tennyson's phrase) because it has become Rome; the only Rome that unites and inspires civilized mankind; the imperial Rome solidly based upon immutable fate, with the godlike mission to govern mankind, striking down the proud and showing mercy to the weak.

This is the Heroic Poem. It is the poem which seeks to declare *all* or the *essential* truth in any age or generation, and it is a uniquely European fact. There have been epics in other lands, though not so widely spread as to constitute a law of

---

* King Alfonso XIII Professor of Spanish Studies, University of Oxford.

cultural progress. The Chinese and the Arabians have lacked this inspiration, and their occurence in India and Tatary as well as Europe is not incompatible with a theory of diffusion from a single antique center. But for the Heroic Poem this diffusion is palpable and historic, for it proceeds from Vergil, and extends so far as Latin civilization. Felt most keenly by the nations of the West, it has extended into Germany and the Slavic hinterland with diminished efficacy, though with notable achievements. By their adhesion they have entered, though partially, into the common heritage of spiral unity, wherein alone humanity can look for peace.

A statement so august must needs be extensive. The form chosen is normally the epic, since its length permits the manifold exploration of the main theme; but both the drama and the ode have, on occasion, served heroically. The dramas of Aeschylus, for instance, grapple with the problems of Greek nationality and human destiny. Dramatic in form, they are also gigantic odes. Paeans and threnodies in solos and choruses thunder through *The Persian Women*, developing the theme of the punishment the high gods mete to overweening pride. In the most modern times the heroic ode has seemed the appropriate means of expressing our disjointed experience; and somewhat earlier, there have been singers, like Milton, who have long hesitated between epos and drama. It is not formal classification which makes the Heroic Poem, but inner intention. The sense of community must be explicit, as the poet strives to reach a statement that will command general assent, and through assent work towards enlightenment.

Such poetry, it is clear, cannot be judged only by its outward form. That form must indeed be consummate if the poem is to shine out above the dusty scribblings of prosers and poetasters; but aesthetic beauty alone will not support its claims. It demands assent in all fundamental ways. The plot is admittedly a fable, but the truth which it symbolizes must be, in the opinion of its public, fecund and essential. If this assent cannot be reached, or reached so imperfectly as by the *Gerusalemme Liberata*, the Heroic Poem proportionately fails. The notion that the poet is "not heard, but overheard" has no applicability to the Heroic Poem, which unequivocally demands a hearing. The idea that poetry can reach only a select minority of souls appears, in the light of the Heroic Poem, as a craven abdication of the highest end of poetry. The Renaissance had lesser forms for the *cénacles*—the occasional epigram, the sonnet, the bucolic idyll—but these served only to give the artist his cunning, to prepare in him "a swan's song to astound the world."

These verse symbols of human experience we owe essentially to the Renaissance and Italy, but they would have failed of their effect had popular taste not been prone to admit their justice. Indeed, in Italy itself, the whole movement was defeated by the actual disunity which no formula could hide or resolve. It was, for Italy, an age of brilliant failures outshining the successes of dimmer lands. But the latter were more sure of their fundamentals. The iron resolve of France had found voice in the *Chanson de Roland*, and a German hero in shining armor gleams through the fog and blood of the *Nibelungenlied*. Spain had her Cid; she had also in her incomparable ballads copious documentation of her national destiny. The Danish *viser* brought all classes into the same communal dance and were a school of Danish character. In the far southeast the warrior's songs of the Serbian highlanders sang of high courage in overwhelming defeat, of sin and purgation and the inscrutable decrees of God. Even in distant Russia, vast and formless as she always has been, there were heroic songs which declared the soil to be holy. England was educated by *Beowulf*, the border ballads, and the Arthurian fable. In all these there was little of reflection, and the expression of common purpose was instinctive rather than intentional; but the terms and purport of the possible Heroic Poem were there to be discerned.

Discernment could be the product only of a thorough discipline. To achieve the heroic a poet must be master of his art, having passed through a proper apprenticeship to its lesser grades. He must know men and cities, both by study in the best authors and by intervention in affairs. His right to speak for all must be conceded on the ground of admitted excellence. He must choose his theme with circumspection, selecting not any subject, but that which is most fundamental. Art must preside over the distribution of its parts, and the whole form a subtle harmony between statement and asides. The ancient models must be followed, but the manner must be modern; and years must be given to the work of the file. Thus the young Tasso defined the heroic task in his famous essays, though it

might have been better for him had he ignored counsels cf perfection and directed his youthful genius to that which, t● live,
must be young as well as old. Camões was happier, since h● conceived and commenced as a youth the work which he perḟcted,
with unabated fire, by the toil of a quarter-century.

Among the forerunners we must reckon the great and solitary figure of Dante, though his achievement is the greatest of
them all. What later became a concerted effort was for ⱨim a
lonely agony. Others have been defeated by the contradi☰tions
of our worldly life; but with Dante for a brief moment, tʰanks
to the great Thomistic synthesis, the poet held the key ⸱o the
riddle. Thought had converged from many distinct directions,
and it was to fly asunder again as doubts increased; bⱨt for
the moment it was uniquely simple, and Dante expresseᵈ that
simplicity. Passionately devoted to his own narrow m◌ther-
land, his temper of mind and the generosity of meḏieval
thought raised him above gross nationalism. He thougⱨt of
peace and justice for all mankind, as an extension of thᵉ love
of God; yet he knew as none other the desperate evil of men's
hearts. In his fears and his confident aspirations he beⱨtrides
the centuries, and is our own contemporary, though iⱨ the
serener air of his immortality.

Men have always recognized their own portraits aⱨmong
Dante's sinners, but in happier times we may have thᵒught
their sufferings exaggerated. Now we know them for plain
truth. Storm winds of passion whirl us round, and a rⱨin of
fire falls on our bodies made gross by ignorance and ⱨreed.
The great destroyers rise, each in his fiery tomb, and lⱨunch
curses against the living, and at the heart of earthly thⱨngs is
the chill desolation of hate and treachery. But beyonᵈ this,
when we have plumbed the depth of despair there is a nⱨrrow
crack, "whereby we climb to see again the stars." Then ☰omes
the long laborious ascent of the soul, which is at first ⱨaffled
and painful, but gains in speed and joy as each cornⱨce is
passed: the painful rebuilding of our wrecked lives, the ⱨiece-
meal recovery of our peace. So far we have been the cⱨnters
of our own experience, but in the last cantos there is ⱨa tri-
umphant reversal of our ideas. We learn that not hate buⱨ love
is omnipotent: "the love that moves the Sun and the ◌ther
spheres." Love, intertwined in mystic rings, is life and light
and spirit. Timeless and placeless, it glows with energy vⱨich,

by extension in place and time, becomes the majestic rhythm of the universe. With defect of love comes sin; with loss of light, darkness; with failure of spirit, gross mass subject to pain; but these negatives, though so present to us, represent no ultimate reality. Goethe has attempted to express the same thing by contrasting the song of the Archangels and the earthy sneers of Mephistopheles; but with how much less amplitude and power than Dante! I do not say that Dante has, in fact, solved the puzzle of the universe; far from it. The logician may find flaws in all his cantos. But he has felt more deeply the desperation of the human plight, and he has seen more clearly than any both the necessity of hope for our salvation, and the certainty of ultimate love.

With him, as so often among the great heroic poets, the supreme message is one of many delivered to the same end. The *Divina Commedia* is consummated in eternal Love; but the extension of this love to terrene society is justice. The *Monarchia* speaks of justice, positing an "emperor" who is no mere dynast, but the embodiment of all men's need of peaceful order. Law is the effect rather than the cause of such order. It requires perfect understanding, such as the great law school of Bologna was affording in the Italian language. Thus the discussion of this language in the *De vulgari Eloquentia* contributes to the program of peace, which is itself an extension of the heavenly order. There is but one message in so many different spheres.

When Dante died there was no man left to bend his bow. The cord of his metaphysic had snapped, and his formidable strength seemed stiffness. He was admired for the allegorical framework which was his least admirable trait, but he left no veritable successor. The great Renaissance quest of the Heroic Poem arose from a new beginning; a disconcertingly trivial beginning. A lady was bored; something must be done to amuse her. So Luigi Pulci remembered a drawing-room conversation about Carolingian legends, and busied himself with a polite parody of the long, aimless narratives chanted at street corners in Italy. His *Morgante* keeps too much of his sources: their hackneyed appeals to religion, their crude adventures, their elementary surprises. But Matteo Boiardo took up the theme with his elegant seignorial wit and classical finish, and he determined the characters and adventures which, as he averred,

Turpin had concealed. Then came the consummate Ariosto.
If Boiardo's work lacked an ending, and Ariosto's lacked a beginning, readers less prone to cavil than the Aristotelian critics
saw in them both the literary event of the age. This was something new in art. The easy flippancy of the narrative, its extraordinary variety without the least confusion, the brilliance
of the personages (especially the new sort of women), the full
mastery of humanistic resources, the classical clearness and fullness of the style, its transitions from jest to tragedy—these were
qualities to close an age and introduce a new literary cycle.
There were seen the old motifs of folk-tale which never flag:
magic rings, flying horses, enchanted steeds, ogres, heroes, exquisite ladies. But there were also richly woven tapestries of
the Renaissance: the gardens of Alcina, Angelica's idyllic surrender to the Moorish page Medoro, the portentous folly of
Orlando, and Astolfo's riotously funny expedition to the Moon.
Ariosto had promised and delivered "things never said in prose
or rhyme," but he had given yet more. His wit was not heart-
less (and certainly not blistering like Dante's), but instinct with
regret.

> Oh the great goodness of those antique knights!
> For they were rivals, enemies by creed,
> Still stiff with sorry wounds from bitter fights,
> Sore in each member and their wounds ableed;
> Yet in the darkling woodland ways those wights
> Wandering together, no suspicion heed.

Ariosto deemed the epic to be impossible, and the *Orlando
Furioso* is witness to his want of faith. But he had brought into
being something not only supreme in itself but instinct with
the most flattering possibilities. What he had left undone all
the poets of Europe sought to perfect in an amazing flood of
epic poetry. In Spain alone two hundred such efforts were made.
In England this surge gave us our finest poetry apart from
Shakespeare. France was less fortunate, but in the fullness of
days the flood reached Germany and distant Poland. Italy drew
comparatively little profit from her invention, since much of
her energy was absorbed in a barren quarrel as to the status
of the *romanzo*. There were those who condemned it and demanded a return to Vergil, the true Father of the Epos. So Vida
patiently analyzed the technical devices of the *Aeneid* by way

of instruction to men of taste, and Trissino attempted to transplant the whole Augustan style. Ronsard was to make the same attempt later in his ingenious and strangely exasperating *Franciade*; for with all the cultural significance of France, how had he the patience to dally with the trivial fable about Francion, son of Hector? There were others, like Giraldi Cinzio, who upheld the claims of the *romanzo* to rank with the classical Epos; and Torquato Tasso devoted his laborious youth to composing six books on the Heroic Poem, when he might have been better employed in giving the freshness of his mind to verse. Verses are best written with the freshness of youth; they can be perfected later, though only by those who have retained their youthful warmth beneath the snow. In the end Tasso's *Gerusalemme* hardly qualified for any specific category. It dealt with a hero and theme admirably chosen for both poetical and historic significance; but it propounded a thesis of Christian unity that was a flat contradiction of the contemporary facts, and it developed a well-known event among incongruous fictions. The lightness and modernity of Ariosto had been sacrificed, and yet Tasso, having failed to achive the epic dignity and veracity, had to appeal through romance.

To the writers of the Spanish Peninsula it seemed that Ariosto had failed for want of truth. There were achievements in the Americas and the East Indies which, they knew, eclipsed in heroism and strangeness anything "said in prose or rhyme"; and they averred that the poet need only transcribe plain facts. That was what Alonso de Ercilla attempted in his *Araucana*— still *the* great poem of the Americas. On bits of paper and scraps of leather he scribbled octaves forged in the heat of battle; they are uniquely vigorous and realistic, and behind them rises the stern, heroic, loyal and chivalrous phantom of their author. But the facts were, he found, no more than a thin coating of our full experience, and he clutched desperately at the skirts of Ariosto for the redeeming grace of variety. His fault did not lie solely in the selection of a modern and transitory theme, since the life of Christ itself did not yield better results uder the skillful hand of Hojeda. Every possible subject and style were exploited in the search for the perfect Heroic Poem. The Carolingian theme was nationalized in the vast *Bernardo* of Bernardo de Valbuena, a poem rich with the tropical splendor he had known in Mexico and Puerto Rico, exquisitely phrased, but long, and exasperatingly dull where it might have been witty. There were catalogues of all the American worthies, lives of Cortés as the typical captain, colonial memories (in which Nereids had too much to do with the founding of Buenos Aires!), saintly biographies, triumphs of baroque religion. But none of these themes gave the desired Epos, so rare is its attainment!

None of these themes, that is, save the national theme of Portugal. Camões' *Lusiads* is probably the only heroic poem of the age which entirely accomplished its purpose. He proposed to sing of the heroic soul of Portugal, and his verses are the intimate pulsations of that soul. Portuguese history was marked by an epic simplicity, since it was directed to the advancement of her freedom and her faith. In the discovery, navigation and conquest of India (as the high phrase went) she had performed a deed more singly significant than any since Greek faced Persian on the shore of Marathon; and by treating Gama's story as a symbol, Camões solved a difficulty that had baffled all Vergilian imitators. It was the difficulty of the "fable," the symbolic action which is the poet's ostensible subject. Such "fables" were normally significant fictions, and embarrassing as such in what was intended for a statement of fundamental truth. Camões found an historical narrative capable of receiving the attributes of a symbol. Above and around the Portuguese travelers the immortals wage their war, as the might and grace of Western civilization bore down upon the treacherous secretiveness of the Orient. The *Lusiads* is ablaze with patriotic passion, with sensuous loveliness, pathos, and flashes of searing despair.

The triumph of Camões was due partly to his limitations. He had found the formula still valid for Portugal, her empire, and the future Brazil; but he had not solved the problem of his age or quieted the dispeace of his soul. His lyrical poems are expressions of an exasperated discontent; he writhed but could do no more. The contradictions of the age had been sensed by Ariosto, who shrugged his shoulders and recited a lovely dream. They were expressed by Cervantes in *Don Quixote*. Cervantes did not admit that the accident of prose disqualified his work from taking a place among heroic poems, and in his plan, theme, attitude, and narrative technique he was own-brother to Ariosto. His optimistic temperament and his Erasmian convictions constituted an irresistible upward thrust, though experience had been for him a catalogue of squalid disasters. His immortal Knight pursues the highest ideals; he is absolute in valor, in chastity, in justice. He is forever overthrown, but when is he defeated? He is defeated only when his ideals have snapped, and he then returns, full of hard realism, to die. But so long as the spirit is high within him he is not defeated, though often cast down. On the contrary, he imposes his will on all he meets, and they revolve round him. He addresses wantons as ladies, and they act as ladies for the nonce; an innkeeper, a barber, a priest, a peasant are forced into chivalrous rôles by the power of his enthusiasm. He compels country gentlemen, nobles, clergymen to reflect seriously upon great themes: public service, the function of culture, the principles of the arts, the duties of government. In short, life puts its own construction on the universe, and dies only through loss of faith. What then is truth? In the exquisite dialogues between the Knight and Sancho Panza, the problem arises in manifold forms, but the solution is never revealed. The essential contradictions of the Renaissance and of all human experience are there adumbrated in a work which brings a great epoch to a sovereign close, sadly but not without hope, defeated but not without honor.

The Heroic Poem in the South has a sensuousness which it never possesses in the North. The bright externals of life were so much more satisfying in Italy, Spain, and Portugal, and the treatment has an immediacy which can never fail of poetic appeal. In the North, under the influence of Protestanism directly, but indirectly of a different path of experience, the Heroic Poem descends within the mind and conscience of men. It is so even with Spenser, though he wrote early enough to come under the direct influence of Ariosto, whom he resembles in verbal loveliness and in the acceptance of fiction. But Spenser demands from fiction not its own external graces, but a revelation of the moral worth of men. "Fierce wars and faithful loves shall moralize my song." He speaks at once of holiness and truth, and goes on to outline the twelve cardinal virtues of a perfect hero. He sought to portray the national hero, Prince Arthur, but, like Tennyson in a later age, struck no answering chord of nationalism in the reader. England has never succeeded in achieving her own spiritual formula, though Shakespeare's historical plays give us its integers. Our highest inspiration has come from somewhere outside the national record and beneath the surface of experience. So Milton must have judged when he turned aside from his project to sing of the Round Table and resolved "to justify the ways of God to man." Experience had passed through morality to become religion.

The religious, puritanical Epos of the North owed much to the initiative of Guillaume de Salluste, Sieur du Bartas, whose pretentious and pedantic *Création du Monde* drew attention to the stores of cosmic poetry in Genesis, to which the story of the Passion was a necessary companion. Vondel, revolting from the disorders which he attributed to Protestantism, gave Holland its supreme masterpiece in his tragedy of *Lucifer*. It is a drama only in name. Two of its acts—the most imposing two —are narratives, the one of Creation, the other of the Fall. His long Dutch alexandrines achieve a melancholy magnificence as they make the heroic counsels of God serve for background to the envy, ambition, and futile calculations of Lucifer and Beelzebub. In his devils he had aptly caricatured the attitudes and projects of contemporary politicians, each seeking his own advantage at the expense of the peace of unified Christendom. He defends that ideal in its bodily form of the Holy Roman Empire, though thereby he seems to condemn all that his country had so heroically accomplished. There is too severe a narrowness in Vondel's conception of orderly rule; he can show that rebellion leads only to disillusionment, but he cannot formulate the bases of the larger order. His God is pedantic, and his Gabriel merely seeks to temporize and rebut. The same is true of Milton, who wrestled with the same theme a few years later. He is so far from "justifying the ways of God to man" that for the most part the reader sympathizes with Satan, the leader of a heroic, forlorn hope. I am not sure but that he pardons him the disruption of Paradise, that lovely idyll which had ceased to be real when the veins of the universe were pouring forth their fire. As between Milton's intention and his effect there is such a gap that one turns with relief to the *Samson Agonistes* for his presumable meaning. Samson is a better Satan; he has sinned and is being punished; but he has not abated his courage, he perceives the evil thing, and he summons all his desperate strength to strike one last blow for conscience' sake.

> He, though blind of sight,
> Despised, and thought extinguished quite,
> With inward eyes illuminated,
> His fiery virtue roused
> From under ashes into sudden flame.

A more gentle pietism reigns in Klopstock's *Messias*, which carried the Heroic Poem from Milton's hand to Germany. One is reminded of Goethe's admission to Eckermann that "our own literature is largely derived from theirs [the English]. Our novels, our dramas, whence have we them save from Goldsmith, Fielding, and Shakespeare? And even today where shall we find in Germany three literary heroes to be placed beside Lord Byron, Moore, and Walter Scott?" The examples might have been chosen otherwise, but the passage shows how far the greatest of Germans was from wishing the "total annihilation" for which his successors clamor. The history of the Heroic Poem, like that of folk-verse which I have treated elsewhere, is proof that the spiritual life of Europe is one strenuous endeavor for which are indispensable the varied gifts of its free peoples. So it was in the case of Goethe, whose *Faust* is not merely his own book of confessions, but the epic of the whole Age of Reason. The moral and religious inspiration had flagged even by the time of Klopstock, and it had been replaced by a more intense interest in Man. Dryden had reduced religion to intelligible human analogies, and Pope had proclaimed that the proper study of mankind was Man. Dogma and sectarian division seemed to have been devices in the hands of the unscrupulous to prevent Man from reaching a solution of his own problems by the light of reason. The narrative epos, whether exoteric or esoteric, had given way to a more discursive treatment, which Pope or Johnson molded into didactic poems, and Goethe into the appearance of a tragedy. His thought was more powerful and wide-ranging than that of his English predecessors or contemporaries, and his scientific curiosity was unlimited. He relied on human reason, but his mind embraced a great world of unreason, swayed by the Spirit that ever denies.

What can we say of *Faust*? It inspires respect as the last attempt to embrace the encyclopedia of experience within one statement, and massive are the commentaries that reveal its penetrating wisdom. But their very bulk inspires a suspicion that the poet has not conveyed his meaning, nor had always a precise meaning to convey. We may sympathize, on the sensuous side, with Faust's disgust at the failure of science to console, and with Gretchen's childlike faith and suffering; but we cannot take so confirmed an egoist as an apposite symbol of the human mind, nor read, without violence, a transcendent moral into an episode rather pathetic than tragic. The trivialities of the puppet play entangle the first part, and in the second Goethe so often mistakes intellectual assent for the total sympathetic response demanded by the highest poetry. It may be that evil is shown to be negative; that not the sensuous riot but beneficence gives to the moment the qualities of eternity; that Mephistopheles, though he denies, is an instrument for the working of Good. But are these demonstrations *fe t* by the reader who comes, as he is entitled to do, without a battery of commentaries? The myth of Euphorion and the marriage of Science and Beauty, lovely though it be, is a private rather than a public truth, like Robert Bridges' *Testament of Beauty*; and the sense of the whole poem is obscured by the pageantry of nonsense, breaking in at intervals. As an encyclopedist Goethe belongs to an age that was passing. His faith in reason and science is of the eighteenth century, but it was crumbling on the threshold of the nineteenth. The great poem splits into disjointed fragments, and bears a meaning scene by scene and not as a whole. The widening of scope for the Heroic Poem menaced its cessation.

It would seem that the nineteenth century—so busy, so rich, so prosaic, so manifold—never succeeded in catching a glimpse of itself. Heroic poetry did not cease to be cultivated, but its themes were no longer contemporary. The successful poets were of two minds: either they thought with longing of an unattainable past, or they endeavored to proclaim the message of the future. The contemporary scene they left as a jumble of uncorrelated particulars.

The poetry of retrospect is exemplified by Tennyson and Longfellow, by Mistral's *Mirèio*, Lönnrot's *Kalevala*, and Mickiewicz's *Pan Tadeusz*. The verses of the Provençal, Finn, and Pole were the more successful because the truth they had to define was more restricted. The language and customs of old Provençe were a lovely memory—an interlude in the rapid development of modern France. It was sufficient to recall that memory through the mists of a loving, wistful poem. The Finns had as yet not entered the stream of modern life, when Lönnrot gathered their rich native resources into one felicitous statement. The case of Mickiewicz is more interesting because more complex. For him patriotism was enough, but that resulted from the simplification due to an irreparable disaster. His earlier poems have not the serenity of *Pan Tadeusz*. In them he shows extreme agitation, culminating in despair. In Poland, invaded, crushed, divided, there could be no straightforward patriotism; but the hero must arm himself with the enemy's strength, and wear for a time the garb of a traitor. It was the spirit of resistance that was essential, and Mickiewicz strove to develop this temper of the soul; but in the famous *Improvisation* he recognized that not passion, but cold knowledge of power, seems to give triumph. These problems appear in the Father Robak of his *Pan Tadeusz* as a reminder of stern realities; but the poem as a whole is a vision of felicity viewed through the window of the poet's pain. It is this yearning which gives virtue to the minute particulars which he brings so vividly before our eyes, recovering in modern times the Homeric freedom to eternize the infinitely small. The quaint formalism of public officers who have only the shadow of a public function, the patriarchal order of the great estates, the loyal subordination of the classes, the buildings and excursions, the woods and forests, gardens and paths, the birds and insects and sounds and scents—Lithuanian Poland floods back into the mind with the pellucid cool green clearness of the Lithuanian folksongs.

The gigantesque Victor Hugo was the coryphæus of the prophets. He was resolved to present, in the *Légende des Siècles*, "successive imprints of the human profile at different dates, from Eve, mother of men, to the Revolution, mother of peoples," so that one would find *quelque chose du passé, quelque chose du présent, et comme un vague mirage de l'avenir*. He carried out his project in sonorous rhythms of exuberant eloquence, with a hand that creates the forms and contours of ideas. The *Légende des Siècles* is merely the culmination of an epic urge which inspires all his best verse, and it is therefore, though obviously a partial achievement, the fullest declaration of Hugo's mind. That mind was the obedient servant of the idea of Progress. Though his epos takes its subjects from the past, it presents a parabola reaching into the future, and it is from the future that its justification should come. Though unified in this way, the mirror of experience was fragmentary, and the poet's meaning is declared by picture after picture, but not by one grand composition. His *petites épopées* might also be called heroic odes, and it is the ode which is the characteristic outlet for the heroic inspiration throughout the nineteenth century. It was so especially with his direct imitators, the innumerable *victorhuguitos* of Spanish America, whose native experience was necessarily one of promise rather than of fulfillment. With a brief and obscure past their eyes necessarily sought distant prospects ahead, as they wrestled with such themes as *Atlántida,* or the future of America, and *Prometeo,* or the future of the human race. We have recently had an epic of the Pacific, beside which Walt Whitman's claim to be the United States seems modest. For with Whitman the heroic touches American life with a more authentic hand than that of Longfellow:

A Phantom gigantic superb, with stern visage accosted me,
Chant me the poem, it said, *that comes from the soul of America,*
    chant me the carol of victory,
And strike up the marches of Libertad, marches more powerful yet
And sing me before you go the song of the throes of Democracy.
(Democracy, the destin'd conqueror, yet treacherous lip-smiles every-
    where,
And death and infidelity at every step.)

I have endeavored to paint for you a picture of European civilization—which is your civilization—in the light of its own revelations. Some of those lights have gone out; all are flickering. But they have revealed the One behind the Many, and I doubt not they will be reillumined. We have passed through a generation of poets who have, somewhat insolently, abstained from making manifestos; but we are now told by younger men that the poet is a specialist in the art we all practise. The poet will again become the mouthpiece of his community; will again make ready "a swan's voice to astound the world." The heroic themes are thronging upon us: infinite violence, infinite heroism; the spirit that destroys gripping the throat of the spirit that believes and builds; a great simplification is teaching us "what men live by." The work of reconstruction may pertain to statesmen and men of affairs; it may be that in recent years we have hampered them by the clamors of our inopportune idealism. But their work will be ill directed and barren unless the poets, in the widest sense conceivable, unless the "unacknowledged legislators of mankind" once more light the beacons. Nor is it unfitting that a great university, rich with two hundred years of knowledge and seeking fresh laurels, should take cognizance of this need. Have we university men been too modest in our claims? The great heroic poets have been teachers, philosophers, schoolmasters—in short, our own blood-brothers—and it has been in the execution of their teaching mission that they have uttered these "thoughts that wander through eternity." We have encouraged in ourselves and our pupils little thoughts and little achievements, since only the little admits of percision. Ought we not rather to think big thoughts, study large maps, and, like our kinsmen the poets, seize the secret which Nature holds, oh, such a little way beyond our grasp?

Unifying Factors in the Development of Modern Ideas

By

JOHN H. RANDALL, Jr., Ph.D.*

To DWELL today on the continuity of a European culture once more in the midst of profound transformation is both irony and wisdom. It is irony, for there are many to tell us that the continuity has at last ended: it is an autopsy we have come to perform. It is wisdom, for there are others, with longer perspectives if no less touched by the tragedies of men, who recall how often civilization has died in Europe in the past, and wonder if this can truly be the end. For the history of Europe is the tale of one crisis and radical transformation after another. In contrast to the stability of other great civilizations, Europe has never crystallized, but has remained flexible in the face of the new problems its energies have created. It has been the very essence of its culture to be revolutionary. That is at once its tragic destiny and its chief glory. It is what gives promise that Europe will yet learn how to meet the conditions of its marvelous power over the forces of nature, that it will manage to organize and control the industrial machine its genius has invented. And it points to the method by which alone its problem may be solved. For out of its very experience of continuous change European thought has won its highest achievement. It has devised in its science a conscious method for the radical change of ideas. In science the twin strands that run through human histories, continuity with the cumulative achievement of the past and adaptability to the changes the present insistently demands, are woven into a single harmonious fabric. Science is both the cardinal illustration and the most effective instrument of continuity in change.

Today, what doubts we have concerning the continuity of European culture are over the end we fear, not over the be-

* Professor of Philosophy, Columbia University.

ginnings we know. And that is but natural. For men live and act always in an age of transition and revolution. It is the present that is problematic and uncertain, and only the past that reveals a clear pattern. The choices we must make tomorrow are always momentous, for they will determine the future. So it is not strange, but rather the very nature of human history, that today we should find European thought confronting the most serious and tragic crisis in its long career—as men have so often found it before, and will so often again.

Men are aware of the changes, not the continuities in the present; for it is not continuities that demand the decision in which living consists. It is only in the past that they emerge, in the backward look of the historian. He can take the most revolutionary idea, that came to its discoverer with the insistent compulsion of novelty, and lay bare its long history, the gradual stages by which men slowly worked it out. In their revolt against the tyranny of intellectual authority, the pioneers of seventeenth-century science were conscious as few others of making a sharp break with the past, of wiping the slate clean and starting afresh with reason alone. Yet every one of them, we now know, was influenced in a thousand ways by the intellectual traditions on which he drew. And the very conceptions of reason they severally trusted for liberation came to them scarred with the battles and worn with the uses of their long histories. Descartes, of them all, had the utmost contempt for the past. Today he has won his fitting reward. For the foremost historian of medieval thought has calmly awarded him the post of the greatest of those who stand in the long tradition that stems from St. Augustine. Especially is this continuity exhibited in the ideas that are so widely shared as to be a social possession. Though human nature be infinitely plastic, and the new-born babe can take on with ease any of the myriad forms of culture man has devised for himself, those institutionalized habits are themselves extraordinarily tough, and even when pressure has grown intolerable change but slowly. This toughness and vitality of intellectual traditions ardent revolutionaries learn to their sorrow, and nostalgic conservatives might well recall to their joy.

So the tale of the birth of modern European culture is a tale of continuity in change. The Middle Ages were invented by intellectual revolutionaries; they have now been destroyed

by the historians and scholars of our generation, who have refused at last to take those boasts at their face value. To their
leaders the Renaissance and the Reformation were desperate
leaps back over the immediate past to the purity of an earlier
and a wiser time. But the historian, soberly examining their
claims to novelty—or to a novel antiquity—has pushed each of
the distinctive ideas for which they stood further and further
back into those very Middle Ages from which they were trying
to escape. After all, we find, there were so many rebirths of
ancient learning, so many reformations of the Church to its
original holiness! The modernity of the Middle Ages has now
been made a familiar story; and so has the medieval character
of modern times. The scholars have pushed continuity ahead
as well as backward. Modern ideas, we discover, did not really
make their appearance till the Age of Enlightenment; what
men earlier so bravely felt and thought was mere compromise
and transition. And now the wise tell us that the heavenly city
the eighteenth-century philosophers worshipped, and even their
adored reason itself, link them, too, far more closely to the
great classic tradition of ages past than to the manifold ir-
rationalisms of the present and the earthly purgatory to which
we soberly look forward. St. Francis, we discover, was fundamentally modern, St. Marx medieval; and though not the whole
truth, what we discover is true. There has been plenty of
change, revolutionary change; but these revelations of our
scholars may serve to illustrate the underlying continuity that
permeates the development of European ideas from the very
beginnings of Western civilization. There has been continuity
in each of the major senses in which we find it exhibited in
human histories. There has been the gradual and continuous
change that, slowly accumulating, finally reaches spectacular
achievement, or wins general acceptance. There has been the
sheer persistence of intellectual materials, of assumptions,
methods, and attitudes. And there has been the preservation
of old ideas bent to new uses in the face of novel experience.

In every field of European culture we find a continuous development in all these senses, with no sharp break, from the
eleventh century on. The dominant force, the steady increase
of the scope and importance of Europe's economic activity,
began with the revival of agriculture and the coming of trade
and town life. It has continued ever since at an accelerating

rate, generating a characteristic type of social experience fundamental in modern times, and quite unlike the experience of
the ancient world—the experience of an expanding society, out-
growing its older forms of organization, and desperately trying
to escape them. It is this that lies back of the long drive for
emancipation from constricting bonds, intellectual and institutional, that has embedded the idea of Freedom so deeply in the
European heritage. Intellectually, there is the same story of
growth and expansion, the eager appropriation of more and
more of the materials of the ancient world to meet the needs
of new experience and the demands for a more potent method.
All the problems of medieval and modern thought have arisen
from the conflict of new knowledge and experience with traditional thought and values. The first clash came with the impact
of Aristotelian science on the Augustinian wisdom in the twelfth
century. The problems it generated, and the solutions with
which men met them, have ever since remained the central and
organizing problems of modern thought. The story of natural
science, chief glory of modern times, once began in 1543 with
Copernicus. It has been pushed back through the Paduan school
of the fifteenth century, through the Masters of Paris in the
fourteenth, to the Oxford group of the thirteenth and the
School of Chartres in the twelfth. And modern philosophy,
which every schoolboy knew sprang full-grown from the brow
of Descartes, has revealed the potent traditions of later medieval
times, which controlled the assumptions and dictated the methods of the seventeenth-century system-builders. Today the first
modern philosopher is no longer Descartes, it is St. Thomas—
unless indeed it be St. Augustine! Without a knowledge of
those two intricate and subtle bodies of ideas, the subsequent
course of the most modern European thinking grows quite unintelligible.

Now that the hitherto unknown domain of late medieval
thought has begun to be explored, so assured is the intellectual
continuity between the ideas of the Middle Ages and of modern
times that I shall not here try once more to prove what a generation of scholars has established. Rather, assuming that continuity, I shall attempt to illustrate it. For whatever strand one
singles out of the intellectual life of Western civilization, it
proves to run back to what we still name the Middle Ages. No
longer do we find a great gulf between the thirteenth century

and what we used to call *the* Renaissance. The Middle Ages form the essential prelude to the development of modern ideas. They have become for us the first stage in modern times, even as that era—the Age of Nationalism—will seem to those who come after the first stage in the new world that Europe will yet create.

In these harsh times, when European nations seem bent on destroying each other in a conflict over differing methods of meeting their common problems, there is one continuity that asks for special emphasis. We have heard much of the unity of medieval civilization. That heritage too was not lost: European culture remained a unity. Despite all the centripetal forces, despite the destruction of the ecclesiastical bond that served to give formal expression to the earlier unity of Christendom, despite the building up of distinctive national traditions, so consciously fostered for ulterior ends in the last century—despite all we know so well of the tragic failure to achieve a European government able to organize the forces of her incomparable civilization—despite all this, Europe has continued to enjoy a common intellectual life. It has not been a unity without differences, it has not been a uniformity; and the differences have been important, fascinating, and vital. But neither was the unity inherited from medieval culture a uniformity without differences.

For unity, like continuity, never is, but always has been—or shall be. It is not something we possess; it is something we look back to with longing, in our lost innocence, in the hope that we too may introduce a little more order and consistency into the multiplicity and diversity in which we forever find ourselves wandering. I would not quarrel too seriously with those who contrast "thirteenth-century unity" with the "intellectual chaos" of modern times. And I yield to no man in admiration for the architectonic synthesis of St. Thomas. But I wonder whether even those in his own order, who so vigorously fought to condemn his theses, were fully aware that they were face to face with a supreme synthetic achievement, and enjoying a unity of thought forever to be denied their successors—to say nothing of the other eager and diverse partisans who made the life of the medieval universities so tumultuous and boisterous a battleground of ideas.

In sober fact, modern culture has been fully as unified as

medieval. Doubtless it might well have more of unity than it has: we need perspectives and foci today. But it could so easily possess too much, as the unhappy nations of Europe witness. Europe needs unification, God knows; it must organize its economic and political life, or perish in suicide. But it is not its ideas that need unifying. Those who are calling today for a unifying social faith, for a new synthesis of knowledge and aspiration, can already contemplate abroad the only kind of synthesis likely to prove popular or effective.

The unity of modern culture has not been such a unity of belief, of creed and dogma—though the Great Tradition, coming down through the Middle Ages from Greek thought, has given it a direction and a backbone in the midst of all the criticisms and extensions that moderns have made. It has not been a unity of faith—though there has been a persisting core of common and shared ideals and values, whatever the devices to which men have turned to give them social embodiment. The unity of modern culture has been a unity of problems confronted, of novel experience to be assimilated and understood, of novel beliefs to be worked somehow into the accepted pattern of living. European thinkers may have wandered into far lands: but again and again they have been called back to meet the same insistent difficulties. And those common problems have repeatedly forced divergent ideas and intellectual methods to face the compulsions of a common world and a common life. Starting with the same heritage of ideas, men developed them in diverse ways as their experience differed. Characteristic traditions, so widely shared as to be almost national, took form as early as the fourteenth century, when the philosophies the later world was to use as its tools and methods first received clear-cut expression. Their subtle but inescapable differences in attitude and approach reappear in the efforts of the intellectual pioneers of the seventeenth century to meet their new problems; they have persisted to this day, coloring political, religious, scientific, and philosophic thought.

Yet time and again these differing intellectual traditions have confronted the same fundamental problems of European social experience; and confronting them, have been led, each by its own route, to converge once more. There have been the problems of economic life, with a different incidence, to be sure, in different lands, but still with a common pattern—the growth of commerce, the rise of business, the new ideals they generated, the new demands for an altered political control. There have been the common problems of industrial and technological civilization, which have forced all lands, each in its own way, to resort to the same devices, and to wage the same bitter quarrels over the same alternative methods. The same expanding commerce broke down the medieval social synthesis, and rendered both its institutions and its ideals inadequate; it provoked the same individualistic reaction, the same demand for the cardinal freedom to build up the modern world. All medieval and modern thought has been colored by the necessity of vindicating an ever growing individualism against the earlier medieval collectivism. The great intellectual movements—the Thomistic protest against Platonic realism, the rebellion of nominalism against Thomism, the Renaissance, the Reformation, the scientific thought of the seventeenth century, the Enlightenment, the Romantic rebellion, the liberalism of the nineteenth century—all have been successive waves of individualism in conduct, religion, and thought. Now that machine technology has built up a new social structure within the ruins of the old, quite irrelevant to the whole ideology of freedom and individuality, Europeans have had to reverse the whole current of their intellectual tradition to get back somehow to a collectivism adequate for a common industrial age. This helps to explain why the task is so hard, why it often seems easier to try to wipe out the past completely, instead of remolding it to meet new needs. Terrific pressure has called for heroic remedies.

And always there has been, for every tradition, the steady advance of science, with its new knowledge to be somehow reconciled with older beliefs, and its new methods to be assimilated and employed. Of all the factors unifying modern ideas, the inescapable fact of science has been the most influential. Just so in the thirteenth century it was likewise science, in the body of Aristotelian thought, that made possible the medieval synthesis. In its continuous if wayward advance, ever injecting new concepts and new methods into some painfully won adjustment, science has been the chief begetter of common intellectual problems, and the chief source of common intellectual methods. And even today it forms the main body of ideas that still remain a common possession of a divided Europe, the principal legacy

of the rich achievements of the modern era to those in the future
who have the wit to wield it.

Both the continuity and the unity of European thought I
wish to illustrate in terms of what has persisted during the entire
medieval and modern period as the central unifying problem
of all. It arose as the major issue in the thirteenth century: the
differing positions taken determined the main outlines of the
distinctive philosophies left as a heritage to modern times. It is
still the basic intellectual issue in the European conflict today,
lifting it above a mere struggle for power to a genuine conflict
of method—or, if we prefer, of ideals. It touches on and involves
in the end every one of those major ideas that have formed the
core of European intellectual life.

The thirteenth century knew it as the problem of the relation of reason to faith, of science to wisdom. In our sophistication, we are apt to phrase it differently. We call it the problem
of the relation of science to human values, of our knowledge
of the means and mechanisms by which we wield power over
nature and over ourselves to the ends of action, the social ideals
to which that power is directed. It is the question of the relation of Truth to Good. In what way is truth a means to the
social good? What is the good which knowledge must serve,
whose good is it in the end, and by what means is it to be
determined?

This is the basic problem of a dynamic culture, one whose
knowledge and therefore whose power is increasing and expanding. What it can do is forever coming into conflict with
what it thinks it ought to do, with its accustomed pattern of
behavior. Its faith—its inherited ideals and goals—is forever
being upset by new knowledge, bringing the power to do new
things. That new power carries with it the opportunity to realize old goals that had formerly seemed unattainable: it liberates
from the bondage of ignorance and weakness. But it has its
own compulsions: much that men had done with impunity it
now makes impossible. To act in the familiar way with magni-
fied power is become far too dangerous; or it is excluded by
the other things men must do to fulfill the promise of their
new resources. For the knowledge that is power is no mere
instrument for effecting accustomed ends: it brings with it new
goals of its own, and imposes its own conditions and responsibilities. It raises inescapably the question of the uses to which

it can be put. Science, far from being irrelevant to values, impinges upon them at every turn. A society that lives by science is bound by the conditions and responsibilities of its power. Upon the strategy of its purposes depends whether it uses its power to achieve new heights, or to sink to new depths. We cannot forget these days that Europe has learned to master the air.

Now the Middle Ages inherited from Greek thought two major traditions, two basic ways of dealing with this central problem. There is the way we may broadly call humanism, which makes of truth a means to achieving the good of man. It subordinates science to values, and takes knowledge as an instrument of power. And there is the way we may call naturalism, the way of scientific understanding. It finds truth no mere means, but an essential part of human good. For it, science is itself a supreme value, and there is no greater power than understanding itself. It is the glory of the medieval synthesis that it succeeded in uniting these two ways, in bringing together humanism and naturalism, in identifying science with wisdom and truth with good. It is the tragedy of Europe that since then the two ways, save for a brief coöperation again in the eighteenth century, have parted company. Wisdom has been divorced from science, truth from good, to their mutual confusion. The central problem of European culture has been to create a scientific humanism that would bring them together once more, as they were united in the thirteenth century.

Humanism the Middle Ages found in the philosophy of St. Augustine—the Platonic Augustine of the medieval thinkers, not the Manichaean of the Reformation. Science and naturalism it found in Aristotle—a science which made the problem easier than it has been in modern times, for it did not exclude man from its scope, and it saw human life not as something divorced from nature, but rather as the illustration of the fullest development of nature's processes. In the solution of St. Thomas, Aristotelian naturalism was nicely inserted within the framework of the Augustinian humanism, subtly transforming it at every turn, and creating the pattern of a scientific humanism as the central core of the European tradition.

Augustine set wisdom above science, as its source and criterion. He made truth depend on good, and subordinated knowledge to the control of values. Science in the end is of worth only in the measure that it contributes to the beatitude that is salvation. And that good which is the object of wisdom is also the object of faith; in the last analysis it is faith which supplies the goals which knowledge must serve. In contrast, St. Thomas made the vision of truth itself the highest good, that truth which is the source of all other truths. In understanding he found man's true well-being, and in knowledge the supreme excellence. The goals of human living are not furnished by a faith imposed upon knowledge from above; they are found rather through the scientific analysis of the proper function of a rational animal.

Both Augustine and Thomas shared the common methods of reason and experience; but they meant quite different things by them. For Augustine, experience was something inner, private, and immediate; it was found by turning away from the world to the soul. And reason likewise was to be reached by analyzing the soul to discover the Master within. It was an object of intellectual intuition, of faith and loyalty. For Thomas, experience was open and public, the operation of man's powers in coöperation with the powers of his world. The starting-point of analysis was not the inward vision of the soul, but rather common observation and the obvious facts. And reason likewise was common to all; it was found in that most public of all human functions, language and communication. It was man's expression of the structure of his common world. The Augustinian philosophy of experience is the ancestor of all the idealisms of modern times; and, in its Ockhamite versions, which embraced a positivistic vision of science, of all the empiricisms. And all, in the end, fall back on faith to determine the goals of living. The Thomistic philosophy of being is the ancestor of all science, of all appeal to observation and testing, and to the rational principles by which facts are rendered intelligible.

In the seventeenth century the content of science changed: it now brought an understanding of nature rather than of human life, in terms that left life unintelligible. And the salvation men sought was no longer beatitude in eternity, but frankly the power and the glory of this world. The power to which the way of humanism made science an instrument became dominion over nature's forces; the end of knowledge was now to extend the bounds of human empire over nature. No longer was science the servant of wisdom, of human good. It was the handmaiden of a power aimed indifferently at good or ill—to the effecting of all things possible. Francis Bacon is the prophet and the consummate spokesman of what the humanist way made out of the new science. That science must indeed aim at "truth in speculation," but it must be a truth that will bring "freedom in operation"—the sheer power to do. And the understanding which the way of naturalism made the supreme value likewise ceased to be the understanding of human good. It became the sheer knowledge of what is, and of man as a part of the great Scheme of things. It might, in a Spinoza, still bring a power, a power over the passions, through the resigned acceptance of what must be; but the power to do what we must and to accept our own destiny remained none the less an impotence. Spinoza has come, somewhat unfairly, to stand as the consummate expression of that other great modern idea, the idea of a pure and disinterested science—the science that studies nature, and man's life in nature, but has no eye for human good and is content with knowing while it lets others do. To the humanist modern science brought the freedom of power, to the naturalist the freedom of understanding; but both it robbed of the treasure they had enjoyed during the Middle Ages, the freedom that is the service of the Good.

Yet the great and insistent problem all men were forced to face was the problem of Freedom, of finding liberation from the institutions of the medieval world, religious, economic, political. And since the goal of emancipation was so clear, the absence of wisdom did not at first prove serious. Men knew what they wanted, and proceeded to secure it. The good was given; the major question was how to secure it. By the eighteenth century the individualistic values were so widely accepted that a new synthesis proved possible. They were firmly established by both reason and experience. Because no sober man of common sense would presume to doubt them, it was not realized that only the intense need of liberation supported the generous and humane ideals of that Enlightenment synthesis. Men forgot that Reason supplies no premises of its own, but depends for the principles it so nicely elaborates on some accepted values: it binds men together only when they already share a common faith. And they forgot also that experience can unite men only when it is common, when it is the shared tradition of a group.

So long as Europe overwhelmingly demanded emancipation from the past, the fact that its intellectual methods of reason and experience were impotent of themselves to unite men in a common wisdom was of little practical moment. But the difficulties broke out so soon as men passed from mere emancipation to the harder tasks of constructing new institutions. Even before the coming of industrialism, the major problem of European thought had begun to shift from Freedom to Organization. At first, it was the need to integrate the national cultures of the post-Napoleonic world. Then, with ever increasing pressure, came the problem of organizing economic life to realize the promise of technology, and to enable it to continue functioning. Freedom was no longer enough; there was need of wisdom once more. Where could men find the necessary wisdom? By what ideas could they be reunited? In a culture drenched with generations of struggle to achieve individualism, how could they enlist the coöperative support of men to effect the necessary social control and directions of technology?

The common need of unification turned men again to their two inherited methods of achieving wisdom. Following the way of humanism, they again sought a wisdom that would control and direct science and its terrifying power over nature. Science was irrelevant to human good, the moderns had taught; it was disruptive and chaotic. It must be brought to order by a unifying social faith in some other superior good. In that good was to be the true embodiment of reason and experience.

In its desperate search for social organization, Europe has tried a number of different unifying ideas. In the aftermath of the French Revolution, it appealed to the Church once more, to the Christian faith; and there are still those who hope that Christianity can perform again in the modern world the miracle of organization it accomplished in the Middle Ages. Reason divides, preached de Maistre; faith alone can unite. But alas, the Church has united its enemies as well as the faithful. Men appealed to the mighty and potent idea of the Nation, strongest of all unifying forces in modern times. Hegel showed how the Nation might be the very embodiment of the World Reason; a host of others have found in it the deepest and most profound reaches of human experience. The idea of Freedom itself was won from the liberals and enthroned in the national state. And men turned to the idea of the Working-Class, of the Toiling and Oppressed Masses; Marx has convinced millions that it is the most rational of all ideas, the true locus and seat of the dialectic of history.

These are all potent ideas, rooted in the very core of European culture; their power for good or ill seems still inexhaustible. They form the several unifying faiths to which Europe has fled in its bitter struggle to escape centuries of individualism. They are the social goods set up to control all knowledge, the wisdom that is to overcome the anarchy of science. That truth is not true which does not derive from them and their strength; that knowledge is false which does not lead men to their Truth. They repeat, in our day and generation, the pattern of the old Augustinian solution, the ministry of all science to the power that can bring salvation.

Over against them is set the other method, the method that founds wisdom, not on some social faith external to science, but on science itself. For it, the good that will unite men in its service is not to be imposed on knowledge from without. It must be itself determined by knowledge, and it must embrace science, not dominate it. The understanding and power of science, it holds, are essential to wisdom: truth is the source of good. The values that will bind men together are not to be found in a superior Reason that can be reached only by faith, or in an Experience that is an appeal to a limited and divisive tradition. They are discoverable only in a common and public reason and experience indissolubly married in the critical methods of scientific inquiry and verification. This way, the way of a scientific humanism, repeats today the wisdom of St. Thomas.

These two ways of relating science and wisdom, truth and good, were struggling in the Middle Ages; they are still in conflict today. They are the legacy of centuries of European thought upon its most profound problem. They are the two ideas between which men can choose in their common need. The goal is set: we must learn how to organize our society so that we may live with technology, and with those peoples who have already taken its demands seriously. The issue that still remains open, the great question at stake in the present tragic conflict, concerns the method of achieving that organization. We too can resort to a unifying faith that will raise some social good above truth, the good of the nation, or the good of a class. Already is heard the call for an American faith; already the idea of national defense has revealed its power to effect the organization we need. We too can turn to the wisdom of Augustine. Or we can adopt the fuller wisdom of Thomas. We can learn from the great Augustinian tradition, the great tradition of humanism, that science must be bent to the service of the Good: in disinterested science, in a science that disdainfully refuses to take account of values, in a science that deliberately eschews wisdom, there is no salvation. But the Good to which science ministers must be a good itself determined by scientific methods, a good of which science is an essential part.

The new faiths are powerful enough; they can unify nations and peoples. But they cannot unify Europe; and until that unity is achieved, all the organization they make possible within national boundaries will serve but to increase the power of the forces of division. The faiths that set good above truth are notoriously negative and intolerant, exclusive rather than inclusive, and bitterly directed against each other. The synthesis that can unify Europe will be comprehensive rather than exclusive, and it will focus its faith, not on empty slogans and hatred for other groups, but upon the critical methods of science and intelligence. Such a faith is fortunately no novelty for Europe; it is its central idea, the core of the Great Tradition. It is the faith that St. Thomas created for the Middle Ages; it is the faith that Europe must recreate today, or perish.

Some Sceptical Observations (While They Are Still Possible) on the Relationship of Economic and Political Developments in Modern Europe to Contemporary Political Totalitarianism and Economic Determinism

By

CARLTON J. H. HAYES, Ph. D., LL.D., L.H.D., Litt. D.*

In the period of modern European history, conventionally dated from the fifteenth or sixteenth century, just as in earlier periods, it has been, of course, not so much the general run of events as particular selections and interpretations of events which have attracted attention and exercised influence. In other words, the raw stuff of history never of itself makes any pattern of the past; this, which apparently humans crave, they get from historiography, and historiography, we know, reflects a contemporaneous, rather than an antecedent, *Zeitgeist*.

If a symposium analogous to the present one had been held when the University of Pennsylvania began in 1740, the participants in all probability would have reviewed man's culture under the spell of the prevalent historiography of the seventeenth and early eighteenth centuries, and the audience would have been spared an address certainly on economic and probably on political developments of modern Europe. Any address on modern Europe would surely have been adorned on that occasion with classical allusions and humanistic phrases; if coming from an elderly conservative scholar it would have been concerned primarily with religious and ecclesiastical matters, while a younger, more up-to-date scholar would have oriented it toward the rising sun of natural science, natural law, and intellectual progress. Now, two full centuries later, we are the

* Seth Low Professor of History, Columbia University.

heirs—and in a sense the products—of two great intervening gestations of historiography: the liberal political of the nineteenth century, and the deterministic economic of the twentieth. At the present celebration, accordingly, a conservative "authority" on modern Europe is expected to concentrate on the political state and its functioning, while a radical may pain but not surprise you by dwelling on economic and sociological statistics and interpreting them according to the dogma of economic determinism. This last, I need hardly suggest, is as different from the assumptions of Montesquieu, Voltaire, and Hume, when the University of Pennsylvania was young, as those were from the viewpoint of the Magdeburg Centuries, Cardinal Baronius, and Bishop Bossuet. As different, and perhaps of no greater validity.

Yet I must make obeisance to the economic interpretation of history. For not even a sceptic can afford to deny it at least a respectful curtsey. Since the days of Marx and Buckle it has inspired the researches and conditioned the conclusions of innumerable social scientists of all sorts, and gradually it has been accepted consciously or unconsciously by an ever widening public, until it has come to supply not only an elaborate creed for a vast and expanding Union of Soviet Socialist Republics but also a central presupposition for multitudes who indignantly reject the appellation of Communist. It is in the spirit of economic determinism that an eminent editor of the *New York Herald-Tribune* has ascribed American participation in the World War to the machinations of bankers and the financial interests of Wall Street. It is in the same spirit that college and university students in the United States, including a large proportion from stalwart Republican homes and conservative private schools, have perceived in that ascription the whole truth and a practical justification for stubborn and militant pacifism.

And what contemporary student of modern European history would not expect me, on an occasion like this, to indicate at least the major landmarks in the re-mapping of that history which the economic interpretation has latterly effected? There is, first, the rise of modern capitalism, starting with the exploitation of peasants by landlords and of apprentices by master guildsmen, and swiftly developing as a new profit-motive brought on and was enhanced by the European religious upheaval and the overseas commercial expansion of the sixteenth century. The confiscation of church property and the secularization of ecclesiastical institutions provided substantial bases for the modern capitalistic state, just as "unequal trade" with distant lands and enslavement of Indians and Negroes further enriched the governing groups within such states.

Then, second, as capitalism overleaps the narrow confines of aristocracy, in which it has originated, and spreads out among urban commoners, enriching them proportionately more, these latter emerge as a self-conscious and ambitious bourgeoisie, determined to play the leading rôle in government and to free themselves from economic and social trammels of the past. Wherefore they invoke principles of individual liberty and enshrine them in Petition of Rights, Bill of Rights, Declaration of Independence, or of the Rights of Man; and for their own political advancement they precipitate and are the chief beneficiaries of the English revolutions of the seventeenth century and the American and French revolutions of the eighteenth.

Third, there is the Industrial Revolution, the utilization of science and technology to speed up and multiply the production of goods and hence of private profits. It assures the final triumph of bourgeois capitalism and the ascendancy of the liberal state in which industrialists and commercial magnates enjoy political preference and by means of which they reduce to a minimum governmental and other interference with their competitive buying and selling abroad and their exploitation of the laboring masses at home. The Industrial Revolution is strikingly dynamic; it runs from one industry to another, and from one country to another, until the quest which it prompts for regions where raw materials can be bought most cheaply, manufactured goods sold most profitably, and capital investments made most lucratively, ends in a material Europeanization of the whole world.

But the Industrial Revolution which magnifies capitalism and conduces to a world-wide imperialism has also given rise to a numerous class of propertyless wage-earners—the "industrial serfs" or "proletariat"—whose gradually successful struggle against exploitation constitutes the fourth and last of the great landmarks of modern history. Against the individualism of capitalists, the proletarians promote a socializing trend, which leads to political democracy, popular education, the feminist movement, collective bargaining, social insurance, regulatory legislation, and all those experiments in municipal and state socialism which characterize the present age. Contemporary differences between dictatorships, and between them and democracy, represent different stages reached by the socializing struggle in the several countries.

England, whose primacy among the nations has been a purely modern phenomenon, is usually cited as the most perfect illustration of economic determinism. There, an early decay of guilds and other restraining institutions of the middle ages, a relatively complete sequestration of ecclesiastical property, and peculiarly favorable opportunities for piracy, freebooting, and slave-trading, combined to engender in high degree the capitalistic spirit and to foster the far-flung commercial enterprise responsible for the attainment of naval supremacy and for the construction of the largest imperial domain the world has ever known. There, too, the accumulation of bourgeois wealth and consequently of bourgeois power produced the first of modern political revolutions and the ideal constitutional liberal state. There, too, began the Industrial Revolution, and hence free trade and a century of England's unquestioned predominance as workshop and banker of the world. There, finally, has emerged the proletariat with its ample socializing ambitions and achievements. And if England is now on the wane and her empire about to be dissolved, it is simply because a Continental power like Germany has at last outstripped her in economic competition.

Such, in broad outline, is the economic interpretation of modern history. I fear, however, that it looks better to the sociologist who deals in broad outlines than to the historian who tries to fill in details. For as soon as one particularizes about it, one encounters contradictions and seemingly quite insoluble problems. The profit motive is no novelty of modern history—it may even inhere in what is called "human nature"; and "modern capitalism" certainly existed before "modern times." Nor was England more "capitalistic" in the sixteenth century than Italy or Germany, the Low Countries or France. Both Spain and Portugal had earlier, and until the nineteenth century much larger, empires than England; and after reading numerous treatises on the Industrial Revolution I for one am thoroughly dissatisfied with any economic explanation yet offered for its how, why, or where. It obviously did not originate in the invention of some cotton machinery in the 1770's, but long before; and its prime development in England rather than on the Continent, say in France, may reasonably be attributed less to any general economic circumstance than to a specific person, Napoleon Bonaparte.

Moreover, I am very sceptical about the bourgeois paternity of modern liberalism. Oliver Cromwell was a country gentleman, and so were John Locke and Thomas Jefferson; Montesquieu and Mirabeau were privileged nobles, and so were Stein and Humboldt, Russell and Palmerston, Cavour and Rudini, Kossuth and Déak. For that matter, does the word "bourgeoisie" really describe any single coherent "class" in modern times, whether "capitalistic" or not, or is it mere dialectic which, by lumping together different occupational groups, conceals the conflicting interests and mutual antagonisms of industrialists (big and little), traders, bankers, shopkeepers, white-collared employees, and professional men—physicians, lawyers, engineers, artists, clergymen, teachers, etc.? One has only to peruse the French or German parliamentary debates between 1870 and 1914 to appreciate how little was the coöperation, for example, between industrialists and traders; and one should not forget that the chief and most telling critiques of "bourgeois capitalism" were the work of "bourgeois" intellectuals like Marx and Proudhon, Kautsky and Jaurès. But if "bourgeoisie" lacks precise meaning, how much the more does "proletariat"! This, as commonly employed, is surely not synonymous with the "working class," unless you suppose that farmers and peasants do not work, or master mechanics or clerks or proprietors of little businesses; and even if you arbitrarily limit "proletariat" to urban wage-earners, it still includes quite incompatible elements of "skilled" and "unskilled" labor, of persons who are "class-conscious" and more who are not.

Besides, the latter-day socializing trend has been promoted no more by "proletarian" trade unionists than by combinations of bourgeois industrialists and agitation of bourgeois intellectuals—or nationalistic aristocrats. By no stretch of imagination can Joseph Chamberlain or Bernard Shaw or Prince Bismarck be regarded as "proletarian"; yet such persons have been somewhere in the vanguard of "socializers." Indeed, the trend of the last sixty years is but a reversion to, and extension of, the mercantilist and cameralist policies pursued by the pre-industrial and aristocratic régimes of the seventeenth and eighteenth centuries—Louis XIV's in France, Frederick the Great's in Prussia; just as contemporary liberalism is a survival, albeit a declining survival, of the political philosophy of such upper-class ornaments of the seventeenth and eighteenth centuries as Milton and Locke, Leibniz and Montesquieu.

Let me express, further, the gravest doubt about the applicability of economic determinism to what is perhaps the most distinctive phenomenon of modern times—the vogue of nationalism and the making of frontiers of language into state boundaries and tariff walls. On purely economic grounds, anyone could reasonably agree with such "bourgeois" capitalists as Cobden and Bright, or with such a magisterial spokesman for the "proletariat" as Karl Marx, that the political (and intellectual) evolution of Europe ought to be toward internationalism and cosmopolitanism. A narrowly local economy had produced the city-states and feudal states of the middle ages. A broadening economy, resulting from commercial expansion, gave rise in the sixteenth century to national states. Why then, should not the world-wide economy, which was ushered in by the Industrial Revolution, lead to a world-state or at least to a coöperating league of nations? It should, but actually it hasn't. Free trade within a town or a province has been succeeded by free trade within a nation, and both Cobdenite liberals and Marxian socialists presumably have had a common economic interest in pressing for the capstone of international free trade. Yet the capstone is still not in place; and though perhaps some day it will be, right now in 1940 (which is as far as the historian can go) it is more spurned and rejected than it was in 1740. What matters most now is the subordination of trade, industry, agriculture—all economic life—to the totalitarian national state. Of this outcome there must be other explanation than economic.

It is my personal conviction that at least in modern Europe political action has directed economic developments far more than these have determined political action, and that therefore politics, if conceived of in the Aristotelian sense and treated as an expression of psychological and cultural as well as material concerns, is much more revealing than economics. For an understanding of contemporary totalitarianism, totalitarian history is requisite, and the central and coördinating feature of both is **the state.**

One can scarcely exaggerate the importance of the modern state, or the significance of its evolution during the past four hundred years. It has been, of course, no creation of merely modern times. It arose out of medieval feudalism and the humanistic revival of Roman law. Dante penned the *De Monarchia* and Marsiglio of Padua the *Defensor Pacis* over a century before the Turks took Constantinople; Machiavelli's *Prince* antedated Luther's *Theses*; and prior to the discovery of America, Ferdinand and Isabella were constructing the modern Spanish state, Louis XI the French, Henry VII the English. I have no doubt that the rise of the modern state was aided by economic factors, but still more by its association with the psychology of nascent nationalism. For flitting beneath the cosmopolitanism of Roman Empire and Catholic Church, and yet hovering over the practical localism and provincialism of ordinary life, were the disembodied spirits, so to speak, of more or less self-conscious linguistic groups which we term nationalities; and in the modern state these finally became incarnate and assumed form and substance. The state of Henry VII was the English state; that of Louis XI, the French state; that of Ferdinand and Isabella, the Spanish state. Even that relic of antiquity and early Christendom, the Holy Roman Empire, tried to be the "Holy Roman Empire of the German Nation."

The nationalizing of the state has been a very gradual and halting process, involving at the outset more of accident than design, and long affecting some parts of Europe more than others. But however and wherever accomplished, it has resulted in arousing an intense popular enthusiasm for the national state and hence in endowing it with extraordinary solidarity and potency. It was nationalist England which held the imperially minded Philip II at bay, and nationalist Holland which successfully rebelled against him. It was nationalist England again which despoiled Bourbon dynasts of much of their dominion and commerce. It was nationalist France of the revolutionary era which overran the Continent and taught all its peoples to be nationalist and to strive for national states of their own. It was her aptest pupil, nationalist Prussia, which ousted imperial Austria from Germany and which now in the twentieth century, with unexampled solidarity and potency, runs amok.

Since the fifteenth century, when the modern state was taking root, a variety of developments—factual and psychological—

have favored its growth and spread, and have nourished the dark fruit which in the twentieth century it abundantly yields. One of these, to which I have just referred, and whose psychological significance cannot be overestimated, is the exhaustless bubbling up of popular nationalism and its canalizing from cultural fields into political (and economic) irrigation of the national state. I would mention five others, in all of which economic considerations have doubtless played a part, though only a part.

First has been the multiplication of things for the state to do. Progressively since the sixteenth century it has taken over previous functions of the church: the maintenance and direction of educational systems from elementary school up to university, the stimulus to and subsidizing of the arts and sciences, the support of charitable institutions, the guardianship of women and children, the care of the poor and the insane. Since the seventeenth and eighteenth centuries, moreover, it has absorbed the local judicial and police powers of the traditional "second estate"—the nobility—and likewise it has fallen heir to the regulatory powers of the traditional merchant and craft guilds whose decay and destruction it hastened. Thus, whereas the business of the secular state was once confined pretty strictly to military protection of its citizens against foreign invasion and domestic disorder and to appellate jurisdiction in certain legal cases, it now embraces a veritable totality of functions—economic and social, cultural and intellectual, provincial and local. No longer does it recognize any principle of plural sovereignty; no longer does it share authority with church, class, or corporation. What rights remain to trade union or religious body are exercised by sufferance of the state and subject to its restriction or prohibition; and it is to the state above everything else that the ordinary man looks for the dispensing of favors.

Second has been the increasing substantiality of the state, the perfecting of agencies for effective discharge of its multiplying functions. I refer here not merely to modern progress in military art and science, important and revolutionary as this has been—the supplanting of feudal armies of bowmen by state armies of gunmen, the transformation of relatively small professional armies into huge conscript armies, the development of general staff, corps organization, and service of supply, the utilization of the latest technology for totalitarian preparedness with machine guns and blasting artillery, tanks and submarines, airplanes and explosive bombs—the whole redounding perhaps to a state's bellicosity and certainly to its ability to suppress internal tumult and revolt. I refer more especially to the gradual transition from royal "court" government of the sixteenth century to professional "career" government of the eighteenth century open to men of talent and frequently of university training, and thence to the elaborated bureaucracy and civil service of the nineteenth century and our own day. Political and civil administration is now characterized by "red tape" but also by an *esprit de corps,* an ambitiousness, a devotion to duty, and undoubtedly a technical expertness without previous parallel. Thereby it is enabled to do vastly more, to do it with much greater efficiency, and to keep on doing it regardless of change of titular sovereign or in external form of government. And however numerous the armed forces of a national state may be, its civil service ramifies still further among the masses and provides a larger number of them with an assured livelihood and consequently with special cause for gratitude and loyalty.

Third has been the intensifying influence of frontiers and frontier psychology. This may sound a bit cryptic, and it is ambiguous in that I attach two different meanings to the word "frontier." On the one hand, I mean the political frontiers— the interstate frontiers—on the European continent. If you look at a contemporaneous map of fifteenth- or sixteenth-century Europe, you will be struck by the lack of clear-cut boundaries. For instance, you will note that the map-maker of that time has inscribed the good old Latin word "Gallia" all over a hodgepodge of local districts vaguely labeled Brittany, Languedoc, Burgundy, Alsace, etc., some of which, you are left to find from other sources, were within the German Empire and ruled by the French King, while others were outside and ruled by him personally or in bewilderingly different degrees of feudal dependency. In other words, you cannot discover from such a map just what were the boundaries of France, and it is safe to say that the ordinary Frenchman did not know or care. Not until the Revolution of the late eighteenth century did the general run of Frenchmen become acutely conscious of national frontiers, and cartographers begin to accentuate them by employing different coloration on either side. By this time, however, the modern national state was fairly well developed; and its exclusiveness, centralization, and belligerence combined to give reality to sharply contrasted colors on the map and to focus attention on those lines where colors met. And as everybody was put in school and taught national geography, something like a disease of "mapitis" seized upon the citizens of every state and rendered them feverish about guarding or acquiring their "rightful" frontiers. Which confirmed the military character of the Continental European state and further inspired the loyalty of its citizens and the efficiency of its civil service.

On the other hand, I use the word "frontier" in a sense analogous to that made famous by the late Professor Frederick Turner. For Europe no less than the United States has been powerfully affected in modern times by a pioneering frontier. Indeed, while the United States has felt the influence of one such frontier—a western frontier—Europe has been simultaneously influenced by two: a *western*, overseas, through the British islands, across the Atlantic and America; and an *eastern*, overland, through Russia, across the Urals and the Siberian steppes, to the Pacific. Among myriad reactions of these westward and eastward movements, since the sixteenth century, on Europe itself, I here hazard generalization only about a curious political reaction and one that has had remarkably divergent effect, depending upon whether its stimulus was from the east or the west. The expanding eastern frontier, perhaps because it was pushed by a power whose heritage was Byzantine, or because it proceeded along lines of Genghiz Khan and Tamerlane, or because it eventually reached the entrenched despotisms of Turkish Sultan and Manchu Emperor, or for whatever reason, certainly served to reinforce Tsarist autocracy in Russia, and, through accompanying access of Russian might and prestige, to buttress absolutism in central Europe. At the opposite extreme, the expanding western frontier, pressed on particularly by a power whose insular position freed it from imminent danger of foreign invasion and hence from need of strong-arm government, gave back to western Europe an idealized picture of the state of nature and the natural man, *le bon sauvage,* and with it some of the democratic and liberating spirit of American frontiersmen. From the eighteenth century until today, this part of Europe has been "free" and "democratic" Europe, while most of the remainder has had continuous experience with auto-cratically minded princes and their natural successors the Bolshe-vist and Nazi dictators. But whether it be easternizing despotism or westernizing democracy, it has been strengthened by the extra-European frontier, and in either case it has strengthened the modern European state. For democracy, no less than dictator-ship, can be totalitarian.

A fourth development has been the conscious and purposeful inculcation of a supreme loyalty to the state. It began with intellectuals of the late medieval and early modern period who dethroned theology as "queen of the sciences." I am aware that some of my contemporaries believe with Comte that sociology is now "queen," and, as I intimated earlier, the claim of eco-nomics to that distinction has been extravagantly urged. Yet if you consider what kind of serious speculation and writing has been most generally prevalent throughout the whole course of modern history, you will conclude, I think, that the "queen of the sciences" since theology's deposition has been political sci-ence, who reigns in ever gathering glory. Theology was espoused by St. Thomas Aquinas; political science, by that vigorous bridegroom, Machiavelli, and then in succession by younger brethren almost as vigorous—Luther, Hobbes, Hegel, Treitschke, Rosenberg, to mention only five of the polyan-drists. By such masters of political science have been begotten an enormous brood of modern textbook writers, journalists, and other popularizers who carry to the masses the gospel of state omnipotence and state omniscience; and once the schools are monopolized by the state, they become its servants and the most effective propagandists of its gospel. State schools are really state temples, and the children's crusades which they foster have sublimated medieval Christian enthusiasm in an ultra-modern and fiercer nationalist enthusiasm. Youth does not count the cost, and its idealism, susceptible of no economic explanation, supremely serves the state.

Finally, the modern age has witnessed, as no previous age, an emergence of the masses, an upsurge of the multitude, from relative quiescence and respect for an élite of brains or wealth or both, to self-conscious and commanding importance. It has been in progress a long time, certainly since the rise of radical religious sects in the sixteenth century, but it has gathered great momentum only since Jean Jacques Rousseau and his disciples romanticized the common man, since crowds of peasants and slum-dwellers found they could exert decisive influence on the French Revolution, and since English workmen discovered in trade unionism a potent means of alarming their employers. For a hundred and fifty years now, the tide has been flowing ever fuller and stronger: here a wave of urban labor combinations, benefit societies, and coöperative stores; there a wave of agricultural unions and agrarian leagues; here a wave of political democracy and popular schooling and universal military service; there a wave of "popular fronts" and "soviets of workers, peasants, and soldiers." The immemorable age of patricians has closed with Bismarck, Cavour, Nicholas II, perhaps Winston Churchill, and the age of plebeians is definitely ushered in by the porter's son Hitler, the blacksmith's son Mussolini, the cobbler's son Stalin, and who will it be in England?

The mentor of my own graduate studies, the late Professor James Harvey Robinson, used to attribute the decline and fall of the ancient Roman Empire to the disintegrating and destructive violence of the barbarian world outside; and, enlightened optimistic soul that he finely was, he used greatly to edify my generation by concluding that, inasmuch as the whole world was now becoming civilized, there would be no outside barbarians to arrest modern progress and introduce another "Dark Age." Alas, he overlooked the emergence of the masses and the danger that at least in some countries they might be agents of renewed violence and barbarism. Perhaps, after all, it was not the Germanic invasions from without that brought ruin to antique civilization, but the existence within of a Roman proletariat intent only on having free bread and free circuses. In contemporary Europe, free circuses seem to count more than free bread, and demagogues who provide superlative (and bloody) spectacles, even if they stint the food supply, can climax all the other developments of the modern state—nationalism, étatisme, bureaucracy, "mapitis," propaganda—with unquestioning mass support of personal dictatorship and repudiation of traditional morals. For the evolution of the modern state represents much more than the operation of economic forces. It represents a popular psychology and a popular religion, and illustrates once more and in supreme degree the truth of the dictum that man—at any rate the common man—does not live, or die, by bread alone.

Three centuries ago Thomas Hobbes prepared the blueprints of the state called Leviathan. Today we have Leviathan actually built and launched. Any shipwreck it may suffer in the future will be shipwreck of much of modern political and economic progress, just as its continuing successful voyaging on the high sea of politics involves ever wider and more grievous depredations on personal liberty and all historic culture. It is still possible, here in Philadelphia, a nursery of liberty, to be as sceptical as one desires and to say whatever one is minded to say. But already one may not question economic determinism in the eastern half of Europe or political totalitarianism in the greater part of the remainder. I speak here while it is still possible.

The task of the next two or three centuries, I venture to guess, is not so much to destroy Leviathan as to tame its captains and crews. To be sure, it took over six centuries to tame the barbarians that took possession of the Roman Empire and to train them for the resumption of civilized life in middle ages and modern times. But however long it may take to tame the barbarians that are now infesting Europe, it must be done unless man resigns himself to a permanent Dark Age, and, inasmuch as men have never so resigned themselves, it will be done. Education in right philosophy and psychology, education in right religion, this, far more than acquaintance with technology or with statistics, is vitally requisite.

As over against the supreme importance of right education throughout the world, the military and imperial collapse of France in the twentieth century, even of Great Britain, may well appear in the long vista of history of relatively slight significance—no more, and no less, significant than previous collapses, in modern times, of Spain, Sweden, or the Dutch Netherlands. One cannot be sure, and something must be left to say at the four hundredth anniversary of the University of Pennsylvania. Doubtless the contemporary struggle between Great Britain and Germany can be viewed as one of imperial power-politics, just as was the struggle between ancient Greeks and Persians. But just as we rejoice in the triumph of Greek power-politics because it was crucial for the development of our whole Western type of civilization, so to our distant descendants it may matter enormously which rival in contemporary power-politics comes off best. But even should Great Britain (and the United States) be eventually degraded to provincial status in a totalitarian and despotic world empire, a liberally minded student of world history may derive some consolation from this final observation, that the forceful incorporation of Athens into the ancient Roman Empire led to the propagation of Greek culture among the conquering Romans and the barbarians in their midst. As the Greeks thus had their revenge, so too may the modern European peoples that have cherished not only economics and politics but philosophy and science and the arts.

UNIVERSITY OF PENNSYLVANIA
BICENTENNIAL CONFERENCE

England's Contribution to Constitutional Government

By

CHARLES H. McILWAIN, Ph.D., LL.D., L.H.D.*

THE general subject I am to try to treat today is the contribution of England to the theory and practice of constitutional government in the modern world. In order to make that subject perfectly clear I must in the first place define some of the terms I shall have to use, at least the most important term I shall have to use: constitutional government itself.

In the last analysis a government that we may truly term constitutional is one so restricted by a law which it cannot change that it lacks the authority legitimately to infringe those rights and liberties of the governed deemed generally to be essential to the fullest and freest development of the individual subject. In a word, constitutional government is the antithesis of arbitrary government; it is the subjection of governmental will to a superior law. This constitutionally limited government is not necessarily self-government, although self-government has come to be its typical form within the last three centuries, and self-government may possibly be found to be its surest safeguard for the future. The point is that self-government is not an end in itself, it is only a means, we believe the best means yet found, of ensuring something far more important than itself, the sanctity of individual and minority rights, the fullest opportunity for individual initiative consistent with the rights of all. Now there were safeguards of these rights before self-government developed, and they form the background of all constitutional history. It was only when these safeguards were proved by experience to be inadequate that our modern democratic state replaced the former monarchical one, and this modern democratic form is still on its trial. Its history covers barely three hundred

* Eaton Professor of the Science of Government, Harvard University.

years. It was practically non-existent in any large unified state before the seventeenth century.

This brings me to a second point: namely, that the threat to this limited government, the tendency toward absolutism which gave rise ultimately to a popular opposition and a form of popular or self-government, is a modern development rather than a medieval one. I hope I shall be one of the very last to fall in with the sentimental view of the Middle Ages now prevailing in certain quarters which decries everything modern and holds up the medieval world as a golden age. If the sentimentalists who hold this view would only turn aside for a moment from their study of the glories of medieval architecture to the actual records of the courts of law in that period they would find a much needed corrective of their one-sided views. And yet, there is another view of the Middle Ages more widely spread than the former but no less distorted, which habitually applies the adjective "medieval" to all the unspeakable barbarities now occurring every day on a scale never approached in the Middle Ages and probably never equalled before in the world's history.

It is the constitutional aspect alone of our medieval development, and especially the English background of our own particular form of constitutionalism, with which we are immediately concerned; and if we restrict our attention to that, our Anglo-Saxon contribution to modern liberty turns out to be the retention of ancient limits to arbitrary government maintained and extended by a representative parliament. The real glory, the unique character of England's political institutions lies not in her representative parliament itself, but in the fact that through it England practically alone of the European monarchies was able to retain, to safeguard, and ultimately to extend to all classes of the people the limits to arbitrary rule which the Middle Ages had transmitted to the modern world.

If this be true, the outstanding contribution of England seems clear. It is not the origination of constitutional liberty, it is rather the unique retention of it.

Half a century ago the study of our constitutional liberties was restricted almost exclusively to their origins rather than their development, to their Germanic origins. Herbert Adams and his pupils at Johns Hopkins popularized in America views that had spread over Germany and had been largely adopted in England. They were concerned with the *gau* and the *sippe* and the primitive local institutions of the Germanic peoples almost entirely. Whole libraries were written to clear up the obscurities of the *Germania* of Tacitus. "Germanic origins" were everything. They furnished the explanation of the whole subsequent development of constitutional liberty. It was not then as clear as now that nearly all Germanic peoples save England had lost or were to lose these ancient liberties; that England almost alone, together with her colonies, or her former colonies, was to be the one great country to retain the institutions that had once been common to all. Historians were engrossed with these common origins, they neglected the more important fact of their persistence to modern times. For if all Germanic peoples once enjoyed these liberties, and if all but England had lost them, it is clear that Germanic origins cannot be the sole source of modern constitutionalism. Even before the tragic disappearance of individual liberty on the Continent in these last twenty years and especially within the last twenty months, or even weeks, the comparative study of political institutions had already done much to weaken the theory of Germanic origins as the sole source of our modern constitutional liberties. There was no question of the origins, but there remained the far more significant problem of the disappearance of the liberties. The very facts adduced by the Germanic school itself to show the wide distribution of these Germanic institutions only serve to accentuate their striking disappearance everywhere except in England, and to place in bolder relief the real problem of our constitutional history: Why did England alone retain these ancient institutions?

As to the wide distribution of the Germanic institutions there can of course be no doubt. As to the disappearance of these institutions throughout western Europe an illustration can be found in Spain. If we adopt the only possible contemporary interpretation of the English Great Charter, for example, it is clear that the rights it asserts pale into insignificance compared with the claims repeatedly insisted on and actually enforced against the monarchs in the *Cortes* of the Spanish kingdoms in the thirteenth and fourteenth centuries. There were at that time far greater limitations on government and probably a stricter observance of them in Spain than in England. As early as 1283, for example, it was provided in Catalonia that no general constitution for the kingdom should be made by the king without the consent of the *cives* as well as of the barons and knights—or at least of the consent of the *major et sanior pars*. Nothing of the kind can be found in England for many years after. In definition of organization and regularity of procedure Spain is equally in advance of England, and nothing in England can compare with such organization as is found in the Spanish kingdoms at the opening of the fourteenth century. Likewise the records of the *Cortes* and the *fueros* enacted there show a legislative activity by the representatives not equalled in England till much later. The same is true of the *gravamina* or complaints of abuses presented by the representatives in the *Cortes*. Possibly above all in importance is a comparison for England and Spain of the application of the principle that taxation can be exacted only by the consent of those taxed. It has always been admitted that the "power of the purse" has been the most important practical factor in preserving English liberty. If we confine our attention to the period before the end of the fourteenth century, the operation of this principle was probably more continuous and effective in Spain than in England. On the whole, therefore, the maturity of the Germanic institutions in Spain is a conclusive proof that these institutions themselves furnish no explanation of the retention of constitutional liberty to modern times. For, in Spain, strong as they were, they ultimately disappeared entirely as compared with England. As the Spanish historian Rafael Altimira says,

In England, apart from some episodes of fluctuating movement, the tendency of national liberties becomes continually more marked from 1215, and soon takes a decisive and progressive direction. In Spain, notwithstanding her priority in this kind of political activity, privileges are lost without any compensating gain to the common rights of the subjects; for the absolute power of the King dominates all privileges, and destroys that which had been attained in the Middle Ages; nor is the loss replaced by any analogous guarantees of equal extent.

Thus, if we adopt the only possible contemporary interpretation of Magna Carta, its guarantees are for the time slighter than those in Spain. There is, however, one aspect of Magna Carta, and that the most important, which Altimira also recognizes. As the late Sir Paul Vinogradoff says, the true importance of Magna Carta—and I may add of all English constitutional limitations as well—lies not in its true meaning when written in 1215 but in the meaning read into it in later times. No Spanish constitutional document ever assumed the importance or received the interpretation given in England to Magna Carta in the later Middle Ages and in modern times. It is that later influence and interpretation that differentiate the English constitutional development from the Spanish. In the thirteenth century England and Spain were probably more alike than unlike. They had much the same institutions derived in all probability from much the same origins, and of the two the Spanish seem on the whole the more mature. But two or three centuries later the liberties attributed to Magna Carta are still alive in England, while in Spain practically all such constitutional limitations have ceased to be remembered except by historians of the distant past. The historian Mariana repeats them in his *De Rege* written as late as 1599, but the historian's theories had long ceased to square with the actual fact.

Spain is but one illustration of the difference between the development of Germanic institutions in England and elsewhere. A comparison of English and French political institutions corroborates the impression one gains from comparing England and Spain. If, for example, we take the centuries from the eleventh to the thirteenth, we find here also institutions and practices more like than unlike. Toward the end of that period rights were defined and protected in France in courts called parliaments as those of England were. But unlike England those parliaments had lost their representative character and had become closed corporations of jurists. It is true that they exercised and long continued to exercise a great influence in preserving some constitutional limits to the king's government through their refusal to register royal ordinances which they considered *ultra vires*, but such restraints were small in comparison with the invariable practice in England in the later Middle Ages under which no statute defining the rights of subjects could ever be legally enacted by kings without the advice and consent of a parliament consisting of representatives of those subjects themselves. It is little wonder that in France kings in time found means to coerce their parliaments and compel them to register even "unconstitutional" acts. It is the most striking fact in constitutional history that in England alone kings never acquired such a power.

If I am right in all this, and if we are truly to estimate facts in the long perspective of history, the great and lasting contribution of England stands revealed. It is not the inheritance but the preservation, of private rights once respected over most of the western world but later surrendered to kings and their governments everywhere except in England alone.

Surely this, if true, requires a change in the emphasis we shall put on later development as compared with mere origins. Surely this, if true, should bring home to every sincere believer in constitutional government today the overwhelming debt he owes to England, and to England almost alone.

And this, if true, now imposes on me two or three further obligations: In the first place, briefly to show if I can how and why constitutionalism was thus retained in England, to indicate the debt we in America owe to that retention, and finally, to summarize the successive struggles and sacrifices required to maintain this liberty of the subject against the great and growing forces of despotism.

The first of these topics is one of the most obscure, most important, and most fascinating parts of English constitutional history. Possibly the best short summary of it all is in the words of one of the greatest of French constitutional historians of the last generation, Adhemar Esmein:

England, after the Norman conquest, began in a monarch almost absolute, and it is perhaps for that reason that it has developed by the seventeenth century into a representative monarchy. Feudal France began with a kingship almost wholly powerless, and it is probably for that reason that it ended in the seventeenth century in an absolute monarchy.

You will notice that this statement attributes the English constitutionalism of modern times to no Germanic or other origin; it attributes it to the conditions existing in England shortly after the Norman conquest; and paradoxical as it seems at first sight, this statement seems true. Conqueror though he was, in actual fact William claimed the right to rule as the legitimate successor of the Anglo-Saxon kings, and the more powerful he was the more effectively he succeeded in doing so. Among the rights he claimed was the right to receive "counsel" from all his subjects from whom it was feudally owing. Thus it was the very strength of the feudal monarchy in England that ensured the attendance at frequent meetings of parliaments in which the service of counsel was rendered. Professor A. B. White has summarized it all in the phrase "self-government at the King's command." In France kings were too weak to compel this attendance and meetings were rare. Thus in England the strength of the kingship itself preserved parliament as a regular organ of government to which new and representative elements were in time to attach, when the time was ripe. This is an interpretation of this important period vastly different from the glowing German democracy of the English historians of a generation or two ago, such as Freeman, or Green, with their rooted hatred of feudalism. Yet I think it is the interpretation now adopted by most competent constitutional historians. And what was thus true of central institutions was equally true of local. Of all local institutions the county court was probably the most important, and it was undoubtedly of Germanic origin. Yet one can hardly study the contemporary documents of Norman and early Angevin England without concluding that its maintenance and its continuance are of equal importance with its origin on any general view of the history of constitutionalism, and that this continuance was the work of the Norman and early Angevin kings and the remarkable administrators they employed. But for the strong government of these kings and such measures as the administrative reforms of Henry II, I think it safe to say that no possible foundation would have existed on which a later representative parliament could ever have been erected. The first critical period of English constitutionalism is in the two centuries immediately following the Norman conquest, a period of strong but not arbitrary rule. The famous Chapter 39 of Magna Carta asserted few new rights. On the whole it is a statement of rights already existing, of limitations on the will of the king, enshrined in a feudal custom which had been made "common," through the administrative reforms of Henry II and his predecessors. Bishop Stubbs does not exaggerate when he says of Henry II,

The constitutional historian cannot help looking with reverence on one under whose hand the foundations of liberty and national independence were so clearly marked and so deeply laid that in the course of one generation the fabric was safe forever from tyrants or

conquerors. . . . He stands with Alfred, Canute, William the Conqueror, and Edward I, one of the conscious creators of English
greatness.

This is the first of the great critical periods in the history
of our liberty. Another came at the end of the Middle Ages
with the development of the Renaissance monarchies, the
period of the loss of that liberty in Spain and France and elsewhere and its unique retention in England, though only after
a long and bitter struggle and a bloody civil war. For England
this period embraces the two centuries beginning with the establishment of the Tudor monarchy and ending with the
Revolution of 1688-89.

But the latter is the period also of the beginnings of English
colonization, the time when our ancestors brought over here
or adopted as their own the English traditions of individual
liberty, won in the earlier struggles I have been trying to re-
count. We received them then and have kept them since, not as
a borrowed thing, as English institutions were copied so widely
in the nineteenth century on the Continent of Europe. They
are bone of our bone, and as much our rightful inheritance
here as in England herself where they were first won. On the
Continent these borrowed articles never took root, and we have
been witnessing in the last few years and months how one country after another that loudly professed the liberalism of her
institutions in the last century has now renounced this liberalism and can say nothing too violent in its condemnation.
Germany, the country that her nineteenth century historians so
proudly hailed as the very cradle of all modern liberty, in 1935
officially adopted the general principle that one can be punished for an act against which no law exists. She deliberately
substituted governmental will for settled law. Compare for a
moment that sweeping adoption of despotic rule with the provisions of our Federal Constitution and its Bill of Rights for the
protection of individual liberty against despotic power; against
ex post facto laws, for example—the direct prohibition of the
central principle of present-day German criminal procedure—
or a dozen other safeguards of fair trial by "due process of law"
to every one accused of any offense. Almost every one of these
safeguards can be traced back to the English struggles of the
seventeenth century or before. The very term "Bill of Rights"

which we apply to them is copied directly from the great Statute of 1689, and most of the specific safeguards included in the constitutional amendments so called have the same origin. The important Eighth Amendment is copied almost *verbatim* from the English Statute: "excessive bail shall not be imposed, nor cruel and unusual punishments inflicted." The first article, guaranteeing the right of petition, has the same origin, as well as the second, concerning the militia. The third article, against the billeting of soldiers, probably goes back further, to the English Petition of Right of 1628. And so we might go on. For there is scarcely one of these fundamental safeguards that does not epitomize the results of some desperate earlier English struggle for individual liberty and a hard-won victory against oppressive government. The provision in the body of the Constitution defining treason is clearly a derivation from the English Act of Edward III, and its safeguards as to evidence mainly a reproduction of a statute of Edward VI. These specific limitations have proved more effective and more lasting than the grandiose declarations in the European constitutions of the nineteenth century, most of which have in our own day become waste-paper.

In the earlier English struggles for the maintenance of these rights which have thus become our common heritage, I mentioned three great periods of crisis, the two centuries just following the Conquest, and the two centuries immediately after the establishment of the powerful Renaissance monarchy of Henry VII in 1485. But what of the third? Need I give an answer? No one of us who has lived through the first year of this present war can doubt that we are at this very moment face to face with the most serious of all the crises in the whole history, not only of constitutional England, but of all constitutional government. Never before in recorded history has such force been enlisted to destroy our cherished rights of the individual, a force employing every engine of modern science in an orgy of systematic but indiscriminate butchery.

If England turns back that force now, or even if she should fall before it—which God forbid—the struggle she is making at this hour with "sweat and tears" will stand forever beside Marathon and Thermopylae among the grandest achievements of the heroic spirit in the annals of mankind. It is England's highest contribution to the cause of freedom in her long history, greater far than that of the thirteenth century or the seventeenth; for this is a struggle to the death, not alone for the survival of a nation, but that human liberty may not perish from the earth.

World Currents in American Civilization

By

ARTHUR M. SCHLESINGER, Ph.D., Litt.D.*

On the day Hitler marched into Austria Mrs. Anne O'Hare McCormick reported an Italian friend as saying,

This is the way Europe acts. . . . In two thousand years we have learned nothing. . . . Europeans talk of how easy and simple your problems are compared to ours. The truth is that you have done everything we have failed to do: you have made a United States of Europe; you have taken our serfs and made them free, our poorest and made them rich, our most irreconcilable strains and given them peace. Using the same seamy stuff we all employ, and starting from scratch, no country has gone so far to remake the world.[1]

This tribute to the innate wisdom of the American people lays flattering unction to our souls. From the earliest colonial days we have believed ourselves a unique species endowed with unique intelligence. As the Reverend William Stoughton of Boston declared in his Election Sermon in 1668, "God sifted a whole Nation that he might send Choice Grain over into this Wilderness."[2] Neither he nor the countless others who have echoed his sentiment deemed it relevant to mention that, though the grain may have been choice, it also enjoyed the incomparable advantage of being sown in a virgin soil three thousand miles away from the troubled neighborhoods of Europe. Moreover, except possibly to the theological mind, grain seems a poor analogue for people since, unlike human beings, it did not bring with it inherited preferences, emotional attachments, and cultural possessions.

It was necessary, however, for the colonists to believe in their dissimilarity to other breeds of mankind if they were to develop a sense of their own fundamental nationality. The more they were unlike others the more they could feel themselves

* Francis Lee Higginson Professor of History, Harvard University.
[1] *New York Times*, July 11, 1938.
[2] William Stoughton, *New-Englands True Interest* (Cambridge, 1670), p. 19.

alike. And once free from England, they insisted on the difference as a matter of survival. In launching a republican government they were defying the ideologies of the Old World. If their experiment was to work, they must keep Europe at arm's length while they maintained their own liberty of action. Hence, in taking the step of independence, they proclaimed the irreconcilable nature of their own and the English principles of government. Twenty years later President Washington expanded the concept of irreconcilability to include all European nations. Warning his countrymen against political entanglements with them, he declared, "Europe has a set of primary interests, which to us have none, or a very remote relation."[3] And before the generation of the Founding Fathers departed the scene, President Monroe in 1823 extended the idea still further. Europe, he stated in effect, must not violate the freedom or the territory of any republic in the Western Hemisphere.

These three basic pronouncements of policy—the Declaration of Independence, the Farewell Address, and the Monroe Doctrine—have been repeatedly stressed by historians who, envisaging history as mere past politics, have conceived of our foreign relations solely in terms of the doings of diplomats and warriors. To the original natural bias against the Old World was thus added the weighty verdict of the historians. Little wonder that, when the English scholar E. A. Freeman visited the United States sixty years ago, he reported:

Some people in America seem really to think that the United States, their constitution and all that belongs to them, did not come into being by the ordinary working of human causes, but sprang to life by some special creation or revelation. They think themselves wronged if it is implied that they are not absolute *autochthones*, but that they are the kinsfolk of certain other nations. They think themselves wronged if it is implied that their institutions did not spring at once from the ground, but that they were, like the institutions of other nations, gradually wrought out of a store common to them with some other branches of mankind.[4]

Indeed, one may add, it is generally forgotten that two even of the three fundamental formulations of national policy were tainted at the source. For the Declaration of Independence

[3] George Washington, *Writings* (W. C. Ford, ed., N. Y., 1889-1893), XIII, 316.
[4] E. A. Freeman, *Some Impressions of the United States* (London, 1883), p. 279.

embodied a philosophy and phraseology borrowed from the Englishman John Locke, while the essence of the Monroe Doctrine had been suggested by the Englishman George Canning, and for many years the enforcement of the Doctrine rested on the British navy. Thus even from a political point of view the conception of the American nation living sternly to itself is unwarranted.

The fact is that, when the colonists cast off the yoke of England, they acted with mental reservations. Not only did they retain the British national anthem, but they also retained many of the governmental principles and practices of the mother land. Just as they set new words to "God Save the King," so also they adapted their political borrowings to their special needs; but in both cases their indebtedness was paramount and abiding. As modern scholarship has shown, the United States Constitution, far from being (as Gladstone said) "produced by the human intellect at a single stroke," was a structure built of materials quarried from English experience. The copied features of the Constitution far outnumbered the original. Likewise, in the domain of private rights, the common law was accepted as the cornerstone of the American system of jurisprudence. Even if the people had willed otherwise, a clean break with British precedents and methods would hardly have been possible because for many years after 1776 the United States was governed by men who had been born and bred as English subjects. Not until Martin Van Buren was elected in 1836 did a President enter the White House who could claim American citizenship from birth.

In appraising foreign influences on American development, however, it is easy to overestimate the English connection. The fact that the two peoples speak the same language and cherish similar political institutions obscures more truth than it discloses. The Americans are not, as is sometimes implied, Britons in exile. On the contrary, they have been from earliest times an amalgam of many stocks. Even as colonists they formed the most cosmopolitan community in the world. The founders of the Republic were not blind to this diversity, for when the Continental Congress authorized John Adams, Benjamin Franklin, and Thomas Jefferson to contrive an official seal for the new government, they recommended a design made up of the national emblems of England, Scotland, Ireland, France, Germany, and Holland, in order, they said, to point out "the countries from which these States have been peopled."[5] Fortunately this synthetic device failed of adoption, but the fact it was proposed by leading patriots, themselves of English lineage, is deeply significant.

The foreign colonization of America did not stop with the so-called colonial period, but continued with accelerating pace until a decade ago. In reality, by far the greatest number of European settlers came in the period after 1776. Thus, in the years from 1865 to 1900, over thirteen million immigrants landed on our shores, a number greater than the total population in 1830. These newcomers penetrated all parts of the country, filling up the thinly settled regions and speeding the growth of towns and cities.

Arriving at different times, representing different nationalities and races in constantly shifting proportions, they subjected the blood of the nation to an unceasing process of change. Recent statistical analyses give us, for the first time, a clear picture of the transformation. In 1790 more than three out of every four white Americans were of English, Scottish, or Welsh stock, with the remainder consisting of German, Irish, and other nationalities.[6] One hundred and thirty years later, in 1920, English, Scottish, and Welsh ancestry accounted for less than half (41%) of the white inhabitants, the German and Irish admixture had nearly doubled, and the peoples of Southern and Eastern Europe had an appreciable representation.[7] The typical American today, while still more British in descent than anything else, is less British than he is a conglomerate of other European nationalities. This is a point of more than biological interest. This continuing transfusion of new blood has had an important modifying effect on American folkways, has influenced our material growth, and has contributed vitally to American intellectual and cultural life.

Undoubtedly, too, it resulted in rendering American thought and practice more responsive to the *Zeitgeist* of the nineteenth century and, in so doing, helped to make the national develop-

[5] Gaillard Hunt, *History of the Seal of the United States* (Washington, 1909), pp. 7, 10.
[6] Report of Committee on Linguistic and National Stocks in American Historical Association, *Annual Report for 1931*, p. 124.
[7] President's Research Committee on Social Trends, *Recent Social Trends in the United States* (N. Y., 1933), I, 20.

ment in most essential respects resemble that of the lands from which the bulk of the immigrants came. This parallelism has been overlooked by American scholars, who have tended to attribute the major trends of American history to the recurrent westward migration and the influence of the frontier. Unquestionably the long-time persistence of pioneer conditions did much to shape a distinctive national character and give an authentic American coloration to political life, but the evidence indicates that the salient developments would have been much the same had no frontier existed.

Thus, students of Western history usually echo with approval the sentiment: "Democracy came out of the forest." But history plainly shows that democracy has been cradled by old settled civilizations as well as by simple primitive ones. What really came out of the forest was a special American brand of democracy, one based on the notion that the best good of all was served by letting everyone look out for himself. If the continent had ended at the Appalachians, if no zone of generous opportunity had existed to relieve the growing tension between rich and poor in the East, it is improbable that the democratic advance would have been retarded. On the contrary, had the opposing forces been obliged to fight out their differences at close range, we may suppose that the movement would have taken a less individualistic turn and, as in Europe, pressed more rapidly toward the goal of a social-service state.

The essential likenesses between American and European experience become manifest when superficial differences are stripped away and attention is fixed on the ground swell of history. In nineteenth-century Europe the great formative factors were: (1) the extension of democracy; (2) the consolidation of nationality; (3) the onrush of imperialism; (4) the advance of machine industry; (5) the rise of humanitarianism; and (6) the growth of culture. Even a little reflection suggests that beneath the varied surface of events these, too, formed the central themes of American development.

The significance of this parallelism becomes clearer upon closer examination. Take, first, the progress toward greater democracy on the two sides of the Atlantic. As is well known, the principal extensions of the suffrage in Great Britain occurred in 1832, 1867, 1884, and 1918. The first date corresponded with the peak of the movement for white manhood

suffrage in America, the second and third almost exactly co-
incided with the successive grants of the franchise in the United
States to the Negroes and the Indians, and the fourth brought
the ballot to English women only two years before their American sisters received it from the Nineteenth Amendment. In
other words, every important democratic victory in the one
country was matched by an equally important one in the other.
The correlation with the Continental states is less marked, but
even there the trend nearly everywhere was toward larger popular participation in the government.

Americans contemporaneously were fully aware that the aspiration for democracy transcended national boundaries. Thus,
John Greenleaf Whittier, the Quaker poet and humanitarian,
saluted the English Chartists (1843):

> God bless ye, brothers! in the fight
> Ye 're waging now, ye cannot fail,
> Far better is your sense of right
> Than kingcraft's triple mail.
>
> . . . .
>
> The truths ye urge are borne abroad
> By every wind and every tide;
> The voice of Nature and of God
> Speaks out upon your side.
> The weapons which your hands have found
> Are those which Heaven itself has wrought,
> Life, Truth, and Love; your battle-ground
> The free, broad field of Thought.[8]

Thus, also, James Russell Lowell addressed Louis Philippe
when the democratic tide swept him from his throne in 1848:

> Vain were thy bayonets against the foe
> Thou hadst to cope with; thou didst wage
> War not with Frenchmen merely; no,
> Thy strife was with the Spirit of the Age.[9]

It was to this same Spirit of the Age that President Wilson
appealed in 1918 when he urged on Congress the equal-suffrage
amendment. "We cannot isolate our thought or action in such
a matter from the thought of the rest of the world," he said.

[8] John Greenleaf Whittier, *Complete Poetical Works* (Boston, 1894), p. 354.
[9] James Russell Lowell, *Poetical Works* (Boston, 1890), p. 93.

"We must either conform or deliberately reject what they propose and resign the leadership of liberal minds to others."[10]

Throughout the nineteenth century the United States took an almost proprietary interest in the recurrent democratic upheavals on the Continent. News of the overthrow of a king and the triumph of the people occasioned public celebrations, banquets, parades, and sometimes official holidays. Everywhere in America the need was felt to display a "popular front" against monarchy and despotism. President Jackson in his message to Congress in December 1830 complimented the French revolutionists upon their "courage and wisdom," and told them that their course had "naturally elicited from the kindred feelings of this nation" a "spontaneous and universal burst of applause."[11] In a similar spirit the national convention of the Democratic party in 1848 sent "fraternal congratulations" to the second French Republic, and rejoiced that the spirit of popular rule was "prostrating thrones and erecting republics on the ruins of despotism in the Old World."[12]

Two years later Daniel Webster, then Secretary of State, dispatched his famous note to Austria, justifying the right of the American people "to cherish always a lively interest in the fortunes of nations struggling for institutions like their own," and declaring grandiloquently that, compared with free America, "the possessions of the house of Hapsburg are but as a patch on the earth's surface."[13] In line with this sentiment, President Fillmore sent a warship to convey to the United States the exiled patriot, Kossuth. When he arrived in December 1851, Kossuth was tendered public ovations in the Eastern cities and was dined at the White House and formally received by each house of Congress. There can be no doubt that the democratic movement aboard was constantly heartened by the encouragement and example of the American republic and that, in turn, the flattery implied by foreign imitation refreshed the democratic spirit in the United States.

The European uprisings, however, usually involved not

[10] Woodrow Wilson, *War and Peace* (R. S. Baker and W. E. Dodd, eds., N. Y., 1927), I, 265.

[11] J. D. Richardson, ed., *A Compilation of the Messages and Papers of the Presidents* (Washington, 1896), II, 501.

[12] T. H. McKee, *The National Conventions and Platforms of All Political Parties* (3d edn., Baltimore, 1900), p. 61.

[13] *Senate Executive Documents*, 31 Cong., 2 sess., no. 9, p. 7.

merely a striving for popular government but also for the consolidation of nationality. Here again the Old World and the New were moved by a common impulse. In America, just as in Europe, the principal problems of statecraft centered in the firm establishment of nationhood, and in many of the countries the highway to accomplishment lay through bloody battlefields. It was no coincidence that the triumph of the nationalist elements in Italy, Germany, and Austria-Hungary came at about the same time the Civil War decided that the United States should remain a geographic unity. Lincoln the American had his counterparts in Cavour the Italian and Bismarck the German. Nor should it be overlooked that later years beheld, in the United States as elsewhere, a steady enlargement of political authority in the hands of the central government.

The third of the world movements, imperialism, assumed at first a different guise in the United States from that in Europe. In America for many years it was possible to appease the acquisitive spirit with adjacent lands, sparsely inhabited and therefore still subject to settlement. This process, known as expansion, usually involved the addition, through peaceful negotiation, of territory belonging to European powers, thus Louisiana from France, Florida from Spain, Oregon from Great Britain. The years 1846-48, however, brought a foretaste of genuine imperialism when the Republic of Mexico was forcibly shorn of two-fifths of her area. In the next half-century the imperialistic bent became more explicit. American industry and agriculture now had a growing surplus to market, and American capital was seeking foreign outlets for investment. In 1898 during the feverish excitement of the Spanish-American War the nation definitely chose the path to empire, acquiring dependencies scattered in two oceans and occupied by peoples alien in race and tradition.

Meanwhile, from 1870 to 1898, the British Empire had grown by about five million square miles exclusive of spheres of influence, while France had added three and a half million and Germany a million square miles to their possessions. If America was somewhat slow in adopting the frank imperialism of European powers, it was only because she had not earlier had the same incentive. She could satisfy her craving for territory, raw materials, and markets without leaving North America. Today the American political system bears every appearance of an empire, though the term is carefully avoided. In addition to the central cluster of free states, it consists of colonies in various stages of self-government, such as Hawaii and Puerto Rico; of other dependencies autocratically ruled by representatives from Washington, such as Tutuila and the Canal Zone; and of still other possessions, such as Baker and Penrhyn islands, with no resident government at all. Besides, for long periods we have maintained political and economic protectorates in the Caribbean. It is a tribute to the flexibility of the Constitution that these developments, utterly unforeseen by the founders of our federal system, have all been sanctioned by the Supreme Court simply through waving the magic wand of judicial interpretation.

No less powerful in its effects on our national destiny has been the fourth of these great international trends, the rise of modern industrialism. As in the case of imperialism, however, the United States made a slow start. While the country was still being settled, agriculture was the all-absorbing interest, but gradually, as the nineteenth century wore on and surplus capital became available, the Industrial Revolution reached America from England. Vainly Parliament enacted legislation to keep the vital technological processes a national secret. By hook or crook Americans mastered the principles of the new machinery and set up their own factories along the northern Atlantic seaboard. After a time our people began to reveal inventive powers of their own and, aided by extraordinary natural advantages, made up for their tardiness in entering the race. The records of the Patent Office shed some light on the situation. With less than 62,000 patents granted in all the years before 1865, the number during the remainder of the century approached 638,000. As late as the 1880's agriculture continued to be the chief fount of national wealth, but the census of 1890 gave first place to manufacturing, and ten years later the value of the output of factories was over twice that of farms. By the mid-nineties America had leaped from fourth place, her rank as a manufacturing nation in 1860, to first in all the world. At that time her production exceeded the combined total for Great Britain and Germany, her principal competitors.

The Industrial Revolution, as it has moved on from country to country since the eighteenth century, has been the most potent international force in modern history. It has flouted political boundaries, shrunk the dimensions of the globe, re-cast the relations of nations to one another, and profoundly altered the character of their domestic problems. The resulting network of economic ties and rivalries has increasingly en-meshed the United States in the world fabric of affairs, diplo-matic and commercial. Internally, the spread of industrialism has injected into American politics the typical problems of the older European countries: the tariff, the regulation of railways, trusts and banking, the rights of labor, the farm question and the like. Most striking of all is the fact that every major eco-nomic crisis in the last hundred years afflicting one shore of the Atlantic has also afflicted the other. The Great Depression of our own time is merely the most recent example.

The fifth of these mighty world-wide phenomena, the growth of humanitarianism, presents an interrelationship fully as im-pressive. Nearly any example would serve to illustrate the unity of purpose that inspired reformers regardless of geography, nationality or creed. Thus in 1815 the first peace societies sprang up simultaneously in London and in three different parts of America.[14] On both sides of the water they represented the reaction of a war-weary mankind to the prolonged period of Napoleonic conflict. In the next third of a century the Brit-ish and American groups worked in close coöperation, exchang-ing speakers, reprinting each other's pamphlets and, finally, organizing international congresses that drew other European pacifist bands into the movement. This early and promising effort, unhappily, was halted by the Crimean War and the American Civil War. Later years, however, witnessed a revival and extension of such collective endeavors.

The agitation against intoxicating drink was more dis-tinctively American in its inception.[15] Yankee temperance tracts in the 1830's were reprinted in Europe, and prompted the formation of total-abstinence societies in Norway, Sweden, and the British Isles. The Crown Prince of Prussia sponsored a group of this kind, and King Frederick William III ordered societies to be formed in every province. In return for Ameri-can assistance, James Silk Buckingham, long active in Parlia-ment as a foe of intemperance, toured the United States from

[14] M. E. Curti, *The American Peace Crusade, 1815-1860* (Durham, 1929), esp. chaps. VI-IX.

[15] J. A. Krout, *The Origins of Prohibition* (N. Y., 1925), pp. 178-181, 218-222.

1837 to 1839, reporting the success of temperance efforts in his own country. A little later Father Theobald Mathew, who had espoused teetotalism in Ireland, journeyed to the United States to convert his many Irish coreligionists to the reform. Ever since, the battle against the liquor traffic has transcended political boundaries.

If it were desirable to multiply instances, it could be shown that many other movements—such as those for penal reform, for abolishing debt imprisonment, for popular education, for women's rights, and for the humane treatment of the insane—were, in the same sense, more international than national in character. In fact, has there been any generous aspiration for helping the underprivileged that has not found simultaneous expression in a dozen different countries? Americans have been particularly blind in realizing the extent to which the abolition movement was world-wide in its sweep. Even historians generally treat Negro slavery as an exclusively American problem, failing to note that it was American only in the sense that the United States lagged behind all other civilized nations in expunging the evil.

British interest in American antislavery efforts proved especially active.[16] In 1807 the two countries, as though obeying a common inspiration, took steps to end the further importation of Negroes from Africa. By 1833 sentiment against slavery had reached such a pitch that Parliament inaugurated a scheme to terminate the system in all the English colonies. This triumph abroad energized American abolitionists to redoubled activity and caused British humanitarians to broaden their interest to include the United States. Pamphlets that had aided the reform in England were reprinted for circulation in America. From time to time William Lloyd Garrison, Frederick Douglass, Harriet Beecher Stowe, and others lectured in Britain to raise funds for the cause, and the English abolitionist George Thompson, among others, took personal part in the American agitation. It was, of course, this common bond of antislavery sympathy that so angered Northerners when the British ministry considered recognizing Southern independence during the Civil War.

America's indebtedness to English example deepened as the

[16] Annie H. Abel and F. J. Klingberg, eds., *A Side-light on Anglo-American Relations* (Lancaster, 1927), pp. 1-51.

increasing complexity of her economic life generated new social problems. Slower than Britain in becoming industrialized, the United States has invariably turned to the older country for instruction. The spreading sore of poverty and chronic unemployment is a striking example. In the interest of a more intelligent system of poor relief, the Charity Organization movement was introduced into America in 1877 by an English resident of Buffalo who had been active in the London Charity Organization Society. Similarly, the social settlement in the United States stemmed from Toynbee Hall in London, where Jane Addams and other American pioneers had served an apprenticeship. The labor movement was as intimately connected, for the American Federation of Labor, formed in 1881, consciously modeled its organization on that of the British Trades Union Congress, and Samuel Gompers, its guiding genius during the formative years, was a native of London. Moreover, it is from British sources that have come most of the ideas which have found embodiment in American legislation for protecting men, women, and children in factories.

Likewise, the various movements to adapt religion to an urban and industrialized society had their roots in England. Thus, both the Y. M. C. A. and the Salvation Army were importations from that country. The institutional church was another instance of borrowing, and in the 1880's the Christian Socialist movement, founded by Charles Kingsley, attracted nearly as many adherents in the United States as in the land of its birth.

If one were to pursue the effect of these international currents in yet other fields of thought and action, it would appear that no phase of American civilization has remained untouched. Our educational system sprang originally from English models, but its modern features derive rather from German sources. Every level of instruction from the kindergarten to the graduate schools attests this influence. American painting evolved through its English, German, and French periods. Our more serious musical efforts have been largely the work of German-trained composers, our symphony orchestras and grand-opera companies are manned by performers with unpronounceable foreign names, and even our popular music contains strong Negro and Hebrew elements. Similarly, American sculpture went to school to Italy before it grew to manhood under the aegis of France. Our literature and, in less degree, our architecture disclose not one but myriad alien influences, oriental as well as occidental. Even our sports life has been, in considerable measure, an outgrowth of the great athletic revival in England in the mid-nineteenth century.

You may well ask, "Why dwell at such tedious length on these world influences on American civilization?" My purpose is less to adorn a tale than to point a moral. Though our historians have written countless volumes on foreign relations, they have told only of the occasional contentions of governments, not of the interdependence of peoples. For example, Great Britain is impressed on the reader's mind as an enemy in two wars and a diplomatic antagonist on numberless other occasions. Germany hardly figures at all until under Kaiser Wilhelm II she suddenly emerges as a monster of ruthlessness. Our three thousand miles of unfortified boundary with Canada receive the barest notice, while our temperamental neighbor immediately to the south gets full and invidious attention. In other words, our historians have compiled case studies of abnormal and exceptional behavior. Diplomatic history has been an undiplomatic account of the distempers of nations.

But, as the record has shown, this is not the whole or even the most important part of the story. It is truth seen through a distorting lens. Though friction and strife have sometimes interrupted our intercourse with other countries, deeper forces have irresistibly and continuously bound us to them. To a wholly disinterested person, say the fabled visitor from Mars, probably the most striking thing about the modern history of Europe and America would be that all peoples have been so nearly alike, not that they have in certain respects been different. If this is so, historians who have been stressing national differences to the exclusion of essential national likenesses have done an ill service to mankind. Voltaire's view that history is a bag of tricks we play upon the dead comes uncomfortably close to the mark.

At this moment of world crisis it is well to remember that the rulers of all the belligerent powers invoke the muse of history in justification of their course. Unhappily, it is a spurious shrine at which they worship. The secret of international peace is elusive, but if war is ever to be banished, a fundamental condition is an understanding of the mutual dependence of mankind. Peoples must not continue to learn of one another only as dreaded rivals or armed foes. They must come to think of themselves as collaborators in the grand enterprise of advancing civilization. When this is achieved, they will reject false prophets who summon them to desperate adventure. The emotional disarmament of nations constitutes the best guarantee of enduring peace.

A Century of American Poetry

By

CHARLES CESTRE, D. Litt., LL.D.*

BEFORE the beginning of the nineteenth century, there were versifiers in America, but no poets. The eighteenth century was too much ruled over by the intellect to allow the artistic and spontaneous faculties to assert themselves. Freneau, even where he is not a mere polemist, cannot be called anything more than a tolerable craftsman of verse. America had to wait till the English literary revival, known as the pre-romantic movement, made itself felt, with due delay, on her shores, to see poetry worthy of the name grow and come of age.

The initiators of poetry in America, Bryant, Whittier, Long-fellow, to whom must be joined Lowell, their junior by a few years, were a New England group. It is an important fact. The stern creed of the old Puritans had been battered by philosophy and science and overrun by the new wave of sentiment. But religion, considered as the stay of morals, still formed the basis of thought. Christianity, with a broader outlook, still molded the minds. It was impossible for that group of Americans to conceive God, in the manner of the English romantics, as the informing Spirit of Nature, and the human soul as freely linked to the divine. They still harbored the notion of the Deity, throned in Heaven, of Paradise promised to the elect in after-life, of angels flying down to the earth and comforting the humans by their invisible presence. This conventional imagery prevented them from yielding to the suggestions of the higher imagination. They acquired qualities of sensuousness and sensi-bility which, to some extent, enriched their descriptions, wid-ened their sympathy, enlarged the scope of their similes and metaphors, touched to life the expression of the feelings. But they were too near the theology of old not to retain much of its rationalistic and didactic bias. They kept a distant allegiance to the intellectual poetry of the neo-classics, with its parapher-

* Professor of American Literature and Civilization, University of Paris.

nalia of Greek mythology, trite figures of speech and poetic diction.

Only a great independent genius could overleap the boundaries of the past. The first New England poets were cultivated, refined, talented, and did honor to the literature of their country, but did not stamp on it the mark of unquestionable power.

Bryant was a proficient disciple of Gray in his descriptive and lyrical verse, and a successful rival of Blair in his meditative poetry. After he had discovered Wordsworth, he rather imitated his moralizing habit than emulated his spiritual contemplation. The nature that he describes is genuinely American. He loves animal life and feels esthetic joy in the flowers' bright hues.

He was precocious, which is a sign of virtuosity rather than of genius. He leant toward the artificial mood of "melancholy," without mawkishness, owing to the quality of his images and of his style. His sensibility assures moving force when he expresses intimate feelings. The seriousness of his thought, supported by his power of vision and his sense of form, enables him to invest death with stately dignity. His lyrics are musical and his blank verse sounds like solemn organ peals.

His fame rests on undeniable merit and on the fact that he was the founder of American verse, not unworthy of the great achievement that was later to place America on a level with England in poetical creation.

Whittier was deeply moved by the political and moral struggle that divided the North from the South, although his anti-slavery pieces ring too much like polemics. The son of a farmer and an apprentice in a shop, when a boy, he might have become the bard of American labor, had his *Songs of Labor* been instinct with truer realism. His ballads lack commanding pathos, except a few which treat of the persecutions of the Quakers in old times. The sincerity of his faith in a tutelary Providence was not sufficient to raise his religious homilies to great poetry.

Late in life, his love of nature, of rural simplicity and homely virtues made him, in *Snowbound*, the moving painter of New England farm life. There is a local flavor, a veracity of feeling, a thrill of immediate experience to his picture of old days, which give them a ring and overtones of their own. At the end of the poem, he expresses the wish that even distant or foreign friends of poesy may feel in his pastoral chant the beating of a human heart.

May I be permitted to say that French readers respond to Whittier's vow. They love in him the poet of the hearth and of agricultural New England, so much like the French country-side. They revere in him the singer of family feelings, heightened by the moral ideals of their sturdy ancestors, and by the hope of human kindness in all men.

Longfellow has become, in Europe as in America, a classic of the schoolroom. This has somewhat weakened his claim to higher praise. All prejudice apart, his poetry seems tame. He ministered too much to the predilections of the contemporary audience. His natural gift for tuneful lines and vivid images was to some extent impaired by too facile writing. Feeling, with him, verges toward sentimentality; pretty and musical style runs into monotony; reminiscence crowds out creation; moralizing crams description; inappropriateness of tone spoils themes that might otherwise be felicitous; namby-pamby religiousness and cheap optimism wrap too many poems in rosy colors skirting the commonplace.

But a selection can be made of a few memorable pieces. He made himself the mouthpiece of noble moral idealism. Some of his ballads ring true. He was sensitive to the beauty or terror of the sea. *Hiawatha* is not unpleasant reading in small doses. He contributed to the development of autochthonous literature by taking subjects from American history, Indian lore, and foreign legend.

As he grew in age, his talent ripened. His later sonnets are finely wrought and closely knit. "Victor and Vanquished" forms a moving conclusion to a life of steady endeavor.

James Russell Lowell, as a young lyrist, introduced into love-poetry a more outspoken tone than had been heard before in New England. Later in his manhood, when he was afflicted by dire bereavements, one might have expected from him a happier expression of personal grief. His imagination is of indifferent quality and his taste uncertain. In his dealing with nature, the fancy predominates. His descriptions are exercises in clever disguises. As an official poet at commemorative functions, he wrote solemn plausibilities, interspersed with passages of noble emotion. His satiric vein in the fields of literary criticism or political controversy has pungency and mordant humor.

His forte is meditative verse. He crowned his career with the composition of "The Cathedral," which contains sound reflections on religion, politics and literature, and rises at times to impassioned eloquence. In that domain of sustained thought, he opened a new vista which broadened the New England outlook and announced further developments in the future.

The primacy of the New England spirit lost its prestige in the eyes of the southern poet E. A. Poe. Here was a sensitive, dream-haunted man, victimized by fate, ignored by his contemporaries, driven by poverty from place to place, who longed for love and could never secure a return to his feelings, because the women he worshipped either died soon or averted themselves from his haggard face and unsteady gait. He was doomed to indite love-songs to half-real beloved ones. Nature he could envisage only when transmuted by his feverish brain into a filmy vision. Life was a torture, which he cherished, while he poured euphonious plaints, as one wandering in the fulgid gloom of Nightland, sinking to a phosphorescent city under the sea, visiting dear tombs, once shut in a grave whence he addressed to Annie a love-plea from the dead. Out of such dismal themes, by dint of devotion to imponderable beauty, he made lyric poems which often bewitch the mind and enchant the ear.

Poe proclaimed himself the poet of immaterial values. He wished us to believe that he snatched from the empyrean shreds of luminous mist. In fact, he polished, by a busy use of the file, sweet-sounding melopoeias. I cannot ward off the suspicion that his pretty effects are obtained by clever tricks. He came back again and again to the same motifs, to similar phrases and recurrent metrical patterns. The repetition, repetend, and refrain became a mannerism. Many of his stanzas are skilfully combined out of reminiscences from Keats, Shelley, Thomas Moore—or himself. His Poetic Principle, vaunted by Baudelaire and the French Symbolists, was largely borrowed from Coleridge.

His claim to spirituality must be taken with reservations. He refines matter to tenuous and transparent thinness, but fails to transcend it. He is more of a dexterous craftsman than of a creative artist. The singularity of his temper does not tower to a commanding personality. He is a master of fantastic imagery and of pleasing melody—a limited field of no small value.

The "jingle-man," such was the hard judgment passed on Poe by Emerson. Why this scathing stricture? Poe had declared his unconcern for truth, and, in the eyes of the poet-philosopher, spurious other-worldliness, morbid emotion, and flights into the strange were not enough to make great poetry. Emerson's earnestness stands in sharp contrast to Poe's attitudinizing. Poetry, for Emerson, was the supreme attempt of the divine in man to find itself and express its relation to the World-Soul. Images were to be introduced, not as pretty ornaments, but as symbols offered by Nature to intimate the omnipresence of the Informing Power. Words ought to spring spontaneously from the depths, where the correspondences between things and thoughts are hatched under the wings of the Spirit.

What if a syntactic construction creaks, a line halts, a rhyme grates? Above such superficial jars, there is the effulgence of God-communicated truth, which melts into the illumined expanse. Emerson may not have been always inspired. The intellect within him is apt to interfere with the soaring of the higher imagination. Too many of his compositions are mere pieces of bare and dry statement. But he had his moments of ecstasy, in which he felt deeply the splendor of the outward world and traced it to its spiritual source in the Heart of the Cosmos. Ringing words then and majestic lines flowed from his pen, attuned, it seemed, to more than human harmony. His best poems teem with meaning, enhanced by resplendent beauty; they overbrim at times with mystic rapture, as if the visionary bard had been missioned to deliver the oracles of the Infinite.

The stress implied in such soul-exertion could not be sustained long. The poetry of Emerson is uneven. As he despised technique, he did not know how to fill the intervals between the fits of inspiration with what Coleridge calls "neutral verse." Such poetry as his is not to be judged by the quantity. With him, for the first time, appears in American poetry unquestionable genius. He bears the sign of the mysterious inner force which molds creative minds.

He was not cold, as has been maintained. He was only hampered by a temperamental shyness, which prevented him from venting his feelings in ordinary intercourse. But there was in him a romantic fervor, remote from passion, akin to the transports of the mystics. Love for him had nothing to do with infatuation for women, but he interpreted the movements of the individual heart, as Plato had done, as preparations for outbursts of universal admiration and worship. He was not at ease when treating of human affections. Even paternal love, intensified by the cruel loss of his little boy, is expressed clumsily in the first part of "Threnody." The second part of the poem, written later, dealing with the comforting influence of Nature, that reveals beyond affliction and regret the far-reaching purpose of God, ascends to sublime serenity.

Intellectual poetry naturally wends its way toward allegory. Emerson discards worn-out mythology and creates his own allegorical figures, powerfully endowed with mysterious life. Thus Uriel, the rebellious archangel, represents himself, ostracized by the celestial host, but awing them by the majesty of his attitude and the calm hauteur of his trust in the future. Merlin stands for the poet, whose breath is the divine afflatus, blown from the spirit-world. The Sphinx, voicing Nature's thoughts, perplexes the common man, but finds her disciple of election in the seer. Once Emerson approached, in person, the World-Soul: he throws away all intermediary and bravely faces the principle of truth; he calls on man, in tragic accents, to exert his will-power to bear the assaults of Fate, and tells of the miraculous "compensation" which is sure to come; the human soul will be identified with the Soul of the universe.

This mystic delight is expressed again, with a wealth of imaginative vision and an irresistible force of emotion, in "Woodnotes." Nature, in this poem, becomes the prophet that discloses the "runes" inscribed on all things by the Creator. Nature reveals the secret meaning of beauty, of universal order, of life. In fine, the poet pierces to such depths of mystery that, overrun by his infectious enthusiasm, our brain reels like Dante's when he was admitted to the Holy of Holies.

Emerson's mind, at such moments, was rushed into a whirl of spiritual ecstasy. He wrote in his Journal: "When my bark heads its way toward the law of laws, I sweep serenely over God's depths in an infinite sea." This mood of intoxicated delight overflows poems like "Brahma," "Mithridates," "Bacchus," and other passages sprung from wells of celestial joy in his pure soul.

This capacity for intellectual glow, joined with imaginative power and metaphysical insight, accounts for the lofty tone, impassioned accent, and colorful sheen of his best philosophical verse. Few poets in England have equalled him in that vein. He surpasses almost all when he expresses the divinity of nature, the spirituality of man, the cryptic significance of the minutest organized forms, the unity of the Whole. Though he achieved musical harmony but seldom, the quality of some of his lyrical stanzas is unmistakable. With him, poetry and worship meet in one current of devotional fervor.

While cultured America produced, with Emerson, a philosophical poet of refined intellect and unblemished character, democratic America reared, with Walt Whitman, a blunt man of the people, of dubious demeanor, endowed with the power to express, at times, in coarse effective accents, the pride of self-trust, to celebrate physical exhilaration, the joy of sensation, communion with nature, and sympathy for man; to praise equality, labor, the American achievement and the modern spirit; and to rise fitfully to mystic exaltation and clothe an instinctive vision of the spiritual in lyric symbols. It was America's portion to give birth, with this rough-hewn son of the Muse, to vernacular poetry, discarding tradition, spurning precedents, despising decorum, laughing to scorn gentility and cant, building a new rhythmic chant on the cadences of ordinary speech, and rising to occasional dignity, graphic vividness, warmth of feeling, splendor of imagery or religious earnestness, There is a large part of incongruity, bunkum or trash in what Whitman wrote, but enough of it has genuine, spontaneous, or spiritual beauty, to make the literary critic pause and wonder.

He shocked his contemporaries by his unashamed reference to sex. This departure from the guarded ways of social propriety came half a century too soon. But it was in the line of the new biological frankness which was destined to prevail first in France, then in England, lastly on this continent. Daring as was Whitman's challenge, it was only a side-aspect of *Leaves of Grass*. Whitman sang his own self, not simply for the naïve satisfaction of boasting, but because he firmly believed that universal humanity could best be known through the consciousness of one representative individual. He had read Emerson. His spiritual insight into the life of things owes much to the Concord Philosopher. His personal contribution to a visionary interpretation of the universe lies in the intensity of his lyrical fervor. He has moments of passionate or awesome commerce with the earth, with night, with the sea. He shares in the life of animals and smoothly passes from sympathy with their ways to symbolical use of them to figure out human feelings. The bird from Alabama sings of love and death; the hermit thrush laments the passing of Lincoln. Plants have a soul. The redwood tree dies with majestic calm; the lilac bends over the bier of the murdered President. Stars shine in the limitless blue to impress on man the sense of the infinite and of eternity.

Whitman redeems too frequent platitudes by splendid outbursts of admiration. Some of his landscapes vie with canvases of nature painters. He was the first to discover the shapeliness of a worker in action. He sketches simple realistic tableaux with much relief and color, in anticipation of the Imagists. He, who so often gushes words in intemperate flow, coins at times ringing formulas with a bold spraying of slang. Mere declamation may unexpectedly rise to fine eloquence. His sluggish, washy, rhythmical prose may warm to lyrical glow, take to a martial gait, irradiate mystic ecstasy. In such exceptional spells, he is a true poet, expressing himself in the untried form of free verse.

One of the crowd, Whitman hid in the recesses of his mind aristocratic distinction. A sensualist, he was capable of refined feelings. A braggart, he could shape just and measured thoughts. His attitude in face of death reaches grandeur. He often let the popular sap freely spurt out of him, but not in such a barbaric way as he would have us believe. After a long delay, he exerted a liberating influence on the succeeding generation, inasmuch as his innovations could be reconciled with the essential principles of esthetics.

Before he became a solitary bard, Whitman had mixed with newspaper men and workers, traveled, served in hospitals. A solitary poetess, Emily Dickinson, shut herself in her Amherst home, conversing with nature within the bounds of her garden, divining rather than knowing mankind. She read few books, trusting her own intuition of poetical values, following her natural bent to romantic emotion, transcribing into spare little poems her reflections on life and death, transmuting through imagery and impassioned transference her scanty experience. There was in her feelings a vehemence sometimes akin to fierceness, in her love of nature a spontaneity bordering on the primitive, in her intercourse with inarticulate creatures a power of sympathy merging them into her own identity, in her worship of God a nearness, together with an awe, which resorted to a mode of expression at once familiar and remote. There was in her mental composition an abruptness, which broke out into short, throbbing flights of lyric verse, unhampered by regular metre, free from exact rhymes. She compelled common words to respond to elevated thoughts, or coined new words out of the plastic dough of the English language. She created for herself a world of images, now borrowed from trifling objects, now broadened to a large relationship with the universe or to religious aspiration.

She conformed to the New England spirit of self-control and contemplative tranquillity, with the one exception of an imperious need of passionate love, purely imaginative, never meant to be communicated, but so intense, either in chaste fervor or in fleshly self-surrender, that her love poems form one of the most revealing, touching, and outspoken confessions of a female heart, balked of tender satisfaction, feeding upon itself, wildly yielding to fits of desperate desire.

Part of her poetry is dimmed by a petit-bourgeois, old-maidenish atmosphere, for which she cannot be held responsible, considering the limited range of her associations. Writing for herself alone, she often lapses into cryptic phrasing. But at her best she is original, tingles with deep emotion, creates figurative expressions entirely her own, and condenses valuable sense into few words.

Nature offered her shelter and solace from the storm of passion that, for a time, raged in her soul. In presence of natural beauty, she revels in color, motion, the numberless sounds that fill the earth with music. She endows birds and butterflies with gentle or frolicsome humors. She personifies dawn, twilight, a storm, the seasons, attributing to them human gestures and feelings. God is present in nature, as the Providence that benignly watches over the created world. The thought of death raises her mind not so much to awful meditation as to confident hope in rest and bliss.

There is great unevenness in her manner of expression. Her four-line stanzas may be rugged, almost vulgar, or they may teem with rich images, ring with sincere emotion, be couched in terse, precise, meaningful words. She works out vivid allegories, constructs felicitous similes, paints lively scenes. Her forte lies in sudden and strong effects produced by one startling word or phrase, which contains as much vision as sense.

We forget that much of what she wrote is inchoate or piecemeal. Her poetry wells up spontaneously under the shock of intense feeling or imaginative compulsion. In her fits of inspiration there was ecstasy. Awkwardness of technique, after all, is secondary. She inaugurated a form of poetry based on greater respect for the essentials and lesser regard for the accessories of verse. We moderns hail creative power, were it in uncouth garb, provided we discover in it elements of human truth and genuine beauty.

Emily Dickinson wrote with no view to any sort of publication. And it was not until after her death that her poems were committed to print. They could have no influence, at the end of the nineteenth century, on the development of American poetry. Quite different was the case of *Leaves of Grass*, whose novelty and boldness made enough impression on some younger poets to urge them to imitate its prominent characteristics.

With Whitman, democracy and the life of the people had entered the domain of poetry. Although tradition and precedent held their own, it was possible now to treat imaginatively subjects which before were not considered as "nice" or as fit to be admitted into the higher forms of literature. Henceforth, along with the current of urbane and cultured verse, there was to settle a stream of realistic, blunt, distinctly American poetry, treating of industry and industrial workers, life in the fields and in the village, the influx of new ethnical elements, or bringing forth some glaring or furtive manifestations of American demeanor, thus far kept in the dark. There was a split in literature, one group insisting, without servility, upon respect for the past, the other looking forward to the future. The latter, which might be styled "the progeny of Walt Whitman," adopted the rhythmical prose period, the free measured line, the irregular paragraph, and an informal way of expression, where slang and popular syntax were often resorted to for peculiar effects.

This school of innovators we shall first consider.

Carl Sandburg, a manual worker and a journalist, before he took to poetry-writing, belongs by birth to the aliens. He acquired education by his own effort, far from the seats of culture, in the Middle West countryside. His mental activity was such that he not only assimilated what he found of proletarian vigor in Whitman, but sought an aliment to his yearning for beauty along lines that were later to be called "imagism" and "symbolism." He showed himself both a painter of rugged, blustering, indecorous figures, and a carver of dainty intaglios. Wherever there are sweating men, lean-faced women, giggling girls, ragged children, we feel that he belongs. In his descriptions of the staring, bantering, grumbling, tossing life of the masses, he tells what he has seen. In his early socialist days, he did not shrink from violent arraignment of present conditions or from cheap melodrama. But he often rose to robust delineation and genuinely moving sentiment, backed by images taken from street life and by a luscious flow of billingsgate, both picturesque and expressive. Whatever his indebtedness to Whitman, he is himself. When he voices his philosophical outlook on life, his lines assume noble dignity. His habit of realistic observation does not preclude elevated thoughts.

There is a delicate artist lurking in him under the mixer with the coarse elements of the Windy City. He limns nature sketches with neat outlines or a vivid splash of colors, distinctly poetical by the figurative meaning and the method of indirection. It may be that on such descriptive, lyrical, and symbolist pieces his fame will rest in the future.

A practising lawyer in Chicago, Edgar Lee Masters, turned to inditing verse and published a collection of short poems, *Spoon River Anthology*, which placed him forthwith among the original writers of the day. The volume was made up of condensed portraits, supposedly engraved on the tombs of citi-

zens of one village. They refer to those who in life suffered
or caused wrong, indulged their passions on the sly or were
severely dealt with for venial faults, to those who cunningly
wriggled through the rifts of the law, or imprudently chal-
lenged solemn fallacies. There floats about those skits a favor
of satire or irony, with now and then poignant touches of
pathos or grim strokes of humor. The use of irregular un-
rhymed lines permits rapid movement, brisk phrasing, sharp
characterization, frequent resort to stinging idioms and racy
figures of speech. We are generally put in presence of naked
grossness with too rare attempts to interpret it in terms of
human complexity. Yet the facts are skilfully handled, often
ending with a shock of surprise. Humor relieves the tenseness
of situations which, faced coldly, would be dispiriting. Masters'
images have an undeniable power of appeal. His manner de-
notes fertile inventiveness and sound workmanship, with not
infrequent dramatic force.

The Middle West again gave birth to Vachel Lindsay the
itinerant bard. There was in him something of a medieval
minstrel and much of the modern boy scout. His poetical inspiration sprang now from a flow of animal spirits, now from
a hankering after the supernatural. He hoped to awake in the
common people the dormant esthetic sense. This glittering
chimera could not but entail disappointment and trial. Lindsay bore them cheerfully, until the stress was too much and
his nerves gave way.

He celebrated the West in the pioneering days, with visions
of sturdy soil-breakers always on the move, and of troops of
Indian horsemen pursuing buffaloes. The modern Americans
he liked to watch driving their automobiles on the Santa Fé
trail, giddy heirs to boisterous ancestors. The poet revels in
onomatopœias, as the honking, tooting horns tear the atmosphere with their clanging sounds.

Lindsay had a sentimental liking for the simple faith of naïve
people, such as Negro preachers and Salvation Army leaders.
There was also in him a power of glamorous imagination,
which appears in two long visionary poems, where China and
India are idealized as countries of beauty, mystery, artistic and
religious aspiration. Nor are thoughts of general import absent

from his poetry. "Sew the Flags Together" is a moving appeal to international amity and peace. "The Perfect Marriage" could be devised only by a clean and loving heart. Religion takes the form of an individual appeal in "Look You, I'll Go Pray."

Further west, beyond the Rockies, a fierce skald borrows from Walt Whitman his long rhythmical line to tell appalling Californian stories of lust and murder, to the screech of the vultures and the pounding of the waves against the granite cliffs of the Coast Range. Shut in a stronghold, built with his own hands of stray rocks, on the shore of the ocean, Robinson Jeffers pores in solitude over the lurid adventures of ferocious natives, with incest, religious madness, or superhuman will-power as the chief motifs. His bent is to excess. In the domain of action, this would mean destruction. Fortunately Jeffers is a poet and can find in art free space for the effervescence of his immoderate desire of passionate fulfillment.

His blood-curdling tragedies are relieved by his sense of natural beauty. He worships the majesty of the Sierras and the vastness of the Pacific. None before him had expressed so powerfully the awe of the mountains, the mystery of the canyons, the divine calm or demoniac anger of the western ocean.

Let us now return, with a pleasant sense of relief and greater literary satisfaction, to the traditional poets, among whom three occupy a towering position. We shall conclude this paper by a review of William Vaughn Moody, Robert Frost, and Edwin Arlington Robinson.

In spirit and by the tenor of his verse, Moody belongs to an earlier age than that in which the date of his birth, 1869, placed him. His tone of passionate earnestness and his magnificence of phrase mark him as a romantic of the era of Shelley. In his first productions, he expressed sentiments roused in him by problems concerning the welfare of the downtrodden and the hope of seeing the end of all wars. Later, having become conscious of his genius, he took flight away from the questions of the day to a realm of visions.

He was to become entirely himself, when he drew his inspiration from subjective sources. His chief motifs, in the brilliant short period between his awakening to his proper mission and his premature death, were love and religious philosophy.

In "The Moon-Moth," he unites his cult of classic Greece (which burns in him with the same flame as in Shelley) with love of woman. The love-passion reaches such intensity that it invades all the avenues of the mind, quickens the sense of beauty, stirs the imagination to call up a magnificent scene, rouses the memory to build a vision of the storied past, fevers the sensory organs into a state of hallucination, and urges the poet to create a perfect symbol. "The Daguerreotype" is based on the striking antithesis of wayward, sensual infatuation and of reverent filial love. By means of resplendent images, Moody pleads that in spite of wanton vagaries his heart is pure, and that he is not unworthy of his dead mother's pardon. Woman, the lover, the mother, the inspirer, is evoked in "I Am the Woman," a bold prosopopœia, which takes as generic theme the abstract idea of woman and vitalizes it by living attributes, to tower above human-sized individuals like a gigantic shape of wondrous proportions and awful meaning.

In this poem there runs already an undercurrent of religious philosophy, which was to rise to the surface and become the prominent feature in a dramatic trilogy meant to present through biblical and mythological figures, acting in boundless space, the poet's ultimate views on man and the universe. Moody could not accept the data of established creeds, divided as he was between pagan love of the earth and Christian reverence for the spirit. He was eager to worship immaterial values, provided they should not attempt to smother the instincts. He gives shape and life to his ideas, with a vigor of imaginative creation, a mysterious depth of thought, a warmth of tingling sensibility, a splendor of form and a majesty of tone, which, in spite of some lagging passages, place him near to the author of *Prometheus Unbound*. He moves with ease in the supernatural world, among huge, fleeting phantoms, beholding the revolutions of the stars, watching the messengers of God on their errands of love or wrath, withal keeping his composure, like Dante, to bring back, in solemn offering, mighty news. His images have a quality of plastic fullness, compelled to express airy immateriality. Romanticism, compounded of such choice and effective elements, rises above the defects often associated with its name. It becomes an auxiliary of eminent thought, a well-spring of rare beauty.

It is a great contrast to pass from Moody, the romantic, to Frost, the realist. It is as if, from a flight to the spiritual world amid sword-bearing archangels and lightning-encinctured Olympians, under the leadership of Shelley, we reverted to a stroll through flower-speckled meadows and cottage-dotted glens, under the guidance of Wordsworth. Robert Frost, self-taught to the best of culture, seems to disregard culture when he writes poetry, preferring, to knowledge derived from books, experience acquired by converse with tillers of the soil and workers at the mill, whose unobtrusive humanity yields to his observant and sympathetic mind the truth of labor bravely done, suffering patiently borne, disappointment shoved away by humor, life simply lived within the compass of daily needs, natural impulses and homely duties.

Part of his work consists of dramatic narratives, taken from rural New England, depicting the ways of farm-life, echoing the speech of the countryside, with such vivid touches of local color and such sincerity of emotion that no unprejudiced reader can remain indifferent. His characters—men, women, farm-hands, artisans, a few shifters, an occasional preacher—form a complete community with various occupations and diversified moral traits. The poet shares in their joys and sorrows, describes their family bonds or irregular liaisons, enters into their secret thoughts and feelings, whether they bow to tradition or claim independence, whether they waddle in intellectual twilight or show keen judgment, liberal views, even esthetic tastes within the possibilities of their condition.

Beyond the features peculiar to New England, Frost reaches universal human nature. His farmers are not essentially different, at bottom, from the peasants of democratic European countries, except where the poet scans so deep that he reveals new aspects of the villagers' consciousness. He opens new vistas into a world where native ruggedness is tempered by the fundamental values of civilization. His condensed, artistically constructed, strongly moving or discreetly humorous narratives unseldom break into outbursts of broad truth, which well up from the depths, like a ground-swell out of a choppy sea.

Another part of Frost's work consists of lyrical poems. He

paints nature with a fine sense of its beauties, of the subtle correspondences of its changing features to passing human moods. A veil of melancholy rests on his contemplative mind, never thickening into gloom. Under trial, he braces himself and stands firm against the buffets of Fate. There is both dignity and tenderness in his picture of love. He sings of steady, devoted love, that keeps its bloom through the lapse of years and the wear and tear of married life.

Frost's form is entirely original. He uses the vocabulary and modulations of ordinary speech, with no loss of literary effectiveness. He substitutes the laws of feeling or of vision for the outer rules of discourse. Stripped of spurious ornaments, his style is that of a true poet by the wealth of images, the force of suggestion and of emotion, the power to throw over the everyday world the glamour of the unusual.

Realism and idealism meet in the work of Edwin Arlington Robinson. He was an observer, not so much of nature (which he sketched infrequently, with brief, sharp, pencil-strokes) as of people, whose inner life he read through outer actions, gestures, face-expressions and soul-revealing speech. He meditated on conflicts of feelings and thought-perplexities in individuals, or encounters of purposes, shocks of passions, tragic collisions of good and evil in social intercourse, and built out of a broad, penetrating view of human behavior moving narratives, raised by impassioned sympathy and imaginative transposition to a high level of poetry. He also reflected on his own mental experience and formed a brave outlook on man's relations to the universe, buoyed up above urgent causes for despondency by an idealism of truth and hope.

A searcher for psychological truth and philosophical verities, he never pandered to vulgar tastes. He appealed to thoughtful and cultured readers. The dominant tone of gentle melancholy in his work is the result of his uncommon penetration. He could not but be sensitive to the blight that settles on many guileless souls. Pregnant and pensive poetry as his could not be popular. Yet Robinson, even under stress of poverty, went on his way, faithful to his interpretation of the world-scene, urged by the intuition of genius that he ought to devote all of himself to his thought and art, at the cost of sacrifice and renunciation.

His first compositions were lyrical, generally not in the subjective, but objective, vein. He interests himself in what happens in Tilbury Town, and, out of materials that in other hands might have been dull, he weaves, through metphor, allegory, or symbol, fabrics of gold tissue. We sense a pulsing personal emotion lurking in allusive utterance or imaginative construction, expressed in pathetic accents. Thus he treats of general ideas feelingly, with impressive wisdom and a peculiar sensitivity to their dramatic impact on man's desperate striving to reach mental equipoise or to erect a barrier against dejection.

Robinson is too modest to state a doctrine. His knowledge of human frailty prevents him from throwing a glamour of optimism over modern society; but, when he speaks in his own name, his tone reflects courageous endeavor to grasp the promise of a higher destiny. Such passages often rise to a degree of spiritual uplift and sensuous beauty that place them at the peak of modern lyrical production.

His delineation of people now takes the form of portraits rich in unforgettable life-likeness or precision, now expands into long interpretative narratives. The latter, either monologues, dialogues, novels in verse, or epic legends, bring out the characters' salient features in their singularity and in their connection with universal human nature. Robinson's keen mind was exceptionally equipped for the exploration of that shifty realm of psychological experience, the subconscious. He chooses the moment when the obscure intimations of the deeper ego emerge to clear awareness. Morbid cases unseldom attract him, not for their gloomy implications, but because pathological dispositions often bring the normal elements into more vivid relief. Intellectual narrowness, egotism, self-indulgence, failure to grasp the higher truth may entail misfortune, ruin, or death. On the whole, his personages are less guilty than overpowered by destructive agencies. If a crime is committed, it is attended by remorse, with such emphasis that the ugly deed is purged of its horror.

He did not shrink from great subjects. He drew the full-length portrait of Shakespeare, the man and the superman, with a power of vivid presentation, penetrating insight, and dramatic movement, that makes it an unparalleled masterpiece. He wrote an epic trilogy on the best-known episodes of the Arthurian legend, conscious of his ability to renew the subject by a personal contribution of thought and beauty. He succeeded so well in modernizing the theme of Tristram, without detracting from its lyrical glow and pathetic force, that it took the readers by storm and at last imposed Robinson's name on the attention of the general public.

His late long narratives introduce a moral or social problem into a story of passion, frustration, or failure, and make the episodes and characters symbols of ideas. The symbols are so finely elaborated, the plot so intimately blends with the intellectual theme, the living beings so subtly impersonate the motifs of the ideological as well as of the affective drama, that the poem is raised to the dignity and significance of a myth. *The Man Who Died Twice, Cavender's House, King Jasper* are modern myths, as artfully contrived, profoundly thought out, and mysteriously involved as the ancient or medieval myths. They are feats of conception and execution, and the meaningful simplicity of the form adds to them a distinction and charm, which make Robinson a classic of literature in the English language.

A country which has produced a poetical genius of this stature, preceded and heralded within a century by a score of eminent talents and a host of non-negligible devotees of the Muse, is assured of a literary future. Whether they sang nature, man, moral steadiness, or spiritual aspiration; whether they celebrated the stately past or the myriad-shaped present; whether they were attracted by the simple life of the countryside or the psychological complexities of urban civilization; whether they sided with democratic forwardness or stood firm in aristocratic poise, most of the poets whom we have passed in review were both staunch Americans and universal-minded thinkers. Their descriptions have more than occasionally a richness, their lyrics a fervor, their self-confessions a discreet intimacy, their polemics a vim, their philosophical utterance a depth, their human portrayals a relief, their dramatic narratives an intensity, which secure them no mean rank in the world community of inspired writers. American poetry, by and large, takes precedence over American prose. American poets seldom expressed passion, as if the tradition of their religious and moral ancestors kept them off the dangerous ground of unguarded feelings; but they have to a high degree the Anglo-

Saxon quality of imagination, with a freshness due to the youthful quality of the national mind, a largeness due to the vast extent of the New World, and a buoyancy due to the benefit of free institutions.

American poems are of shapely structure, consistent in thought or vision, progressive in interest or dramatic force, illumined by clear light or bathed in mystery with a logic of its own. The form is fluid or crisp, weighty or nimble, brawny or delicate, generally with a propriety of terms, a syntactic sweep, a vigor or a charm of tone, which are the fine flowers of taste. Since poetic composition has attained great amplitude in America, it shows there is a public—were it limited in scope —to welcome it.

Poetry goes along with culture. Let those foreigners who frown at American civilization, because they think it is materialistic and mechanized, look at other things than the sky-scraper, the packing factory, Buffalo Bill circus or Coney Island. Let them, if they can, glance at American poetry. They will find in it one of the essential features of the American temper, individualism, transformed by intellectual exertion, fruitful expansion of the imaginative and affective faculties, a sturdy or exquisite relish for style, into artistic individuality. They will find out that the American nation, in the persons of its makers and readers of poetry, cannot be satisfied with the pounding of the sledge hammer, but, best sign of an advanced stage of spirtual and esthetic development, yearns to speak and to understand the language of the gods.

Tradition and Rebellion: European Patterns in the Literature of America

By

STANLEY T. WILLIAMS*

IN A year in which the intimacy of Europe and America is sharpened by anxiety and sorrow, I attempt a scholar's task: to present a tranquil record, to refresh your memory concerning a rich and ancient heritage, to offer, in brief, an outline of European patterns in American literature. Let me be at once explicit. By a pattern I mean, in this particular study, the presence in our literature of one or more of three subtly diffusive elements: first, ways of thought, namely ideas or ideologies derived from Europe; second, ways of feeling, namely moods or states of mind resultant from the impact of European thought upon American writing; and, third, ways of expression, namely European techniques. An example of the first element might be the ideology of the eighteenth-century Enlightenment in the novels of Charles Brockden Brown;[1] of the second, the peculiar mood of veneration for Europe's past in the essays of Washington Irving; of the third, the craftsmanship of the modern novelist, Frank Norris, in relation to the French naturalists.[2] Such elements intermingle, vary in emphasis, are modified by other influences, American or even Asiatic;[3] they are but shadows of the good and great of Europe; yet however shifting or elusive, they form patterns recognizable and even blessed to the American who loves his country's literature.

* Colgate Professor of English, Fellow of Calhoun College, and Adviser in American Literature in the University Library, Yale University.

[1] See, e.g., C. B. Brown, *Ormond* . . . , ed. Ernest Marchand, New York [1937], Introduction, xiii-xvi.

[2] See Marius Biencourt, *Une Influence du Naturalisme Français en Amérique*, Paris, 1933; and Franklin Walker, *Frank Norris, a Biography*, New York, 1932, index.

[3] See, e.g., Arthur Christy, *The Orient in American Transcendentalism*, New York, 1932; F. I. Carpenter, *Emerson and Asia*, Cambridge, 1930.

Now in the selection and study of patterns which seem to be European, I must ask your indulgence for not defining sharply what elements in the pattern are not purely European but composites of many influences. For you may well object, What *is,* in our complicated intellectual development, a *European* ideology, a *European* way of thought, a *European* technique? For example, it is virtually impossible to distinguish with finality in our literature between the records of the European ideology of the rights of man and the records of the American copy with its development of this ideology in our own philosophy of democracy. I shall, therefore, speak today only of currents of American literature in which the European voltage is, so to speak, high and apparent, either from known European philosophies or, more particularly, through direct imitations of European men of letters.

Finally, by American "literature" I mean today belles-lettres, books written and published in America of aesthetic and literary value. Such exist; it is high time that in a civilized reaction against the abasement of our writing to a mere social record, we reëxamine—yes, that we bathe our minds in—this slender but distinguished canon of prose and poetry. On the border line between intellectual history and belles-lettres you and I may quarrel; some may limit our artists to Emerson, Hawthorne, Melville, Poe, Whitman, Henry James, or a few others. Yet there *is* a Pantheon, even a Valhalla, with its quasi-immortal warriors chosen from the slain. And through all these pulsate the currents of European thought and feeling.

To the complex causes for the existence of these European patterns in our belles-lettres I shall refer, but only incidentally. The intellectual historian is vaguely correct: in our economic, social, political, and institutional life may be discovered the seeds of such an essay as Emerson's democratic "Self-Reliance" or such a poem as Whitman's international "Passage to India." The work of art can never be convincingly removed from the life experience of its creator and his people. Yet the literary historian should dig even deeper than the intellectual historian, for whom literature itself often seems but a gigantic hat-rack of illustration; he should explore the genetics of American literature in respect to foreign thought; he should give us grievously needed studies concerning its debts to the

English, French, and German cultures.[4] What, however, interests us in this short moment is *the living presence of these European patterns.* Here they are, today, coloring our literature as distinctly as the familiar American patterns and influences, such as the frontier. Here, in our belles-lettres, these patterns have long since ceased to be social forces; fashioned in art, memorably arrested in essay, tale, or lyric, they seem to enjoy an immortality denied the tides of thought which begot them and then passed into history. Thus Longfellow's poetic drama, "The Spanish Student," is a tangible; its Castilian moods are real,[5] however learnedly we may debate the meanings of that Spanish trend in American culture a century ago. King Boabdil of Granada is in history a tenuous shade, but in the etchings of Washington Irving—not so![6] He is actual. I intend, then, to sketch, for the first time, I believe, the growth and decline of the dynamic European patterns (ideas, moods, and techniques) in our literature; and, finally, to indicate some meanings for these patterns in the history of American belles-lettres. And so I may communicate some meanings for our life of today, for its most civilized essence has flowered in these belles-lettres.

And now, at the outset, we must remind ourselves of the eccentric development of American literature. For us no native body of folklore became nobly articulate in a *Beowulf* or *Chanson de Roland;* for us occurred no thousand years' distillation of primitive thought and passion; for us no slow spiraling into the wisdom and sophistication of a national, modern literature. Instead, the people whose intellectuals created what we call American literature were indifferent to or actually destroyed the cultures (Aztec or Indian) of the new continent. Such cultures, though they later inspired an occasional novelist or poet, were never the vertebrae of our literature. For its main sources were western European, and the indigenous accretions, such as the frontier influence, were grafted upon a European literature written in America, a transplanted literature indeed! Instead of, as in many countries, a core of native culture, expanding, experimenting, refining, and admitting

[4] E.g., H. M. Jones, *America and French Culture,* Chapel Hill, North Carolina, 1927.
[5] See I. L. Whitman, *Longfellow and Spain,* New York, 1927, p. 199.
[6] See *The Alhambra,* London, 1832, I, 157-173.

foreign elements only with suspicion, here the reverse was nearly true: a seasoned literature in a primitive country regarded native intrusions with condescension. We must not oversimplify. The primary facts of space and land, and the secondary but mighty forces of invigorated religious, social, and political thought tempered these European patterns almost immediately. World ideas stride with a free American gait in, for example, the bumptious poetry of Walt Whitman. Yet we begin, I repeat, with a migrated literature, with writing wedded to European patterns.

Through the language and through constant communication with "Our Old Home," the predominant European pattern in our literature, until after the Revolution, was English. This was overwhelmingly true, though the omnivorous Cotton Mather studied French and Spanish; though Dutch was spoken in New York and Swedish in Delaware. In the seventeenth-century poetry of Ann Bradstreet and Michael Wigglesworth and in the prose of the Mathers reigned the influences of Calvin and Ramus,[7] salvaged from Puritan England and France. Unsweetened by the more liberal Elizabethan views of life (few copies, if any, of Shakespeare are known to have existed in the New England colonies), and unenlivened by the sophistication of the Restoration (drama was anathema), this early American prose and verse was a deracinated Puritan literature. Indeed, its complete subservience extended to techniques. For through the thickets of Cotton Mather's prose peers the face of Thomas Fuller[8]; and in the devotional verse of Edward Taylor, the frontier-parson of Westfield, Massachusetts, we hear the accents of the English metaphysicals.[9] In this provincial poetry lumber on the sustained "conceits," and in it sounds, like the surf on Cape Cod shallows, the "fourteener," dear to the metrists of this ponderous age.[10] Such literary history is familiar, but it is necessary to our present story. Here is, indeed, a corner of England, of Puritan England,

---

[7] See *The Puritans*, ed. Perry Miller and T. H. Johnson, New York [1938], Introduction, pp. 28-41.

[8] See J. K. Piercy, *Studies in Literary Types in Seventeenth Century America (1607-1710)*, New Haven, 1939, p. 230, note 500.

[9] See *The Poetical Works of Edward Taylor*, ed. T. H. Johnson, New York [1939], p. 11.

[10] See *Johnson's Wonder-Working Providence, 1628-1651*, ed. J. F. Jameson, New York, 1910, pp. 12-14.

almost without sea-change, except, perhaps, for the somber in-
tensification of religious moods through the menace of the
frontier. Here are history, chronicle, sermon, diary, verse;
here are powerful, but none the less inferior, supplements to
English ecclesiastical writing.

Although it is difficult for us in the volatile twentieth century to credit so concentrated an English influence, we must
realize that it persisted, molding the colossal intellect of Edwards in the temper of Locke[11] and, in due time, shaping his
style by the reformed prose of England, that lucid, workman-
like protest against the cloying richness of seventeenth-century
writing.[12] In Benjamin Franklin emerges the first alien modification, through French influence, but the *Autobiography* reveals his basic English pattern. Franklin wrote with the English
deists in mind; he conned Addison sentence by sentence; he
never wearied of quoting Alexander Pope. His obligation to
French thought suggests a problem recurrent, and insoluble
in our present study, that of separating the direct from the
indirect influence. Were Franklin's or Thomas Paine's debts
to the French encyclopedists immediate or through their English interpreters? We shall see how, later, the New England
transcendentalists channeled off German thought through
Coleridge and Carlyle. Whatever the answer to this question,
there appeared in the years directly after the American Revolution, a challenge to the prevailing English pattern in our literature, not only in the Gallic overtones in Franklin and Paine,
but in the French idioms of St. John de Crèvecoeur, the Pennsylvania farmer,[13] and in the rhapsodical invocations to French
ideas in the poetry of Philip Freneau.[14] The long process of
the erosion of English patterns had begun. Yet until the last
decade of the eighteenth century one sees merely French flowers
budding in the crevices of the English granite. Through the
satires of John Trumbull, inspired by Churchill; through the
epics of Joel Barlow, reëchoing Milton; through the novels
of Brown, rebuilding the Gothic tale; through the regimented

[11] For the influence of Locke upon Edwards, see *Jonathan Edwards, Representative Selections* . . . , ed. C. H. Faust and T. H. Johnson, New York [1935], xxv.
[12] See H. M. Jones, "American Prose Style," *The Huntington Library Bulletin*,
Cambridge, No. 6, November, 1934, pp. 115-151.
[13] See *Sketches of Eighteenth Century America*, ed. H. L. Bourdin, R. H.
Gabriel, and S. T. Williams, New Haven, 1925.
[14] See, in the present work, pp. 186-187.

imitators of Pope, Goldsmith, or Denham, Britain ruled the American literary scene until the turn of the nineteenth century, without real rivals.

Indeed, the English patterns in this latter century still fascinate us into sentimentalism, apparently our incurable vice in literary history. After 1830 occur the full flowering of the Concord and Cambridge writers; the minor enrichment of these patterns by continental influences so outré as the Finnish in Longfellow's poetry[15] and the Russian in Howells' novels;[16] and also the fertilizing interplay of both English and continental patterns with the growing, lusty, native traditions of the frontier and democracy. We may find also in this nineteenth century, besides these parallel or horizontal influences, what may be called the vertical influences from England. Thus there flourished the almost sacred tradition of English literature of the past, persuading Herman Melville in *Moby Dick* to reënact the tragedy of *King Lear*,[17] and in *Pierre* to repeat despairingly the problem of *Hamlet*.[18] Hawthorne knows Spenser and Bunyan; Emerson, the metaphysical poets of the seventeenth century; and Lowell, Keats. The English tradition seems inviolate! Often, however, the American writer hears his contemporaries in the island across the Atlantic and repeats the song or story with a voice fresh and powerful, if less subtle in modulation. On Bryant's lips is the music of Wordsworth; Poe re-dreams the fantasies of Coleridge; Emerson and Whitman breathe new life into the gospel of Carlyle.

So much may be said in general for English patterns in the nineteenth century. Now if we think of these more specifically, as including ideas, moods, and techniques, we perceive at once that in these literary records ideas and moods are often inextricably blended. Familiar liberalisms, for example, reappear as emotional assumptions, as in the poetic assertions concerning liberty in Emerson's "Self-Reliance" or Whitman's "Song of Myself." Of these emotionalized patterns let us glance at three or four. We think first of the concept of the individual,

[15] See K. E. Möykkynen, "The Influence of the *Kalevala* on Henry Wadsworth Longfellow's *Song of Hiawatha*," unpublished Master's Essay, Yale University, 1940.

[16] See, in the present work, p. 189.

[17] See Charles Olson, "Lear and Moby Dick," *Twice a Year*, Fall-Winter, 1938 (pp. 165-189).

[18] See Herman Melville, *Pierre or the Ambiguities*, ed. R. S. Forsythe, New York, 1930, xxix-xxxiii.

free and in his destiny illimitable. There is a fine French in-
fusion here, but the vision in our great representative liberal,
Emerson, is hardly more in debt to continental, classical, or
frontier attitudes than to the English. Emerson's "American
Scholar," vitalized by Plato and also by the "trapper" of the
prairie, includes echoes of the English liberals. Thoreau repeats
the lofty strain in *Walden,* the story of an individualist's experiment in solitude; and Lowell, in *The Biglow Papers,* shows
the free Yankee in action; all these New Englanders rejoice in
the history of English liberty. Whitman chants the divine average man; he is thinking of the American but he hears the words
of Carlyle; and Swinburne salutes him with his "To Walt Whitman in America." Indeed, the humanitarian cast of our nineteenth-century literature is always akin to that of contemporary
England; Whittier's poetry of abolition gains strength from
the victory over slavery in the mother country; Margaret Fuller
is a feverish George Eliot.

Similarly, throughout the nineteenth century the *English*
patterns of scientific and philosophic thought repeated themselves emotionally in American literature. Thus the *English*
teleological adjustment to the implications of science in the
poetry of Tennyson had a parallel development in the poetry
of Oliver Wendell Holmes and Sidney Lanier;[19] and New
England prose bore the stamp of such *English* literary philosophers as Coleridge and Carlyle. It is, indeed, hardly possible to
exaggerate the influence upon our intellectuals of Coleridge's
Aids to Reflection or of his *Biographia Literaria.* The German
influence upon the Concord writers was, in their mid-career,
considerable, but the basic Emersonian point of view contained
in *Nature,* his first proclamation of himself to the universe, is
hardly touched by a direct modern influence from the continent, except his study of science in the Jardin des Plantes.[20]
Emerson's sources were primarily the Platonists and the *English*

[19] E.g., Holmes's *The Chambered Nautilus.* See the references to Lanier's interest in Darwin and nineteenth-century science in *Southern Poets,* ed. E. W.
Parks, New York [1936], Introduction, lxxi-lxxii.

[20] See *Journals of Ralph Waldo Emerson,* ed. E. W. Emerson and W. E. Forbes,
Boston, 1910, III, 161-164. The entry of July 13, 1833, describes Emerson's visit
to "the cabinet of Natural History in the Garden of Plants." He writes: "Not
a form so grotesque, so savage, nor so beautiful, but is an expression of some
property inherent in man the observer,—an occult relation between the very
scorpions and man. I feel the centipede in me, cayman, carp, eagle, and fox.
I am moved by strange sympathies; I say continually 'I will be a naturalist.'"
(p. 163)

neo-Platonists and other *English* interpreters of philosophic systems.[21] More and more the philosophical backgrounds of American literature widened and deepened, admitting continental thought directly. Yet during the first decades of the nineteenth century such influences were primarily English.

Finally, in this brief summary of English ideas emotionalized and arrested in American literature, we may comment on the nineteenth-century dream of man aspiring, man looking back on the past with longing, man reaching out his hands and his spirit toward nature, in brief, we may speak, in its complex manifestations, of the romantic conception of man. It was natural that American literature should develop the current notion of progress (Emerson and Whitman). Less natural seems its adoption of the more artificial aspects of the romantic temper: melancholy, nostalgia for the past, a sophisticated love of nature. Yet such moods were derived, writer for writer, though similar attitudes existed on the continent, from the English: Wordsworth and Bryant; Shelley and Lanier; Coleridge and Poe; the links are innumerable. As if to challenge the practical qualities in the American character, our bookish men of letters sat them down upon the frontier and told "sad stories of the death of kings." In this respect, indeed, was the English influence most stubborn and perhaps most baneful, for such verse, from Fitz-Greene Halleck to Thomas Bailey Aldrich, hinged upon the unhappy theory that our best writing should not concern itself with America's realities. If it did, they asked, how could it be literature? Unhappy belief, indeed, which, with support from many a gifted spirit, enervated belles-lettres in our land for many years. For neither fine writing about Europe nor crude writing about America was enough; neither all silk nor all homespun would do. The importunate need was evident: the cultivated mind eager to write of the America scene. But this heresy the English romantic pattern did not encourage. These English patterns in the conventional romantic tradition are, indeed, distressingly familiar. Even now, despite the rise of nativism in the mighty Mark Twain and his spiritual descendants, this imitative verse, made in the feeble likeness of the standard English poetry, symbolizes for the half-read their country's literature—*American* literature!

As a postscript, the dominance of English patterns in Amer-

[21] See the recent edition (especially Introduction and footnotes) of *Nature*, ed. K. W. Cameron, Scholars' Facsimiles & Reprints, New York, 1940.

ican literature of the nineteenth century is painfully visible in the repetition of techniques. Again and again a character type, a stylized method of narration, a verse form tantalizes the reader sensitive to echoes. Irving is in debt to the essay of the village (Miss Mitford); Cooper and Dana to the novel of the sea (Scott); Brown, Hawthorne, and Poe to the Gothic romance. Bryant is indentured to blank verse; Lowell is enamoured of the ode; and the facile Longfellow plays with every species of stanza and line. Even toward the end of the century we encounter the Byronic narratives of Joaquin Miller and tinkling imitations by Aldrich and Stedman. Why not? These were the sanctioned techniques of the literature which we had kidnapped. Should, then, a new country create new forms? It should, declared Whitman; and he brought them into being, too. No part of our eventual rebellion against European tradition was more audacious than his.

Of this revolt, later. For the present, observe the proud strength of these English patterns: their richness, which moved Lowell to suggest that it was folly to do other than imitate;[22] their susceptibility to modification or adaptation, as in Bryant's introduction of American aspects of nature (instead of the nightingale, the mallard duck);[23] and their authority, as representative of one of the noblest literatures of all time. Yet observe also that this domination counseled by example an exclusion of all that was unique in our civilization; indeed, its continuance meant a kind of death in life. The intellectual history of America has been that of successive renunciations of ways of thought out of tune with the actual development of the country. Calvinism, for example, born of the crowded cities of Europe, could not survive in agricultural America. No more could patterns of literature contemptuous of our everyday America. These English formulas were doomed. Of their fate in the twentieth century I hope to say something at the close of this study. First, however, let us understand how they were, in the nineteenth century, qualified by other factors, namely, the French, the German, and the other continental patterns.

Of all the penetrations of American literature through the

[22] In spite of his strong desire for nationalism in literature, such was probably Lowell's real belief, of which his attitudes towards Thoreau and Whitman appear to be a confirmation.

[23] See "To A Waterfowl," *The Poetical Works of William Cullen Bryant*, New York, 1903, p. 26.

medium of a foreign language, that of the French remains the most provocative; this is partly because the two main periods of its civilizing influence lie a full century apart, in the last years of, respectively, the eighteenth and nineteenth centuries. In the French, as in the Spanish and Italian, to chart too precisely the elements in the pattern (ideology, moods, and techniques) is still a perilous task. One characteristic, however, is as prominent as Henry Thoreau's nose. Whether through blood, as in Crèvecoeur and Thoreau, or through a literary theory, as in the bond between Zola and our naturalists, each appearance of the French influence in American literature has been the signal for lucidity of expression, for a rich and special craftsmanship. This was true in the eighteenth century. What ideas of the Enlightenment in Franklin's essays came directly from the French is, as said, problematical; he was familiar with, to mention only Olympians, the works of Voltaire, Lavoisier, Turgot, Quesnay, and Condorcet; both his bagatelles and his letters in this foreign tongue indicate the French influence on his style.[24] The pattern in Franklin is English, but the finish, the gloss, is Gallic.

Through unkempt Thomas Paine, whose chief literary quality was an overwhelming energy and through Philip Freneau, blessed with a delicate feeling for nature and a love for humanity and through Crèvecoeur, the Pennsylvania ploughman with the Rousseauistic pen, is imprinted on our literature the ideology of the French Revolution. In Freneau, indeed, the concept of liberty is clothed in a passionate eloquence in behalf of French republicanism. He cries, not without sympathy from his twentieth-century readers:

> Ah! while I write, dear France ALLIED,
> My ardent wish I scarce restrain,
> To throw these Sybil leaves aside,
> And fly to join you on the main:
>   Unfurl the topsail for the chace
>   And help to crush the tyrant race![25]

[24] See A. H. Smyth, *The Writings of Benjamin Franklin*, New York, 1905-1907, I, 182-195; 216-217; J. B. McMaster, *Benjamin Franklin as a Man of Letters*, Boston, 1887, p. 276; M. K. Jackson, *Outlines of the Literary History of Colonial Pennsylvania*, Lancaster, 1906, pp. 67, 76.

[25] "On The Anniversary of the Storming of the Bastille, at Paris, July 14th, 1789." *Poems of Freneau*, ed. H. H. Clark, New York [1929], p. 137.

Of French descent, a student of French at Princeton College, an apostle of Rousseau, and an agent for "The French Society of the Patriots of America," Freneau, who was really our first poet, reflects, far more forcibly than eupeptic Joel Barlow, the most Jacobinical of the "Connecticut Wits," the French dream (or delusion) of man's enlightenment and freedom. Meanwhile Timothy Dwight was skeptical; with withering irony, so he thought, he dedicated his poem *The Triumph of Infidelity* to the anti-Christ, Voltaire!

At any rate, the violences of Thomas Paine and Philip Freneau could hardly perpetuate French thought in American literature; in the nineteenth century the disillusionment of the English romantic poets with French libertarian ideas found an echoing sympathy here. On our first belles-lettres, on Bryant or on Irving, France made slight impression; it is pertinent that Irving, that tireless explorer in English, German, and Spanish literatures, brought back from his various stays in France only a trifling sketch or two of Parisian manners.[26] There is some incidental obligation, such as Poe's experiments with French "atmosphere" and nomenclature; and the successive waves of travel literature washed in, among various dilettante studies of French village and peasant, such colorless plunder as Cooper's *Notes on France,* and, in particular, Longfellow's *Outre-Mer.* Longfellow, indeed, was temporarily Francophile; he crammed letters and diaries with allusions to French classical writers.[27] Yet even if the Enlightenment had not spent itself, its skepticism would have been distasteful to the naïve, optimistic thought of growing America. At Geneva in 1833 Emerson alluded almost bitterly to Voltaire as "the King of scorners."[28]

Indeed, the character of French influence upon American literature now became "vertical," resembling that, already noted, of the masterpieces of English literature. As, for example, Shakespeare moved Melville, so Montaigne stirred Emerson;

[26] E.g., "Sketches in Paris in 1825," *The Knickerbocker,* April, 1840, republished in *The Crayon Papers.*

[27] "Il possédait à fond nos auteurs classiques, comme on peut s'en apercevoir aux multiples citations de Molière, de La Fontaine, de Madame de Sévigné qui dans ses lettres, dans son journal, se présentent naturellement à sa mémoire et coulent sans effort de sa plume." Edmond Estève, "Longfellow et la France," *Bowdoin College Bulletin* (No. 146), October, 1925, p. [10].

[28] See *Journals of Ralph Waldo Emerson,* III, 152, June 16, 1833.

some of the noblest recognitions of French thought or feeling
appear in such single works as Emerson's essay on Montaigne,
Henry Adams' study, *Mont-Saint-Michel and Chartres,* or Lafcadio Hearn's translations of Gautier and Loti. These me-
morials reveal the latent French influence upon particular
writers; and such are more important, far, than the feminine
flutter in Concord concerning Fourier, who never, I believe,
engraved himself upon a single passage in American literary
prose or poetry. In brief, the French pattern in American
literature during the better part of the nineteenth century
was fitful, but rich in personal debts, as in this affinity of
Emerson with Montaigne.

The vascular force of Montaigne's speech enraptured Emerson,[29] and we may consider his a typical American experience.
For the French ways of expression continued to allure a civilization never tolerant of the dreadful French ways of heathen
thought. French social and intellectual prestige, French standards of morality, French skepticism have always abashed Americans; and the barriers of race and religion have too often
intervened for a free exchange of ideas.[30] During the last
quarter of the eighteenth century the ideas of the Enlightenment were available to American literature through both
French and English versions. Presumably, then, the matchless
skill in the presentation of these ideas enthralled Franklin and
Freneau. Certainly their interest in the language itself would
argue this. Does not, then, the French influence become most
potent in our literature in questions of style, of literary method,
or of literary philosophy, such as Zola's? This, I have come to
believe, is the essential fact about the French pattern in American literature. Americans in the nineteenth century longed to
add to our belles-lettres some of that luminous, high clarity
of expression, compared with which, it must be admitted, the
styles of other literatures are mildly barbarous! So felt, I am
convinced, Franklin and Thomas Jefferson; so felt Emerson;
so felt Longfellow; and so felt also, at the end of the nineteenth century, many of our realists and naturalists.

The entire nature of the realists' debt to France is challeng-

[29] "It is the language of conversation transferred to a book. Cut these words,
and they would bleed; they are vascular and alive." "Montaigne; or, the Skeptic,"
Emerson's Complete Works, Boston, 1883, IV, 160-161.

[30] See H. M. Jones, *America and French Culture,* "Conclusion," pp. 569-572.

ing, and, as a whole, still unexplored. Evidently a realistic temper and realistic modes of expression developed in America independently, as in the self-contained Stephen Crane. How much is French, how much is Russian, how much is even European, has not been, in 1940, yet determined. We hear vigorous denials, as in Howells' well-known words:

Henry James introduced me to Flaubert and Balzac, and then I read Turgenev and Tolstoy for myself; but I had already grown into my realistic method, and I was authorized rather than inspired by the Frenchmen.[31]

Yet good cases may be made for the cogency of these recent French influences; it is plain to students of the American literature written between 1880 and 1930 that the contribution of French techniques,[32] not only in forms of verse, such as Amy Lowell's, but in prose, such as that of Mrs. Wharton and Miss Cather, is substantial. We must conclude, then, that the French patterns, though less dependent after 1800 on ideologies, retain, with renewed emphasis after 1880, French techniques, that is, French ways of expression. Finally, then, from 1780 to 1940, though less dominant than the English, these French patterns have been precious (perhaps in both senses) enrichments of this transplanted literature of ours.

Possibly because of the generally firm intellectual content of French writing, there is lacking in our literature an emotional identification with France, a kinship of mood. It is completely otherwise in the German patterns, with which we are now thoughtfully concerned. We may omit the body of literature written in German in America, such as Pastorius' eighteenth-century descriptions of Pennsylvania, and we may neglect such influences as that of Pennsylvania German types upon Whittier's poetry (Maud Muller). Let us begin in the late eighteenth century with Gessner's *Death of Abel* and his *Idylls,* with Klopstock's *Messias,*[33] and, of course, through the pioneer playwright, William Dunlap, with the drama of Kotze-

[31] Quoted from a letter of Howells to A. H. Quinn. See the latter's *American Fiction . . .* , New York, 1936, p. 258. See also *The Cambridge History of American Literature,* New York, 1921, III, Chap. XI.

[32] See the discussions of modern American poets in *The Oxford Anthology of American Literature,* ed. W. R. Benét and N. H. Pearson, New York, 1938, pp. 1663, 1676, etc.

[33] See A. B. Faust, *The German Element in the United States . . .* , Boston, 1909, II, 338-342.

bue and Schiller. Gay young Washington Irving, man about town in early nineteenth-century New York, felt the force of the German influence in the theatre and in the popular translations.[34] He wept and shuddered at Goethe's *Sorrows of Werther*, at the tales of terror in the magazines, and at Bürger's *Lenore*. We see him the guest of Walter Scott at Abbotsford; the older author takes down from his shelves, one by one for his American disciple, the volumes of German fiction and poetry.[35] From this time on the story is familiar enough: the introduction into New England of German scholarship by Everett, Bancroft, and others; the study of the German philosophers; the adaptation of the tale of horror by Poe; the translation of *Faust* by Bayard Taylor; the humorous (and oh, how misleading!) caricatures of the red-nosed, bespectacled, beer-drinking Teuton by Charles Godfrey Leland.[36] All these aspects of German influence, making the French pattern, by comparison, somewhat pallid, record themselves upon American literature until the last decade or two of the century, when they become mysteriously—or perhaps not mysteriously—quiescent. In the period of our maturity we turned again to French patterns. Yet it was a kaleidoscopic interlude, not without results for belles-lettres.

For the elements in the German pattern fall naturally into our component parts, of ideology, mood, and technique. This ideology did not, like that of the French, concern social or governmental questions; such blessings were reserved for our own perverse generation! A century ago the truly seminal German ideology was primarily philosophical. This part of the pattern, however, was contributory rather than pioneer. For, as already observed, the philosophical ideas of our humble transcendentalists took form under the tutelage of the ancients and of the British interpreters of these. The German philosophers were ancillary and confirmatory. Indeed, during the first quarter of the century, it was almost impossible to know the originals:

There is no gentleman [wrote Longfellow's father in 1827] in this state [Maine] who is master of the German language.[37]

[34] See S. T. Williams, *The Life of Washington Irving*, New York, 1935, I, 38.
[35] *Idem*, I, 162.
[36] See A. B. Faust (*op. cit.*), II, 351.
[37] Quoted by J. T. Hatfield, *New Light on Longfellow*, Boston, 1933, p. 139.

Whatever quips occur to us about Maine or gentlemen in
this state, it is certain that, during this period of literary
adolescence, the situation was typical of America. We recall
Emerson's painful reading of Goethe at the exhortation of
Carlyle; it is arguable that German was hardly more familiar
to the transcendentalists during their early creative period
than is Swedish to our young scholars today. I find Frederic
Henry Hedge's address before the Phi Beta Kappa Society in
1828 both amusing and informative. Speaking of influences on
American thought, he says:

> Turn we from these to shapes of other mould,
> Let foreign climes their varied stories unfold;—
> See German horrors rise in dark array,
> And German names more horrible than they.
> Amazed we hear of Werke and Gedichte,
> Of Schlegel, Schleiermacher, Richter, Fichte,
> And thou great Goethe, whose illustrious name,
> So oft mis-spelt and mis-pronounced by fame,
> Still puzzles English jaws and English teeth,
> With Goty, Gurrte, Gewter, and Go-ethe.[38]

Mispronunciation, however, has never daunted the healthy-
minded American—witness Mark Twain's struggles with this
language; and it was no augury now; the emphasis upon German studies increased markedly after 1840. The dissemination
of German philosophy, in no small sense due to Hedge himself, who influenced Margaret Fuller and others, left its mark:
in *The Dial*; in Emerson's discovery that Goethe was a "representative" man; and in various essays and poems of the Concord
Group, wherein German transcendentalism blended comfort-
ably with that of Greece, Asia, and Yankeeland. The dream of
God, of the oversoul, and of the "fair apparition" of nature
faded in the post-Civil War America, and with that dream
dwindled the influence of the great intuitionalists of Germany. Yet they still abide in the prose and poetry of our rural
transcendentalists. Emerson's "Waldeinsamkeit" is more than
a pretty title!

Thus the German ideology, ironically enough, fostered New
England individualism! Even more incongruous with thoughts
which may now be in your mind, is another web of the German

[38] O. W. Long, *Frederic Henry Hedge, A Cosmopolitan Scholar*, Portland,
Maine, 1940, p. 16.

pattern; this is the mood, already mentioned, of romantic longing for the Germany of song and story. This sad infection few
of our poets escaped; it reached a sugary apogee, of course, in
Longfellow. It would be worse than tedious to list the German
writers, such as Goethe, Heine, or Richter,[39] who left memorable traces on his poetry; and you will be relieved to know
that I shall not discuss the German backgrounds of "A Psalm
of Life" or *Evangeline*.[40] It would be a half-truth to say that
Longfellow's poetry was conditioned by his susceptibility to
German sentiment; though Poe declared that Longfellow was
"imbued with the peculiar spirit of German song."[41] One may
momentarily entertain this idea of Longfellow's denationaliza-
tion, for the German influence upon this poet was sweetly
insidious. Longfellow's receptivity was, however, a result, not
a cause. The root of Longfellow's attitude toward Germany
lay in his temperament, which owned a capacity for sentiment
about each nation proportionate to the nation's remoteness;
even that bad critic, Walt Whitman, spoke of him as the "poet
of the mellow twilight of the past in Italy, Germany, Spain,
and in Northern Europe."[42]

Longfellow represents, particularly through the German influence, the poets who thought of America as possessed, to use
his own words, by "lethal, deadly influences[43]"; who dreamed
of foreign countries, if only they were distant enough, as glowing in the "mellow twilight of the past." This tendency the
German legends and songs confirmed in Longfellow. For his
facile mind, despite its saturation in languages and foreign literatures, remained pitifully sterile in understanding or recre-
ating the ideas of the civilizations which it knew so well. A
lecturer on Goethe, he never penetrated beyond the periphery
of that titanic mind. He merely created a schoolgirl's dream
of a shining, medieval Germany, a Germany of turreted, red-
roofed cities, of minnesingers and *Gemütlichkeit*, a dream from
which we have recently been roused in dismay! We may even

[39] See, e.g., Otto Deiml, *Der Prosastil H. W. Longfellows. Der Einfluss von Jean
Paul auf Longfellow's Prosastil*, Kronach, 1927, p. 57; and Henry Wadsworth
Longfellow, *Representative Selections* . . . , ed. Odell Shepard, New York [1934],
xxxi; and J. T. Hatfield (*op. cit.*), p. 140.
[40] See J. T. Hatfield (*op. cit.*), pp. 84, 114.
[41] Review of *Ballads and Other Poems*, *Graham's Magazine*, April, 1842.
[42] *The Critic* (New York), II, No. 33, April 8, 1882, p. 101.
[43] *Representative Selections*, xxviii.

find some wit in the remark of the student, with its too glib use of numerals, that Longfellow was the Third Reich's first fifth-column agent! Jesting aside, he set a tone; he fixed this tradition; he drew this hieroglyph in the pattern. He, together with Irving, whose sedulous disciple he was, transmitted to our literature the *Sehnsucht*, the wistfulness for the beautiful past, for something—God knows what!—that never did exist.

So much for ideology and moods; the imitations of German techniques were also numerous. Irving and Longfellow used the romantic autobiographical narrative, perfected by Goethe; and Irving, Poe, and Hawthorne rifled the German tale.[44] One of our classics, *Rip Van Winkle*, is now recognized as virtually an adaptation of Otmar's *Peter Klaus*.[45] We need not, I think, linger over this embroidery in the German pattern. Keeping in mind the philosophic influence, the mood of longing, and the technique of the story, what, may we say in summary, did the German mind transfer to American literature? I think we may say that, in contrast to the influence of the French ways of expression, the German pattern offered primarily ways of *feeling*. Thus the New England transcendentalists admired the German philosophers for their *intuitions* about the universe; indeed, they sometimes called them "the feeling philosophers." These New England disciples were inclined to soften the hard thought of Kant and others into nebulous moral sentiments, perhaps to attack thereby a declining Calvinism or a Unitarianism, which Coleridge had compared with a cowrie; in the shell one hears only the faint murmur of the sea. The conclusions, not the hard thinking, of the German philosophers, communicated a sense of emotional security. I find this sentiment not too far distant from that of Longfellow on the lower levels of his poems of far-off Europe, or of Irving's tales of the supernatural. I do not think that we should press this generalization too strongly; exceptions will occur to you. Yet it cannot be denied, I think, in contrast to the firm pattern of ideas which is English or the pattern of techniques, however few, which is French, that the story of German thought in American literature is, for the

---

[44] See H. A. Pochmann's studies of these influences. E.g., "Irving's German Sources in *The Sketch Book*," *Studies in Philology* (1930), XXVII, 477-507.

[45] See S. T. Williams (*op. cit.*), I, 183-184.

most part, the record of *feeling*, whether about the divine, about the remote past, or about the supernatural.

These three patterns, then, the English, the French, and the German, are basic in American belles-lettres. In each of the three, as we have seen, the subsidiary elements of the patterns (ideology, moods, and techniques) receive different emphases. Even if we have not studied vocabulary, allusion, foreign speech, special characters, or the important secondary influences, such as the French in New Orleans and the Germans in Pennsylvania,[46] it is evident that American literature, like the American civilization, has drunk deeply, and perhaps to excess, of these old European wines. Or, to change the figure, here is our three-centuries-old cathedral, with its English nave, its two French aisles, and its rococo German apse, done in the sentimental manner. In it, too, are the traceries of other foreign architects: the Dutch (Washington Irving); the Scandinavian and Finnish (Longfellow); the Italian (Howells, George Henry Boker, and George William Curtis); and the Russian (Howells). This is filigree work, inferior to that of the three main patterns. Yet I shall ask you to pause, momentarily, over the mysterious, the seemingly alien Spanish.

More than the French, more even than the German, the Spanish pattern took its being from local American sources: not from Cervantes or from Lope de Vega but from Louisiana, whence the novels of George Washington Cable; and from the Southwest and West, where originated the Spanish experiments of Helen Hunt Jackson and Bret Harte, and, recently, of Willa Cather. That melancholy and hauntingly beautiful creation, "Benito Cereno," seems to arise entirely from Melville's imagination. Yet there flourished an old-world Spanish pattern in the nineteenth century, born partly of the antiquarian, patriotic devotion to Christopher Columbus, partly of the unquenchable curiosity concerning the barbaric Peninsula, and partly of the opulent scholarship of Irving, Ticknor, Prescott, and Gayangos. Naturally, this Spanish pattern centered in a way of feeling, not unlike that already studied in connection with the English and German patterns. The transmission to our literature of Spanish ways of thought (the extravagant individualism; the Catholicism; the isolationism) was unthinkable; and only in the born linguist and metrist (Longfellow) or in

[46] See A. B. Faust (*op. cit.*), pp. 357-358.

the trained story-teller (Irving) did American writers lean upon
Spanish techniques. In Longfellow's editions and translations,
and in a few poems under the spell of peninsular literature,
occur, like music from soft Andalusia, Spanish legends, Spanish
names, and Spanish verse forms. Likewise Irving's *Alhambra*
is tinted by the Spanish *articulo de costumbres*, or essay of
native manners, which he had discussed in 1828 with the novelist, Fernán Caballero.[47] And all such borrowings are expressions of the indomitable mood of longing for the remote, this
time for the distant, golden Iberia of history and folk-song:

> What dreams [wrote Longfellow] romantic filled my brain,
> And summoned back to life again
> The Paladins of Charlemagne
> The Cid Campeador![48]

And now having beheld, so to speak, the many-patterned
rainbow, what of its promise? What are its meanings? The pot
of gold we shall not, in all probability, see in our day; we shall
not meet the Shakespeare or the Goethe who, interweaving
these patterns with those of native America, shall create those
timeless masterpieces which we covet for our country's literature. Yet the European patterns suggest interpretations; I direct
your atention to three for brief summaries, and, in conclusion,
to a fourth.

What are the meanings? *The first meaning is color.* I refer
to the enrichment of American literature in idea, mood, and
technique through the magical recurrence of these diverse
European patterns. In contradiction of the commonplace that
our literature is pale and negative, I venture to assert that a
real intimacy with it, which many of us still persist in scorn-
ing, will convince us of the opposite truth. Inevitably it is
richly composite, varied, colorful. This quality it owes in large
measure to the European patterns, to which its peculiar origins
and development offered a hospitable plasticity. These patterns, as we have seen, alternate and cross each other. We find
the English most powerful in the seventeenth and eighteenth
centuries, and dominant until about the last third of the
nineteenth. It then suffers a decline or at least inspires a skep-

[47] See S. T. Williams (*op. cit.*), I, 351-354.
[48] "Castles in Spain," *The Works of Henry Wadsworth Longfellow*, Boston
[1886], III, 103.

ticism concerning its authority, until in the twentieth the signs of its direct control vanish. Meanwhile the French pattern, crescent after the Revolution, loses its force, save upon a few eclectic writers, until its renascence at the end of the nineteenth century. The German patterns, beginning in late eighteenth-century drama, reach their height in the New England transcendentalists and the romantic poets and story-tellers of the first half of the century; then subside into translations and the literary comic strip. We should perceive the solidifying of these patterns, particularly in the cases of the German and Spanish, through the growth of communities and literatures in their respective foreign languages, in, for example, Pennsylvania and the Southwest; and we should consider, too, the occasional concentration of several patterns in one writer, as in the virtually expatriated Irving, in the multilingual Longfellow, or in Lafcadio Hearn, born in Ionia, of Irish father and Greek mother, educated in France and England, and absorber of the cultures of New York, New Orleans, the West Indies, and Japan. Indeed, this literature of ours is a gathering of the nations, a symphony of the races. In it we may hear Bedouin and Scandinavian songs, tales of Granada or Saxony, or the voices of Dante, Goethe, and Calderón. Or we may explore the Rive Gauche, the Mexican hacienda, the Harz Forest, the Italian Apennines. Who, in brief, will deny the shock and brilliance of color bestowed upon American literature by these patterns of old Europe?

A second meaning is rebellion. Almost at once, in the vigorous young republic, the prevalence of foreign patterns, particularly of the English, aroused resistance, creating the vision of an American literature as independent as its political institutions. Most of us are acquainted with this rather naïve transference of our nationalism to our literature;[49] and we recall how this domination by foreign patterns asserted itself in diverse but related ways. For a time it emphasized American subjects, but maintained conformity with European, particularly English, forms of expression, as in Joel Barlow's *Colum-*

[49] See, e.g., R. W. Bolwell, "Concerning the Study of Nationalism in American Literature," *American Literature* (X, 405-416), January, 1939; B. T. Spencer, "A National Literature, 1837-1855," *American Literature* (VIII, 125-159), May, 1936; H. H. Clark, "Nationalism in American Literature," *University of Toronto Quarterly* (II, 402-519), July, 1933.

biad or Longfellow's lyrics. Later it stressed native subjects, proclaiming the need of new forms and of indifference to all foreign patterns, as in the daring techniques of Walt Whitman and the casual, insolent vernacular of Mark Twain. Or, admitting the inadequacy of rebellion based on mere adaptation of American materials to European techniques, such as Barlow's and Longfellow's, and realizing also the absurdity of rebellions, such as Whitman's and Mark Twain's, which minimized mankind's achievements in art, this more intelligent protest went deeper. It valued the past and respected the canons of art; but, making use of native materials and occasionally of original forms, it adhered to the trite but inviolable truth that literature must, in the end, be concerned with the universal experiences of the human spirit. No, it was not enough merely to introduce American themes and characters; to ignore the traditions of the past was fatal. No American literature would survive which tried to solve the problem by describing the Indian in heroic couplets or by showing the noble frontiersman in realistic dialect. Art, too, was important. For a definition of this wiser kind of rebellion we may turn to Emerson's *The American Scholar*, in which the native writer is urged not to ignore, but not to listen "too long" to the "courtly muses of Europe." Emerson begged for eternal issues in American vestures.

Now the virility of this rebellion, in its different and related degrees of wisdom, we owe in part to these tyrannical European patterns. Some historians of literature have deplored their strength; my study teaches me more and more that what is most profound and beautiful in our literature derives from the conflict between these patterns and the native forces. Sometimes within a period, sometimes within a single poem, such as Whitman's "When Lilacs Last in the Dooryard Bloom'd," we may see the old and the new in a regenerative opposition! There are few problems in any literature more deserving of study than the intense struggle by which we have oriented ourselves toward the peculiar heritage of a transplanted literature, and groped our way in this twentieth century toward a literature unmistakably our own. As the social historian studies the hardwon democratic faith, so may the literary historian study the equally arduous and more intellectual battle for a free yet civilized literature. And this victory, really won today, has been made possible by the European patterns.

A third meaning is assimilation. I speak now of twentieth-century literature; it is exactly three centuries since Richard Mather, John Eliot, and other "Chief Divines" issued *The Bay Psalm Book*; we now live in the age of Robert Frost and Willa Cather. What has happened to the European patterns in our belles-letters? They are with us, of course, but they are infinitely less dynamic, infinitely more incidental. That is, they are reduced to perspective; they are assimilated. Just as our young men feel less their responsibilities to the European civilizations, so our writers of belles-lettres are more self-sufficient, disdaining to refer their work to transatlantic criteria. In fact, they even derive in their imitative moments from other Americans: Robert Frost reveres Longfellow; Carl Sandburg and Stephen Benét, Whitman; and Edith Wharton, Henry James. We are experiencing an amazing invigoration of confidence in our own standards. We have lost interest both in the portrayal of the American scene for its own sake and in the repetition of European ideologies, ways of feeling, and techniques. The serene mastery of both European ideals of art and American materials is obvious in *North of Boston, Death Comes for the Archbishop*, or Edwin Arlington Robinson's powerful introspection within the framework of Arthurian legend. How naïve now appears the ancient controversy between native and European impulses: the sharp antithesis between a Whitman and a Thomas Bailey Aldrich; between Mark Twain and the New England writers! Anglophilism and nativism have fled, or are fleeing our literature, and such controversies we now understand to have been merely stages in our march toward a civilized belles-lettres, assimilating all conflicting forces. Indeed, as early as 1888 Walt Whitman foresaw this, declaring in his own inimitable vernacular that

> There is even towards all those ["bequests of the past"] a subjective and contemporary point of view appropriate to ourselves alone, and to our new genius and environments, different from anything hitherto; and that such conception of current or gone-by life and art is for us the only means of their assimilation consistent with the Western world.[50]

[50] "A Backward Glance O'er Travel'd Roads," *November Boughs*, Philadelphia, 1888, p. 10.

Indeed, akin to these meanings of color, rebellion, and, in particular, to assimilation, there exists another meaning so important that I urge you to recognize how vital a moment is this in our intellectual history; that I exhort you to give yourself more generously to the study and understanding of this fullgrown literature of your own country. For is this not the time, two hundred years after the founding of the University of Pennsylvania and three hundred after the founding of American literature, when we may anticipate (not waiting as so often in the past, for the verdict of Europe) the critic of fifty years hence? May we not say with assurance this: *In so far as a precise time may be named for such subtle processes of intellectual development, American literature has now attained, in the truest sense, independence?* What the homespun Connecticut Wits, what Emerson, what Whitman dreamed of long ago has finally come to pass; and it has come to pass, in my judgment, only in the last two decades. Certainly the kind of independence to which I refer did not exist at the death of Stephen Crane in 1900; at the death of Mark Twain in 1910; or at the death of William Dean Howells in 1920. The independence which I have in mind has not come, as those early writers conceived of it, in poetical reflections of a geographic vastness or in indigenous themes or in a new language, although all such have a part in the new independence. Nor has it come through the isolation which this tremendous moment in the history of the world seems to lend to American literature. For it is at least conceivable that some of the literatures to which I have referred may soon be the literatures of subjugated peoples. Even during the past six months our culture seems, through its greater chance of survival, to have assumed a new leadership and a new promise. Such an independence, however spectacular, would in the long run prove factitious. Nor could we, whose literature is a tissue of these other cultures, desire a shallow eminence through their destruction. I refer rather to an independence, affected but not created by war or the movements of peoples, but by the slow irresistible growth of cultural forces. I say rather that American literature has attained independence *in the true sense* because it is now, for the first time, at once American and universal.

It may be doubted whether a great literature can develop without a sense of national consciousness; ours is still American, but—blessed emancipation!—it now lacks that excess of national consciousness, which is provincialism. In our new literary independence the national consciousness is but a pungent flavor, as in the literatures of Europe, within the wider freedom of tested intellectual and imaginative values. Here at last is an independent literature in which neither a European ideology nor a frontier culture is authoritarian, yet in which few of the ideologies, moods, and techniques evolved by man for literature are absent. Thus in the novels of Miss Cather, to whom we may return for a farewell illustration, may be found old-world principles of writing and also our adolescent frontier impulses, adjusted, matured, refined: character types, local color, the frontier, and the influences of writers as different as Balzac and Sarah Orne Jewett. Here they are, all fused within a prose style, derivative but entirely her own. Yet Miss Cather is but one of our present group of civilized writers in this year 1940. Their deeply imaginative treatment of native themes within the disciplines of proven tradition proclaims the nature of our new literary independence—an independence which wears an air not merely of achievement, but of blessed expectancy, suggesting within the next century other books and other authors closer still to the inner spirit of American life and of eternal art, perhaps even books and authors that will shine down the succeeding ages, even as those of Europe have illumined ours.